Praise for *Ho...*

MW01286417

The challenges of discipleship in the twenty-first century seem overwhelming to many Christians. Lakies explores our underlying sense of bewilderment and fear as society changes around the church. Affirming the relational nature of God's reality, Lakies turns our attention to the person of Jesus, demonstrating how His assumption of a self-sacrificing identity shines His light into our lives and through us into the lives of those whom He has made our neighbors. Readers are equipped to embrace those who can only confront and refute in the spirit of acceptance, patience, and humility displayed by the Lord Himself.

ROBERT KOLB, PROFESSOR EMERITUS OF SYSTEMATIC THEOLOGY,
CONCORDIA SEMINARY, ST. LOUIS

What do drums, tar pits, elephants, and a doctor who becomes a patient teach Christians about outreach? Chad Lakies wields these and other storied images to help a post-Christendom church mend her nets. He offers ways to share Jesus in word and deed, especially as our secular neighbors are gripped by their mortality, stirred by a sense of purpose, or roused by the light creeping in through joy and pain. People-fishing is still our calling. Lakies tunes our ears to our risen Lord. Perhaps the time is ripe to cast on the other side of the boat?

MICHAEL ZEIGLER, SPEAKER OF *THE LUTHERAN HOUR*,
LUTHERAN HOUR MINISTRIES

People are deeply hurting in this current age, when the convergence of individualism and the unending quest for personal meaning has paradoxically led to widespread loneliness and despair. The Christian Church, when embodying Christ's mission of forgiveness, reconciliation, and restoration, offers a potent remedy. Dr. Lakies rightly calls the church to lean into this challenge and bring the Gospel to bear, for a relationship with Christ and His church provides what the culture cannot: identity, restoration, hope, and belonging.

MICHAEL A. THOMAS, PHD, PRESIDENT, CONCORDIA UNIVERSITY IRVINE

Dr. Chad Lakies calls Christians back to bold and resilient faith. Exposing flawed responses to a confused and chaotic culture, Lakies helps believers see and articulate the saving voice, wisdom, and ways of Jesus. This book guides readers through the storm of societal upheaval and provides resources for the church to bring Jesus, the friend of sinners, to the world.

REV. MICHAEL W. NEWMAN, PRESIDENT, LCMS TEXAS DISTRICT; AUTHOR OF
HOPE WHEN YOUR HEART BREAKS: NAVIGATING GRIEF AND LOSS

Reading *How the Light Shines Through* was a timely reset for untangling complex topics in the work of the church in uncharted territory. Chad Lakies tackles issues of identity, hospitality, authenticity, and resilience in the framework of loving others. Chad gives clear direction for how my own winsome witness can reflect a discipleship path following Jesus. Using this model, now my complicated life task is to never let an issue prevent a relationship.

CONNIE DENNINGER, COFOUNDER OF VISUAL FAITH® MINISTRY

Chad Lakies invites readers into a stimulating theological conversation about Christian living and faithful witness in our pluralistic here and now, offering insight into both the way things are and how we may engage with confidence, humility, and love. Never does he lose sight of the ultimate—proclaiming Jesus Christ, the light of the world—and never is his tone less than hopeful.

REV. JACOB A. SCOTT, LCMS; CHAPLAIN, OREGON NATIONAL GUARD

Beyond tired outreach programs and scripted evangelism conversations, this book is exactly what the church needs in the here and now into which God has placed us. Lakies diagnoses the hostile culture that surrounds us without calling for a war against it. Instead, his insight into the culture, blended with some of the best practices of the early church, gives Christians a way to talk about the faith authentically with the people in their lives.

REV. GRANT A. KNEPPER, PASTOR,
GRACE LUTHERAN CHURCH, MODESTO, CALIFORNIA

Dr. Lakies has written to the church's heart with this book, speaking to our fears and frustrations as well as to our loves and our very identity as Christians. Through his deep reading of Scripture, theology, and the best of sociology, he has collected critically important insights for anyone who serves our Lord in the contentious present age. Pastors and lay leaders will find herein both keen insight into what we are feeling and helpful advice to guide us in these turbulent times.

PHILLIP BRANDT, PhD, PASTOR, ST. MICHAEL'S LUTHERAN CHURCH, PORTLAND,
OREGON; CAMPUS PASTOR, CONCORDIA ST. PAUL GLOBAL'S ABSN NURSING
PROGRAM IN PORTLAND; AUTHOR OF SUNDAY-SERMON.COM

If all the swift changes in culture have you feeling back on your heels, you owe yourself the chance to calmly think alongside Chad Lakies before reacting out of fear or frustration or even zeal. In his new book, Lakies helps us understand these dark times in nuanced and important ways, and he points out hopeful steps we can take toward embodying a resilient witness.

REV. DON EVERTS, AUTHOR OF *THE RELUCTANT WITNESS:
DISCOVERING THE DELIGHT OF SPIRITUAL CONVERSATIONS*

HOW THE LIGHT SHINES THROUGH

Resilient Witness in Dark Times

CHAD LAKIES

CONCORDIA PUBLISHING HOUSE • SAINT LOUIS

Published by Concordia Publishing House
3558 S. Jefferson Ave., St. Louis, MO 63118-3968
1-800-325-3040 • cph.org

Library of Congress Cataloging-in-Publication Data

Names: Lakies, Chad, author.
Title: How the light shines through : resilient witness in dark times / Chad Lakies.
Description: Saint Louis, MO : Concordia Publishing House, [2024] | Summary: "How the Light Shines Through examines the Christian church's reaction to a changing culture, discusses challenges the church faces while existing in this new environment, and suggests practices and habits to help Christians live out a faithful witness today"-- Provided by publisher.
Identifiers: LCCN 2024022988 (print) | LCCN 2024022989 (ebook) | ISBN 9780758674500 (paperback) | ISBN 9780758674517 (ebook)
Subjects: LCSH: Witness bearing (Christianity) | Christianity and culture.
Classification: LCC BV4520 .L323 2024 (print) | LCC BV4520 (ebook) | DDC 248/.5--dc23/eng/20240613
LC record available at https://lccn.loc.gov/2024022988
LC ebook record available at https://lccn.loc.gov/2024022989

1   2   3   4   5   6   7   8   9   10   33   32   31   30   29   28   27   26   25   24

To my parents,

Brenda and David Lakies,

giants upon whose shoulders I stand

And to my daughters, Anabel and Daphne:

May you, your children, and your

grandchildren meet Jesus

in the winsome witness

of a resilient church

CONTENTS

Foreword

Years ago, I preached a sermon titled "It's a Great Time to Be the Church." Afterward, a woman asked, "How can you say that?" I understood. Her church was struggling. I sensed it. Empirically, things aren't looking good for the institutional church. "Christian" America is gone, and many of us grieve that loss. We're in dark, unfamiliar times. Rev. Dr. Chad Lakies starts this book by explaining how we got here.

But it's still a great time to be the church, because this is the church of Jesus Christ! Yes, we have challenges, but we're the church of the living Lord Jesus. The deciding question for the church today is this: Do we live by faith or by sight (2 Corinthians 5:7)? Faith centered on our risen, ascended, ruling, and soon-to-return Lord is faith that is optimistic about the church. Of course, we must also be realistic. Faith seeks understanding, as Anselm of Canterbury wrote. Unfamiliar times invite soul-searching—who are we? What is, or should be, our being in these times?

In these not-so-cozy times for the church in society, we can learn anew or for the very first time that our identity is in the Lord Jesus Christ. "It is no longer I who live, but Christ who lives in me. And the life I now live in the flesh I live by faith in the Son of God, who loved me and gave Himself for me" (Galatians 2:20).

In dark times, the church knows who we are, and we know where the light is! Jesus says, "I am the light of the world" (John 9:5). Note that He uses the present tense. Right now, as you read this, Jesus Himself is the light to guide and sustain us through these challenging times.

Perhaps we have focused so much upon the work of Christ in His first-century state of humiliation that we don't preach enough, teach enough, to center the piety of our people on Christ now ascended, now ruling and guiding all for the good of the church He has redeemed by His blood, and who will soon appear in glory to make all things fully right. Perhaps we have left people with the impression that the church is a museum of first-century artifacts, a Christ of history. We say Christ will come again, but how many Christians actually believe that in their workaday lives?

The ascended Lord is now with and over His church. "Jesus Christ . . . has gone into heaven and is at the right hand of God, with angels, authorities, and powers having been subjected to Him" (1 Peter 3:21–22). "He upholds the universe by the word of His power" (Hebrews 1:3). "He is before all things, and in Him all things hold together. And He is the head of the body" (Colossians 1:17–18). Present tense!

This reality of Jesus in our lives here and now changes how we act, and Lakies offers suggestions for how the church can live out that present-tense reality. As he writes in chapter 2: "When we live in a manner that aligns with what we say is important, only then will the world see a compelling public witness." Unfamiliar times compel us to recognize that we are called to be a peculiar, countercultural people. We followers of Jesus have an unprecedented opportunity in our lifetimes to offer a resilient witness to the light that shines in today's darkness.

There are signs of hope—if we'll see them. Younger followers of Jesus are bringing Christ into a context that may be unfamiliar to older people but is familiar to them. Equipping their witness is a rising generation of scholars, like Lakies, who are doing faithful theology for the mission of the church in this time. His very practical guidance in this book, all well-researched and documented, can shift our mindset from grief that the church is increasingly on the margins of society to confidence that the church is perfectly positioned to make a difference.

In post-Christendom America, we have a unique opportunity to teach people within and without the church how the love of Jesus forms us for life in our impersonal, uncaring, and often cruel society. A congregation flourishing in worship and witness will be a fellowship gathering around Jesus Christ, hearing Him speak about how to live now in this world as we anticipate His appearing. Our Lord Jesus is present in His church, but as our exalted, reigning Lord, He is also over us in the church. This means He continues to form and fashion us, as Lakies describes, to be people of confidence, humility, and patience in a pluralistic culture. That entails being more intentional about faith-motivated good works to people outside of the church, creating occasions to witness the hope that is in us (1 Peter 3:15). As Luther wrote:

> A Christian lives not in himself, but in Christ and in his neighbor. Otherwise he is not a Christian. He lives in Christ through faith, in his neighbor through love. By faith he is caught up beyond himself into God. By love he descends beneath himself into his neighbor. (*Luther's Works*, vol. 31, p. 371)

Historian Phyllis Tickle has written that every five hundred years, the institutional church holds a giant "rummage sale," when it "cleans out its attic." She writes:

> One of the hallmarks of the Church's semi-millennial rummage sales has always been that when each of the things was over and the dust had died down, Christianity would not only have readjusted itself, but it would also have grown and spread. Never has that principle been more operative than now.[1]

Five hundred years ago, the Reformation cleaned out medieval excesses and bequeathed to us *sola gratia, sola fide, sola Scriptura. How the Light Shines Through* points us to the necessity of Christ-centered faith and works, and with Jesus at the heart of all we do, resilient witness is guaranteed!

Dale A. Meyer
President emeritus, Concordia Seminary, St. Louis

---

1   Phyllis Tickle, *The Great Emergence: How Christianity Is Changing and Why* (Grand Rapids, MI: Baker, 2008), 19, 121.

The Loss You're Feeling Is Real

The world is changed. I feel it in the water.
I feel it in the earth. I smell it in the air.

The Lord of the Rings: The Fellowship of the Ring *(2001)*

These few words, spoken by the elf queen Galadriel at the start of an epic saga, capture what many of us feel as we look back over our lives. The world seems much different now than even a few decades ago. At times, we feel terrified about all of this; in other moments, exhilarated. Change often produces discomfort. We're forced to adjust. But we fit more easily into new realities when we're prepared in some way for the change. Perhaps we've learned something new to help mitigate the adjustment. Maybe we just have a flexible disposition.

Yet those adjustments tend to be increasingly difficult, if only because the world does not cease to change just so we can catch up. The overwhelming nature of how different things seem today than they did just a handful of decades ago often elicits a sense of nostalgia. We look back on some time in the past when things felt easier, when making those adjustments seemed to go so smoothly it was as if we did not have to adjust at all. We want to feel something like that again.

But nostalgia often views the past through rose-colored glasses; rarely do we remember it accurately. We allow ourselves to forget that there were likely just as many hard times in the past as we experience now. The new, more immediate challenges of today seem more difficult—ones we'd rather not endure. If we must endure anything, we'd prefer the old challenges we've successfully navigated. Those are the ones we feel prepared to face. Those are the ones we know how to approach, how to overcome.

Yet God has brought us to today. How do we inhabit this day, this moment in time? How do we face the realities of the present? Galadriel's words are not nostalgic. They are an announcement made as she and the rest of her world face a disconcertingly different reality than what they had known. And face it they must. So also for us.

First, then, we must do it all with the help of God. Second, we must remember that time is not prodding us along from behind, pushing us into these new times and new situations against our will. Rather, God Himself is pulling us forward into the future He has ordained for us. We are on a trajectory, and God is drawing us and all things to Himself. Still, it may be the case that our experience of God pulling us toward Himself feels like being dragged kicking and screaming into the future. The part of us that tends to lean on our own understanding (Proverbs 3:5) resists believing that it is God who has brought us to this new territory, placed us here, even created us for such a time as this: to echo Esther 4:14, God doesn't do things by accident.

We might confess all of this to be true, but our lives reveal that, deep down, we likely believe otherwise. Our habits, practices, routines, and even the way we talk tend to reflect our real attitudes and convictions. As we face this new frontier, we are indeed often nostalgic, but also fearful. Nothing is familiar. What tools do we use to navigate the terrain? Are we really capable of adjusting to this new reality?

AFTER CHRISTENDOM

Yet, what exactly has changed? I think the sense of what has changed, what we feel we've lost, what we look back on with nostalgia, can be captured in one word: Christendom. I want to be clear on what I mean here. Christendom has a long tail, reaching back through history to the fourth century, during which the Roman emperor Constantine issued the Edict of Milan in AD 313, effectively legalizing Christianity in the Roman Empire and ending the persecution the church had endured for three centuries. While the Edict of Milan was a significant turning point, a more important one for our purposes came about half a century later in AD 380. The Edict of Thessalonica made Christianity the official religion of the Roman Empire. Christendom, then, is the coming together and intermingling of church and state.[1]

---

1   I should clarify what I mean when I say that Christianity became the official religion of the Roman Empire following the Edict of Thessalonica. The relationship between religion and the state in premodern society is difficult for modern minds to grasp. When the Edicts of Milan and Thessalonica were issued, religion and government always commingled. This was the way of things in premodern society. For example, Roman emperors, among many others across different civilizations, were considered divine, valorized as gods. It is more accurate to say that the Edict of Thessalonica made a certain version of Christianity (the one authorized by the Council of Nicaea in AD 325, from which we receive the Nicene Creed) the official version within the Roman Empire. Other versions of Christianity, then, became not only heretical in the eyes of the church but also illegal in the eyes of the state and thus punishable. While other religions existed, over time, Christianity became the established religion of the Roman Empire because it was so deeply intertwined with the state through the conversion of its leadership and the influence of Christian leaders upon those who ruled.

For the last seventeen hundred years, Christianity has had a close relationship with state power in the Western world. This is what is meant by *Christendom*. Some scholars use the term *coextensive* to describe the relationship, suggesting that the church and the state have long been mutually legitimating each other.

Yet the relationship between church and state in the West has begun to deteriorate over the last few centuries. Many shifts in Western culture have weakened the ties between church and state, effectively weakening the church's influence in society, while the influence of state or government has increased. Since the middle of the twentieth century, even as the church in North America experienced its highest membership, religion has held less and less sway. As religious influence decreased, we experienced a rise in so-called hostility against religion.

Today, we live *after* Christendom. Some define our era as post-Christian. While there are good things about the decoupling of church and state—a separation and a recognition that the church and state operate as two unique kingdoms with distinct tasks given by God is one of Martin Luther's great contributions to Western Christianity—there are also lamentable changes. Primarily, as society no longer identifies closely with religion, Christianity has become merely one option among many others. Religious influence and the voices of religious leaders in the lives of citizens are but a whisper and thus easily ignorable. The effects of consumer capitalism subtly distract us from religion, such that Christianity is caught in a clash of competing allegiances, each vying for attention and commitment. The comfort of an affluent society makes people less concerned about spiritual things, spurring a growing sense of apathy about faith (and many other religious sensibilities).

POST-CHRISTENDOM AS LOSS

Another significant consequence of the slow disappearance of Christendom is that ministry seems more difficult than it used to be. We don't feel adequately prepared to do ministry in the changed world Galadriel describes. The new challenges can be overwhelming, especially for those of us who have been in ministry for a while. We seem to be spinning our wheels. The harder we try, the more burned out we become. Writer Andrew Root says that it often feels like we're trying to minister to people who don't need a god.[2] Perhaps the best way to describe the nostalgia stirred by the challenges of modern ministry is that we feel a deep sense of loss. We can describe that loss in several ways.

First, we experience the loss of the way things were. We have lost a familiar context and environment in which to do ministry. There were times when we had the right tools, times when our tactics and strategies were effective. Conversations about faith were warmly received. People regularly showed up to Sunday worship. The Judeo-Christian worldview, and its sense of moral norms, was widely shared, even by those who didn't follow Jesus. Yet none of these experiences can be expected any longer. And we feel their loss like a heavy weight that drags us down.

The second way we experience loss is more subtle but perhaps more powerful: we feel as if something has been taken from us. The previous paragraph lists mainly matters of historical experience, which implies that something must have happened to make that former reality fade away. As humans, we often want to understand why something happened. Even more, we want to know why it

---

2   See Andrew Root, *The Pastor in a Secular Age: Ministry to People Who No Longer Need a God* (Grand Rapids, MI: Baker Academic, 2019).

happened the way it did. Knowing this helps us make sense of things and find a path forward. For example, when we try something new and fail, it's healthy to want to know why so we can improve on our efforts and avoid repeating the same mistakes. But that's not the approach we usually take with this issue.

When we ask why the comparatively Christian culture of the past eludes us, we tend to imagine that some entity is responsible for the loss of a situation we once enjoyed. It has been taken from us, we think. And so along with the feeling of loss come other emotions: anger, frustration, outrage, resentment.

Sociologist James Davison Hunter borrows the French term *ressentiment* to capture all of those feelings in one word. *Ressentiment*, he says, includes what we "in the English-speaking world mean by resentment, but it also involves a combination of anger, envy, hate, rage, and revenge."[3] There are also felt elements of disrespect and humiliation that amplify the other emotions since these are especially felt when one is in the losing position. Hunter goes on to suggest that *ressentiment* is never just a feeling or sentiment; it is always attached to and expressed according to a story. When we feel wronged in some way, whether the injury is real or perceived, we use narratives to frame our *ressentiment*.

When we frame our sense of loss in this way, that something has been taken from us, we start to imagine what we must do to recover what we had. Perhaps we'll seek some kind of justice. Perhaps we'll try to remove from power those we hold responsible for eclipsing the cultural situation that once existed in which ministry was easier and our influence more respected and broadly shared. Perhaps we'll seek

---

3   James Davison Hunter, *To Change the World: The Irony, Tragedy, and Possibility of Christianity in the Late Modern World* (Oxford: Oxford University Press, 2010), 107. Copyright © 2010 Oxford University Press, Inc. Reproduced with permission of the Licensor through PLSclear.

vindication with vitriol. Our narrative of loss might even morph in a way that generates fear—fear that we have more to lose and that there is a "them" trying to eradicate "us" and take away our way of life. We will then need a plan for how to protect ourselves. Perhaps this will mean rooting out the perceived rot from within, those who claim to be part of "us" but who really don't belong. Or we might find ways to malign the character of outsiders to the extent that we believe violence against them is justified.

There are two things to note from Hunter's discussion of loss and the *ressentiment* it elicits. First, storytelling has the power to unite people under a shared sense of identity and belonging because they collectively feel like victims. It is always powerful to know that we are not alone in our experiences. Social groups are easily bound together by shared interests (e.g., fans of the Detroit Lions or model train enthusiasts) but even more so by shared experience. Especially if the experience is some kind of pain—and Hunter suggests we experience loss *as* injury—the bond is immediately deeper because those who share it carry similar scars.

Second, if the story we tell about our loss *as* injury enables us to imagine possibilities for recovering what has been lost, then our emotional response to the loss—our *ressentiment*—will affect how we react to the new situation. If something is merely lost, we want to try to find it. But if something is taken from us, we want to get it back. And we might fear that something else could be taken. Both responses are almost instinctual. We have behaved this way since we were children. If we believe that our ministry context has been actively and aggressively taken from us, it's easy to see how our reaction will be either equally aggressive, deeply fearful, or some combination of the two.

VALIDATION AND WARNING

Before we go any further, it's important to understand the point of the previous section. My intent here is simply to acknowledge this sense of loss. It is true that things have changed; it is not as easy to do ministry or live as a Christian in these dark and precarious times. The feelings that attend our sense of loss—the anger, frustration, outrage, envy, humiliation, disrespect, nostalgia—are valid and legitimate. They are to be expected. They are normal. And they are indeed widely shared. You are not alone in feeling this way. You are not entirely in control of the feelings either. They can surprise us, appearing when we don't expect them. At other times, they lurk in the background in ways we can't articulate. It is not bad or wrong to feel *ressentiment* because of the loss we have experienced.

Still, our *responses* and our *reactions* to our emotions are critical. We have agency over our response to emotions in a way that is not quite true of the feelings themselves. Scripture teaches that feelings are untrustworthy. As we live drenched in cultural messages encouraging us to "follow your heart," "do what feels right," and "be true to yourself," we're wise to distrust our feelings at least somewhat. The prophet Jeremiah warns, "The heart is deceitful above all things, and desperately sick; who can understand it?" (Jeremiah 17:9). While the feelings might erupt unexpectedly, how we react is on us.

The consequences of those reactions are most important for the argument of this book. Since the very beginnings of the church, Christians have been observed by outsiders. What outsiders see, their interactions with individual Christians and their experiences with the church at large, constitutes our public Christian witness. We are in the eyes of the world what we have been before the eyes of the world. Our witness is never not on display. In situations where we feel afraid of or injured by others, our reactions matter intensely for our witness. Will people meet Jesus in us if we aggressively respond in kind to the threats we feel? Or are they more likely to meet Jesus in us if we patiently endure the challenges set before us, constantly leaning back in reliance upon Him? Despite how we might be feeling—whether threatened, fearful, or angry—Scripture regularly exhorts us to trust not in our own selves, our own feelings, or our own plans. Instead, Scripture calls us to put our trust in the Lord.

GOD'S PREFERENCE
FOR A WINSOME WITNESS

Concern for the quality of our witness is easily visible in Scripture and the life of the early church. We'll say more about this in later chapters, but at the very least, the New Testament writers make it clear that God prefers a positive, winsome witness. Paul advises the Colossians to "let your speech always be gracious" (Colossians 4:6), and Peter encourages us at length, saying,

> Who is going to harm you if you are eager to do good? But even if you should suffer for what is right, you are blessed. "Do not fear their threats; do not be frightened." But in your hearts revere Christ as Lord. Always be prepared to give an answer to everyone who asks you to give the reason for the hope that you have. *But do this with gentleness and respect, keeping a clear conscience, so that those who speak maliciously against your good behavior in Christ may be ashamed of their slander. For it is better, if it is God's will, to*

> suffer for doing good than for doing evil. (1 Peter
> 3:13–17, NIV, emphasis added)

How people perceive us matters. The New Testament writers continually encourage us to do right by others. Outsiders may still react negatively, but we will maintain our internal sense of having done right according to God's guidance.

The fruit of a winsome witness is increased trust in Christians and the church. And with God's help, more are added to the kingdom of God. While it is the Holy Spirit who generates faith in every person who comes to trust in Jesus, God has chosen to use human relationships built on trust to introduce people to Jesus. None of us who claim to be followers of Jesus has experienced coming to know Him without the intervention of another person (and often many people). This is God's chosen means for Kingdom expansion. Thus, the character of our witness makes possible our ability to "walk in wisdom toward outsiders, making the best use of the time" (Colossians 4:5), such that we can take advantage of opportunities to share the Good News with others.

Regardless of how our cultural position as Christians has changed, consider the life and times of the people to whom Peter and Paul wrote. Centuries before the Edicts of Milan and Thessalonica, Christians in the Roman Empire were marginalized and persecuted. The encouragement and exhortations offered by Peter and Paul always directed those Christians to a posture of winsome witness. The early church fathers wrote similar letters and exhorted the first three centuries of the church to be patient.[4] These exhortations turned out to be remarkably helpful for the growth of the early church. And perhaps we should also note that they were necessary

---

4   See Alan Kreider, *The Patient Ferment of the Early Church: The Improbable Rise of Christianity in the Roman Empire* (Grand Rapids, MI: Baker Academic, 2016).

to curb the common temptations to run away or to react in kind to the persecution they were experiencing. After all, Jesus would not have had to tell us to turn the other cheek or to love our enemies if doing so were part of our natural inclination.

THE PLAN FROM HERE

As we move into part 1 of this book, the first chapter will explore the dangers of responding to our sense of loss and *ressentiment* according to our natural inclinations. The final chapter in part 1 will give a brief account of our so-called secular age, attempting to put a name to what our feelings tell us about this world and how much it has changed.

Part 2 will address various challenges the church faces as we attempt to navigate the new contours of our secular age. First, we will tackle some of our human tendencies that lead to the fractured, splintered, and polarized social dynamics that define our time. We'll learn some strategies to help us be more like Jesus, who never let an issue prevent a relationship. Second, we'll engage in a challenging discussion of hospitality, seeking to live better as the Body of Christ in a world full of others and enemies. Third, we'll examine the common effort to "find oneself" and live authentically, seeking to explain what we're really trying to find when we are trying to find ourselves and how the church offers a story that all of us can confidently live by. Fourth, we'll dig deep into the rise of concerns about identity and explore a better starting point for such conversations. Finally, we'll seek direction together on how to reach out in a secular age, focusing on looking for the cracks in the secular that let the light of God's presence and the Gospel shine through.

In part 3, we'll return to the earlier exhortations that aim the church toward a winsome witness. The final three chapters will help us take note of the reputation of the early church as a means of inspiring us to see what's possible for the church today.

RECURRENCES

Throughout this book, we will bump into a common cast of characters. They are the thinkers I reference most, the giants whose shoulders I stand on. I find wisdom in their work that applies to many situations. Rather than use a wide variety of voices, I will engage some of the same thinkers repeatedly to create continuity (and a more accessible starting point for those who'd like to read further). One such voice is James Davison Hunter, whom we already met in this chapter. Others include Charles Taylor, Yuval Levin, Dietrich Bonhoeffer, Alan Jacobs, Jonathan Haidt, John Inazu, and Luke Bretherton. I am thankful for what I've learned from them and commend them to you for further engagement.

We will also keep bumping into an ecclesiology in a nutshell— that is, a brief doctrine of the church—that I often use to help us understand the role of the church in a secular age and why a winsome witness is vital. We'll explore this more fully in later chapters, but it goes basically like this:

- Dietrich Bonhoeffer called Jesus Christ "the man for others."

- Paul said, "It is no longer I who live, but Christ who lives in me" (Galatians 2:20).

+ If Jesus is the man for others and His disciples are those in whom the man for others lives, then that makes us—the church—a people *for* others.

+ The church, then, Bonhoeffer said, is "Christ existing as church-community." Or as he put it elsewhere, "The church is nothing but that piece of humanity where Christ really has taken form."[5]

If the community called the church is the very means by which God has chosen to make Himself known in the world, then the world will meet Jesus in us. This requires us to trust in God, build trust with others, rely on the Holy Spirit to prepare hearts, and winsomely spread the seeds of the Gospel on good soil, beginning with people we know, one by one. There is nothing fancy, innovative, or flashy about any of this. This is how it has always been. While the world around us has changed, everything I've written here is meant to help the church accomplish its original goals (Acts 1:8; Matthew 28:18–20) in a manner that is sensitive to today's cultural context. I hope that you find help here for this task. Whether you're an interested layperson who feels a sense of urgency to share the Good News, a student in a professional church-worker program preparing to serve and lead God's people, a parent or grandparent who wants to better engage your children or grandchildren with the Gospel, a church worker seeking to lead as faithfully as possible, or

---

5   See Dietrich Bonhoeffer, *Letters and Papers from Prison*, vol. 8 of *Dietrich Bonhoeffer Works*, ed. John de Gruchy (Minneapolis: Fortress, 2009), 501; Bonhoeffer, *Sanctorum Communio: A Theological Study of the Sociology of the Church*, vol. 1 of *Dietrich Bonhoeffer Works*, trans. Reinhard Krauss and Nancy Lukens (Minneapolis: Fortress, 1998), 121; Bonhoeffer, *Ethics*, vol. 6 of *Dietrich Bonhoeffer Works*, ed. Clifford Green (Minneapolis: Fortress Press, 2005), 97.

any other role you might play in the Kingdom, may the Lord use you to faithfully introduce Jesus to those around you.

To God be the glory.

REFLECTION QUESTIONS

1. In what ways has the relationship between church and state changed in your lifetime?

2. How have your country, state, and church reacted to the changing times?

3. As an individual, how have you experienced a community of *ressentiment?*

4. Describe someone you know or have known who has a winsome witness. What characteristics did that person display?

PART 1

The Church in Dark and Unfamiliar Times

CHAPTER 1

Unintentional

Eclipsing the Gospel and the Church's Vocation

I've been playing drums since I was young. When I was in high school, I joined the marching band. My skills advanced more over those four years than at any other time in my life, in part because of my instructor, but mostly because half of each rehearsal was spent on basic drumming exercises. I realized that the right technique allows you to play faster and more accurately, and relaxing is a key to both.

Drumming is a highly physical activity, so if you've never played drums before, you might imagine it requires a lot of tension to control your body and accomplish playing a beat or particular licks. I've taught a few younger players over the years. Sometimes people would visit my home and want to sit down at my drums and try out a few things. They all had the same idea I used to have—that to control yourself and play well, you need to keep your body, and particularly your arms and hands, rigid.

Now, no one had ever taught any of us this. It's unlikely any of us could have articulated this assumption out loud. It's just that, when we started trying to play drums, our bodies automatically took on a tense posture. Through four years of constant exercises and slight adjustments from my instructor about posture and grip, I learned that not only were my previous assumptions wrong, but they prevented me from playing at my best. My body had to unlearn bad habits before I could improve. Whenever I could share this insight with those few students I worked with, they, too, seemed to experience it as a kind of revelation.

In this chapter, I want to serve readers in a similar way. I take it for granted that if you are reading this book, you want to faithfully live and serve in the kingdom of God and make an impact in the world through the power of the Gospel in the lives of people who don't know Jesus. What I will discuss below might feel like learning the same kinds of difficult lessons I had to learn about my own drumming. I had all the wrong assumptions about how to play well, and they prevented my improvement and sometimes led to my drumming poorly. Learning those difficult lessons forced me to adjust and do something different. It was hard to believe those adjustments would lead to improvement, but the proof was in the experience.

The church seems to believe several things about how we should respond to this new time in which we are experiencing loss and feeling *ressentiment*. But these beliefs are preventing us from achieving our true goals, and we end up hurting our own witness. I believe that by knowing clearly what *not* to do, we are better empowered to do what we *ought* to do. This chapter will help us unlearn what hinders us so we can start to imagine better ways to respond.

SCANDAL AND DISTRUST

Since the 1990s, the United States has witnessed a series of high-publicity scandals within the church—from the sexual abuse and pedophilia accusations affecting the Roman Catholic Church to the mishandling of finances and power, rampant emotional and sexual abuse, and marital impropriety in many other church bodies. The actions of many high-profile ministers and leaders have brought great public disdain toward the church.

Churches and Christians are experiencing the lowest level of social trust in nearly a century. The Gallup organization has been polling Americans across a wide variety of issues for decades. In 2022, their research showed that confidence in the institution of the church was at its lowest level since polling on this question began in 1973.[1]

While it's safe to say that social confidence in the church has been deeply damaged by scandals of many sorts, they are not the only reason. Social trust for the church is also affected by how the church responds to the challenges of our new social landscape. The church's reactions to losing its previously prominent social position have contributed to the decline in social confidence.

In this chapter, I will highlight three different ways the church tends to react to its current situation and describe how those reactions undercut the church's witness, damaging public perception and preventing social confidence in the church as an institution. With each reaction, the church is actively trying to stop the decline in membership and recover something of the cultural prominence it used to have. They have each made the church's situation worse. The three reactions are relevance, resignation, and resistance.

The sooner we realize the inherent problems in these reactions, the sooner we can avoid them.

---

1   "Confidence in Institutions," Gallup, https://news.gallup.com/poll/1597/confidence-institutions.aspx (accessed September 9, 2022).

TO BE RELEVANT AGAIN

It stands to reason that if confidence is down, church leaders would want to do whatever it takes to get people to sit up and pay attention to the church again. They believe in the church's mission and that the church has much good to offer to the wider society. The Gospel message of God's saving action in our lives through Jesus Christ is always relevant. Similarly, that God provides our daily bread—and not just ours but everyone's—is a timeless truth. We could argue that there's no reason for the church to *seek* relevance because our mission of proclaiming the truth is never *not* relevant. However, seeing as the church cannot proclaim that message without hearers, we expend additional effort to gain those hearers, to attract listeners who might become followers of Jesus.

Attention is difficult to cultivate in our time. We're constantly distracted by various bids for our attention. Church leaders work hard to win the competition for attention, to draw eyes to the Good News of the kingdom of God.[2] It is often here that seeking relevance inadvertently becomes troublesome.

New programming or practical messages, modern worship styles or the embrace of mystery within ancient traditions and liturgies, even hip and stylish aesthetics in fashion, architecture, and media—these are just a few of the ways churches and church leaders seek to stand out, to be relevant and noteworthy, and therefore to be heard. Even more, churches often end up competing with other

2   Achieving attention through efforts to appear relevant can be exhausting for church leaders. Andrew Root has written helpfully on that topic, noting how many churches are caught up in an effort to provide resources for people who have busy lives. The effort becomes something like living with a machine that always needs to be fed, leading to anxiety, burnout, and depression in leaders. See Andrew Root, *The Congregation in a Secular Age: Keeping Sacred Time against the Speed of Modern Life* (Grand Rapids, MI: Baker Academic, 2021).

local churches, seeking to gain the largest audience. The churches and ministries that are most successful at gaining attention tend to stand as models for others.

Scholar Andreas Reckwitz writes about what he calls our "society of singularities."[3] Singularities are those events, places, people, institutions, goods, or images that our society collectively recognizes as important and worth our attention. Singularities come and go, rise and fall for many reasons. But Reckwitz gives name to our efforts as churches and church leaders to make our church, our ministry, even ourselves attractive and thus relevant: we're trying to be singularities, to have the ineffable quality that characterizes "the Most Interesting Man in the World," made famous as a fictional celebrity in Dos Equis commercials. Whatever it is that makes him interesting, that's what we want.

To be a singularity is to have *it*—whatever *it* is, we seem to know it when we see it. According to Reckwitz, whoever has *it* has an audience. He illuminates this for us when he says, "In the mode of singularization, life is not simply lived; it is curated. From one situation to the next, the late-modern [person/church] *performs* his or her [or its] particular self to others, who become an audience, and this self will not be found attractive unless it seems authentic."[4] For Reckwitz, the attractive and the authentic are effectively synonymous. Thus, when we say "relevant," we often mean "authentic."

For the church, what are the consequences of chasing relevance, of seeking to be a singularity? We end up captive to cultural practices that ultimately undercut our efforts to proclaim the Good News. Despite our motivations to introduce people to Jesus, in practice,

---

3   See Andreas Reckwitz, *The Society of Singularities*, trans. Valentine A. Pakis (Medford, MA: Polity Press, 2000).

4   Reckwitz, *The Society of Singularities*, 3. Emphasis in original.

such concerns become secondary. What people primarily experience from us are the efforts to stand out, to appear relevant, to attract an audience. Eclipsed is the Gospel, the Good News of the kingdom of God for sinners, even when it's proclaimed plainly. The pomp and flash of the delivery, the environment, and the experience all overwhelm the senses, drawing so much attention that the Gospel proclamation goes unnoticed.

In aiming for relevance, the church and its leaders can easily become indistinguishable from many other institutions in our society. This is because the competition for attention leads to competition for an audience. Once we have people's attention, we vie to gain and retain their commitment and allegiance. Gaining an audience is treated as an end in itself, separate from the reason an audience is desired in the first place. The church is unwittingly caught up in all of this.

Yuval Levin, one of our recurring thinkers, helpfully describes the situation when he talks about how many people who occupy public office seem—if you keep up with their social media feeds and major news appearances—to spend a significant amount of time doing something less akin to their actual institutional job and more like performing a particular part in the theater of public politics. Instead of serving the institutions and their needs, politicians, along with journalists, educators, scientists, athletes, artists, leaders of major companies, and even ministers of religion, seem to focus on building a personal brand by leveraging their position as if it's a platform for their voice and personality. Levin points out that, in general, when these individuals raise their voices, they speak in a way that signals their allegiances in the cultural and political battles happening across our society. They're happy to lend their voice of support to the current cultural orthodoxy people are arguing about, taking a side and encouraging their followers to join them.[5]

This extends to the church. Levin is deeply concerned that Christian leaders are leveraging the institution of the church solely as a platform for their own self-promotion, for building their personal brand, for seeking the status of "singularity." Because of this, people have started to view familiar public institutions differently. Rather than molds that shape their members, institutions are being used as platforms to amplify certain voices and display certain personalities. And since this is happening within virtually every institution across society, Levin suggests that each institution is losing its distinction. Any given institution begins to look like every other, each presenting as yet another metaphorical podium from which those voices and personalities can announce their position in our cultural and political battles, joining in the fight.

There are serious consequences when institutions become platforms instead of molds. Institutions, Levin argues, are being undermined by the very people who lead them. He highlights two outcomes that occur when institutions are used as platforms. First, those outside of the institution—those who engage its services or observe its work—stop respecting the institution because it fails at its own goals when it merely serves the self-promotional efforts of its most significant leaders. Second, those who have roles in or are members of the institution lose sight of what it means to serve an institution, with its boundaries and ethos that shape a certain way of being and thus form people to accomplish the institution's goals.[6]

---

5   Yuval Levin, *A Time to Build: From Family and Community to Congress and the Campus, How Recommitting to Our Institutions Can Revive the American Dream* (New York: Basic Books, 2020), 35.

6   Levin, *A Time to Build*, 36.

The church, then, becomes indistinguishable from most other institutions. Those who allegedly serve the church come to be seen as people who use the church to serve themselves. Granted, this is not everyone, perhaps not even most servants of the church. But the misguided efforts of the few drastically impact the social consequences for the many. The result is a damaged public perception and the loss of public trust. Ultimately, the church's push for relevance ends up generating significant distrust, all while ostensibly seeking to gain a hearing for the Gospel.

As a reaction to the loss of a prominent role and voice of influence in society, seeking relevance might initially seem to be the logical avenue for increasing engagement and reaching more people with the Good News. Intuitively, it seems as if this would lead to recovering or reestablishing in some way the prominence the church has lost. But the exact opposite tends to be the outcome.

When the church is merely a platform and when church leaders are merely trying to attract an audience, the primary message and purpose of the church is obscured. The church appears as merely a reflection of the many other institutions that exist in our society. When there's no difference, there's no reason to pay attention. Social trust continues to decline, the loss we experience and the *ressentiment* it elicits are exacerbated, and the reactionary effort to stem the loss only causes further damage and pain, leaving the church and its servants more deeply mired in the conditions we sought to escape.

RESIGNATION: THE OPPOSITE OF AIMING FOR RELEVANCE

If seeking relevance is a problem because it eclipses the Gospel, the opposite problem is when the church resigns itself to the decline in participation, attendance, and social influence.

The first step toward resignation, unwitting as it may be, often comes through complacency. More than once when my family and I have visited churches, looking for a place to worship after moving to a new area, we have had the experience of feeling unwelcome. We've ended up departing after the service without having been engaged by a single person the entire time. While likely unintentional, we got the impression that everyone was "all set"—they had their friends and seemed uninterested in welcoming guests or making new friends at church. Experiences like this, if common, generate for visitors a negative perception of the church and puts a church at risk of stagnation in terms of Kingdom growth. If this posture toward visitors becomes a habit, it will not only be harder for the church to overcome but will also make it easier to resign to shrinkage when it occurs.

Complacency also leads to resignation when people notice an issue like decline and recognize that it's not good but don't believe it is *their* problem. In fact, recent research has shown that in the last quarter century, Christians in America have less and less readily identified sharing their faith as part of their calling as members of the royal priesthood.[7] Rather, American Christians seem to think this work belongs to the institutional leaders of the church—the professionals—and not to those included in the priesthood of all believers. As the thinking might go, if the decline of the church is not my problem, I don't have to do anything about it. And when a problem is someone else's, I can easily become complacent about it, even to the point of eventually ignoring it altogether. We may end up resigning ourselves to decline because we don't think we are able to address the concern in a meaningful way.

---

7   See the report *Spiritual Conversations in the Digital Age: How Christians' Approach to Sharing Their Faith Has Changed in 25 Years* (Ventura, CA: Barna Group, 2018).

Resignation can also take a more insidious form, one that, in essence, denies that decline is a problem at all.

Theologian Oswald Bayer has an excellent little book on the idea of justification—a central theme within Protestant churches. Bayer begins the book by examining a common feature of fallen humans: the need for justification. He gets going creatively with that analysis by pointing out that justification is a feature of our everyday interactions.[8]

He pictures it like this: Someone challenges us about why we said or did something (or neglected to do or say something). Perhaps they wonder aloud why we didn't do otherwise, presumably signaling there was a better, wiser thing we should have done. This kind of confrontation demands an answer. Most often, we try to defend ourselves, and not just defend ourselves but make ourselves appear to have done or said the right thing. Critical for Bayer is the observation that we simply want to be "right"; we want the confrontation to turn back on the accuser, effectively undoing the accusation itself. If we're successful, we make ourselves out to be right and reveal that the accuser has no grounds for making the accusation.

From our earliest days, we start practicing techniques for justifying ourselves—showing ourselves to be right. As small children, it starts off with blaming others, such as our siblings or classmates. "I didn't do it. He did it." We also quickly learn to lie, or at least bend the truth far enough to make our actions seem good and in line with expectations. As we get older, our tactics for justifying ourselves get more complicated and effective.

---

8   Oswald Bayer, *Living by Faith: Justification and Sanctification* (Grand Rapids, MI: Eerdmans, 2003), 1.

If every human is good at it, I suggest that Christians—particularly those with substantial training in the study of Scripture and theology—are better at it than most everyone else. We are the ones who ostensibly know what God expects of us. And we can use and abuse that knowledge, along with our knowledge of what the Bible says and the applications of sophisticated theological arguments, to demonstrate that not only are we right, but we are also morally upright and holy according to Christian standards.

It is this sort of argumentation that comes into play when the church resigns to the fact that it is shrinking in the various ways noted above. The argument tends to go like this: There may be fewer and fewer people who are attending worship and actively participating in the life of this congregation, but that's only because those who are here are the true faithful. Those who no longer attend church with us were probably not real Christians anyway. We are the faithful remnant.

For lack of a better term, let's call this remnant theology. Don't let the language confuse you, however. We're not discussing a remnant in the sense of God's people returning from exile, like we see in the book of Nehemiah. Rather, we're discussing an insidious theological justification from God's people, and particularly its leadership, for ignoring the church's mission to proclaim the arrival of the kingdom of God and call to repentance those who have ears to hear.

Let's look more closely at this remnant theology. Resigning ourselves to decline signals a disconnect with the urgency of the church's call to share the Gospel and make disciples. Practically speaking, fewer people in churches means fewer bodies to manage congregational life and fewer dollars flowing into the church's budget to keep the lights on and pay the salaries of church workers. Despite all this, the decline is reframed and characterized as a good thing. And not just any kind of good thing, but a theologically good thing—a phenomenon that supposedly reveals a congregation's faithfulness most directly.

The issue here is not whether a declining congregation is faithful. It may or may not be, and that is for God to judge. Rather, the problem occurs when it is argued that such shrinkage is a positive thing. To defend this phenomenon is at odds with the church's mission. To understand why, and to get a sense of just how sophisticated we fallen humans can get when it comes to defending ourselves, we need to consider one of Luther's earliest arguments.

Luther made a distinction between a theology of the cross and a theology of glory. This distinction appears in several places throughout his work, but it is most famously found in his Heidelberg Disputation of 1518.

The theology of glory is all about success and growth, "winning" at the Christian life, experiencing God's favor. God is presumed to be responsible for all these things, but Luther pointed out that this theology of glory has no place for suffering. In a theology of glory, God is seen as a champion on the side of sinners; once we become disciples, all things will go well for us. Even if we have a bad experience or two, it will only last for a moment because God will do something about it. Of course, the real trouble comes when those moments of suffering extend longer than anticipated. At that point, we might begin questioning the sufficiency of our faith. Do I really believe? Am I believing hard enough? God Himself is called into question. Does He really exist and is He really good? And if so, is He really powerful enough to deal with this situation?

By contrast, there is the theology of the cross. There is no winning here, for the true nature of taking up one's cross and following

Jesus means the very opposite—that we are beggars burdened by our sins and failures, desperately in need of a Savior. We cast our future upon the suffering of another, Jesus, who bore the burden of our sins on His own cross, dying for them yet emerging victorious from the empty tomb.

Suffering has a place of prominence in the theology of the cross because suffering constitutes the Christian life of repentance. No one likes to admit they are sinners, but this is bad news about ourselves that we must nevertheless accept. We see the theology of the cross in Paul's confession about the "thorn" in his side, which he had asked God to remove several times. Yet God did not act to do so, saying to Paul, "My grace is sufficient for you" (2 Corinthians 12:7, 9). We see Job respond similarly. Despite all the suffering that came his way, Job's faith did not wane, and he nevertheless proclaimed, "I know that my Redeemer lives" (Job 19:25).

And paradigmatically, Jesus Christ did not come as some kind of philosopher-king who kicked out the Romans from occupying Israel's territory to establish His reign according to worldly standards. The way the Messiah came did not meet the expectations of God's people. Instead, He came quietly to people who did not know Him or accept Him, and His reign was established by His being killed, raised from the dead, and seated at God the Father's right hand (Acts 2:36).

The theology of the cross rightly reveals that our suffering is hidden in Christ. The theology of glory, on the other hand, cannot fathom suffering. We can use Luther's distinction to analyze what remnant theology argues—that decline and shrinkage is a mechanism for revealing the faithful, the remnant in which the true Body of Christ is known. Remnant theology makes a sophisticated argument that ultimately suggests that churches experiencing growth do not matter (contra the entire book of Acts, which indicates that church growth does matter). Rather, it is the shrinking church that reveals what it means to win at the Christian life. To be in decline, it is argued, indicates God's work of whittling down church membership to the truly faithful.

We must identify what this argument really amounts to: taking a form of suffering (decline in participation, shrinking in congregational size and Christian social influence) and arguing as if we know God's true motivation and therefore reinterpreting something bad as something good. Yet Luther said in his Heidelberg Disputation that only "a theologian of glory calls evil good and good evil" (Thesis 21). He continues, arguing that humans are mistaken when we claim to perceive what God is actually up to, saying, "That wisdom which sees the invisible things of God in works as perceived by man is completely puffed up, blinded, and hardened" (Thesis 22).[9] Humans cannot fully know why things happen. As Isaiah clearly teaches us, God's ways and thoughts are higher than our own (Isaiah 55:8–9).

In contrast to a theologian of glory, "a theologian of the cross calls the thing what it actually is" (Thesis 21). It's time to call remnant theology what it actually is. It is a heresy that demands repentance. In the language of Luther's distinction, it is a version of the theology of glory. That is, it confidently interprets the church's suffering as a sign of God's favor. But such confidence is merely speculation. We do not know the mind of God, after all. This speculation, then, is no more than a sophisticated move of self-justification. If I argue that my declining church reveals God's favor for us, the obvious conclusion is that my leadership must be exactly right, so I'm going to keep doing what I've been doing. Resignation to the

---

9   *Luther's Works*, vol. 31, pp. 40–41.

church's decline in this manner is simply unfaithful. We cannot defend decline when the church's very calling is to "go . . . and make disciples of all nations" and to proclaim the Gospel "to the end of the earth" (Matthew 28:19; Acts 1:8).

RESISTANCE:
THE CHURCH IN FIGHT MODE

The third common response to the church's new situation—marginalized, shrinking, with minimal social influence—is to mobilize against the perceived cause of our present circumstances.

Journalist Mónica Guzmán tells the story of the ongoing interaction she has with her parents. Guzmán describes herself as a progressive, liberal person. Her parents, on the other hand, are conservative. There is a great deal of discussion in both our country and our church about the differences between people who identify using these categories. A cartoon in *The New Yorker* depicts a father telling his son that he and his wife are separating because he wants what's best for the country but the child's mother, who sits disgruntled on the other side of the room, does not.[10] The cartoon captures well what is happening to many relationships across our society. They are breaking down because of disagreements over things people hold sacred, and such things are often political.

While Guzmán often vehemently disagrees with her parents (and they with her), her story is surprising because she finds it implausible that their association with one another would be called into question because of disagreements. There is no chance the relationship would break down because they cannot agree. Far from

---

10   Frank Cotham, "A Father Explains to His Son," *The New Yorker*, August 15, 2011, https://www.newyorker.com/cartoon/a15905 (accessed April 15, 2024).

it. Guzmán deeply enjoys and values her familial relationships, especially with her parents. And despite the disagreements, she exudes a deep sense of joy about what she learns in conversation with them.[11] The differences between them tend to make her more curious, prompting her to ask questions and dig deeper to better understand their alternative perspectives. Perhaps it's her journalistic instincts, but rather than shy away, she leans in to learn more.

We're not used to this kind of behavior. We're more likely to resonate with *The New Yorker* cartoon and the tendency to break relationships because of disagreement. In fact, we're so used to the fracturing, splintering, and fighting over our differences that we seem to have lost sight of why we're divided at all. As Levin aptly puts it, "'The list of controversies is endless, but the parties to them are remarkably constant and durable. Individually, these fights sometimes touch on genuinely vital questions. Yet seen together they appear as a vast sociopolitical psychosis. They are all one fight, *and the fight is the point.*"[12] Perhaps the "fight is the point" because, as we'll discuss further in chapter 3, having something or someone to be against binds us together with others in solidarity and thus offers us a strong sense of identity and belonging.

For conservative Christian churches that feel under threat, that feel the sense that not only have they lost something but that there are forces at work actively trying to take something away, the fight tends to take a particular shape. James Davison black helpfully describes what this looks like for conservative or right-leaning churches.[13] He observes that such churches tend to see the problem

---

11   Mónica Guzmán, *I Never Thought of It That Way: How to Have Fearlessly Curious Conversations in Dangerously Divided Times* (Dallas: BenBella, 2022).

12   Levin, "How to Curb the Culture War," *Comment Magazine* 40, no. 2 (Spring 2022): 7–17. Emphasis mine.

13   James Davison Hunter, *To Change the World: The Irony, Tragedy, and Possibility*

in general terms, referring to it as "secularization." Secularization refers to the bygone academic argument that as a society modernizes, antiquated things like religion will slowly decline and disappear altogether. Most thinkers who thought secularization would happen have recanted.[14] In fact, they observe, Western societies are as religious as ever. However, the language of secularization is still useful for Christians because their churches continue to experience decline in numbers and influence. For them, this *is* secularization. Their experience sometimes includes feeling a sense of hostility from the wider society. Some Christians see themselves as engaged in a kind of moral combat on behalf of Judeo-Christian values. Both responses—hostility and combat—presume an us-versus-them dichotomy, where those outside conservative churches (especially progressives) are imagined to be the enemy, while members of such churches are on the side of good and righteousness.

Hunter's argument works quite effectively in light of new and surprising research revealing that modern Christians in the West tend to choose their religious affiliation based on their political affiliation. We often presume that once a person settles into a proper Christian worldview (conservative or progressive, respective to the formative theological environment in which they are immersed), they will adopt a correlated set of political values. Instead, what is observable for at least the last half century is that our politics have begun to dictate our religious beliefs. Thus, people are affiliating

---

of Christianity in the Late Modern World (Oxford: Oxford University Press, 2010), 99–175. Copyright © 2010 Oxford University Press, Inc. Reproduced with permission of the Licensor through PLSclear.

14   The most famous of these is probably the late Peter Berger, one of America's most revered sociologists of religion. Berger's recantation is most helpfully captured in *The Desecularization of the World: Resurgent Religion and World Politics*, ed. Peter L. Berger (Grand Rapids, MI: Eerdmans, 1999). See also his *The Many Altars of Modernity: Toward a Paradigm for Religion in a Pluralist Age* (Boston: DeGruyter, 2014).

with churches whose views and values align with their own political perspective.[15]

This shift makes many of us uncomfortable; it seems out of order with how we think things should be. But we must reckon with the observable practices of modern Christians and church bodies that suggest there is often a deeper commitment to certain political values, parties, and leaders than there is to Jesus Christ. Such allegiance is often justified by casting it as an answer to this question: "What would Jesus do?" Yet it often goes unrecognized just how far short worldly politics falls compared to the actual Kingdom politics of Jesus. The true citizenship of a Christian not only supersedes but transcends the concerns of worldly politics. Only in light of the ways of God's kingdom can Christians account for their own weakness and the ineffectiveness of worldly politics at bringing about the kind of society Christians envisage. To say it another way, because Jesus is Lord of all, earthly politics, as Christians have long known, are but a parody of the ways of the Kingdom.

When we live as if our religious commitments (e.g., that Jesus is Lord of all) are secondary—which the data indicates is the case—we rely on politics as a means of power to force others to live according to our worldview. Each side perceives some threat of harm to the country and feels driven to action. This fear over the future of our country signals just how closely the modern Christian imagination tracks with politics. Conservatives and progressives alike attempt to pull the levers of government and legislation to establish shared moral norms and ethical values across society and mitigate the perceived threat. According to Hunter, conservatives see secularization as the threat and thus seek to reverse America's course.

---

15   For a helpful discussion of this phenomenon over the last few decades, see Michele F. Margolis, *From Politics to the Pews: How Partisanship and Political Environment Shape Religious Identity* (Chicago: University of Chicago Press, 2018).

Because country, culture, and faith tend to hang together as one for conservative Christians,[16] when one element is perceived to be under attack, all elements are considered under attack. A sense of injury in one place affects all the others.

As a response, an effort is made to change the country, to "take it back," as it were, restoring it to its proper Christian roots. The way forward is typically formulated in a two-pronged plan of action. Conservatives call on Christians, first, to pray for our country and, second, to take the fight for our future to voting booths and courtrooms.[17] Troubling for Hunter is not the plan itself—for it is arguably good that Christians of all stripes pray for our society and participate as citizens in the political processes appropriate for them—but rather the character of their engagement. Hunter observes, similarly to how he did when he first identified the so-called "culture wars," that conservative Christians harbor a deep-seated intention to regain and maintain a dominant position of political and therefore cultural influence.[18] To have such control is to ensure Americans are legally coerced to conduct themselves on Christian terms.[19] In other words, the goal in this war is winning.

To get a sense of how far off course Christians in America have gone, especially as it concerns their coextensive relationship with politics, it is worth citing Hunter at length. His analysis shows how our response to the deep and legitimate feelings of resentment, loss, and injury has been to lean more and more on politics to accomplish the church's goals. Many of the greatest concerns of the Christian life as it relates to society—fairness, equity, liberty,

---

16 See Hunter, *To Change the World*, 118.

17 See Hunter, *To Change the World*, 121.

18 See Hunter, *To Change the World*, 124.

19 See Hunter, *To Change the World*, 124.

justice, decency, morality, hope, marriage, family, and children—have become meaningful only on the political field of battle and thus lack the distinctive theological depth that has long characterized them as the inheritance upon which Western society was made possible. Hunter considers it ironic that the American church, in its attempts to secure its own existence, has given away the possibility of its renewal by seeking to achieve its goals via worldly power. The church, he argues—whether of conservative or progressive stripes—has unwittingly given up its unique role in American society; by engaging so fully in political power plays, the church has lost the position from which to hold society accountable by critiquing the politics that organize it.[20]

Hunter goes on to render a sharp criticism of the American church, saying that "the consequence of the whole-hearted and uncritical embrace of politics by Christians has been *in effect,* to reduce Christian faith to a political ideology and various Christian denominations and para-church organizations to special interest groups."[21] This is a tragedy that has resulted from a distorted theology—especially of the distinction between church and state, or more to the point, of Luther's doctrine of two kingdoms—and a failure to learn from history.

The cost to the church is an exceedingly weakened identity, since "an identity rooted in resentment and hostility is an inherently weak identity precisely because it is established negatively, by accentuating the boundaries between insiders and outsiders and the wrongs done by the outsiders."[22] Acting from a place of resentment,

---

20 See Hunter, *To Change the World,* 172.

21 Hunter, *To Change the World,* 172. Emphasis in original. Copyright © 2010 Oxford University Press, Inc. Reproduced with permission of the Licensor through PLSclear.

22 Hunter, *To Change the World,* 173. Copyright © 2010 Oxford University Press, Inc. Reproduced with permission of the Licensor through PLSclear.

"many of the most prominent Christian leaders and organizations in America have fashioned an identity and witness for the church that is, to say the least, antithetical to its highest calling."[23] To put it plainly, Hunter relentlessly seeks to make his case, saying,

> The tragedy is that in the name of resisting the internal deterioration of faith and the corruption of the world around them, many Christians—and Christian conservatives most significantly—unwittingly embrace some of the more corrosive aspects of the cultural disintegration they decry.[24]

One could argue that the harm the church has done to itself by embracing the mechanics of politics is worse than any harm we have suffered from our changed society. As an institution, the church's social (not theological) function is to mold and shape its members to live *as* Christ in the world and thus witness to the presence and future coming of His kingdom. Christians formed in this way would inevitably contribute to the greater flourishing of all members of American society.

Yet because of the politicization of the church's values and its simultaneous dedication to an amalgam of country, culture, and faith, the church has abandoned its own responsibilities, seeking power via the established political mechanisms that it ought to be holding accountable. In so doing, the church has foregone its role as an institution that models and witnesses to the politically alternative ways of the Kingdom or that can prophetically call into question the values of society.

23 Hunter, *To Change the World*, 175. Copyright © 2010 Oxford University Press, Inc. Reproduced with permission of the Licensor through PLSclear.

24 Hunter, *To Change the World*, 175. Copyright © 2010 Oxford University Press, Inc. Reproduced with permission of the Licensor through PLSclear.

The result is that society has lost trust in the institution of the church. Our reputation is like a dumpster fire within the theater of American public life, making it easy for outsiders to simply look, shake their heads, shrug their shoulders, and move on. We are irrelevant and ignorable, and we've done it to ourselves.

STILL, THERE IS HOPE

The preceding analysis of three major ways the church responds to its feelings of resentment, loss, frustration, and injury may seem too big of a challenge to overcome. Furthermore, it is a difficult message to swallow because it clearly indicates that we have been complicit in our own decline. Yet, if we do not recognize our part in creating the situations from which we are trying to pivot, we will continue, however unwittingly, to undercut our own efforts.

Christians who gather regularly for worship experience weekly moments when they are invited to repent. Part of that invitation includes considering sins of omission—the things we didn't do but should have. This chapter has tried to point out some sins of omission that perhaps until now we didn't know we had to confess. Nevertheless, the blood of Jesus is just as ready to cover these sins as every other sin. So let us receive God's gracious absolution and stand with confidence that He will empower us to seek and embody even greater faithfulness.

Our witness before the world need not be limited to who we have been; instead, we can reflect who Christ is molding and shaping us to be in spite of our past. He does not erase our past but rather preserves the memory of it for our benefit. We know now what not to do. We know now the cost of these errors. And we also know the God who brings something out of nothing, who can redeem the most broken and bruised because He raises the dead to life. Let us proceed, then, in this newness of life, leaving behind the bitter *ressentiment*, seeking the leadership of the Holy Spirit to help us meet the urgent hunger of the world around us to know the same redemptive hope we have. The rest of this book will explore what a resilient witness can look like in our dark and unfamiliar times. Together we pray that God will use each of us frail, feeble, fickle human beings (not too different from Jesus' disciples we meet in the Gospels) to introduce the people we know to the only One who can quench their thirst for true life.

The next chapter will explore how we came to live in such a time as this, one in which we experience the deep loss and *ressentiment* that engendered these reactions. Parts 2 and 3 will illuminate spaces where the church can live faithfully, adjusting its behaviors and habits to align with the kind of witness we are called to have in the world. To the extent we can do that, we can slowly regain public trust, which will open new spaces for us to proclaim the Gospel.

REFLECTION QUESTIONS

Answering these questions might tempt us toward finger-pointing and blaming others. However, as you consider these questions, seek with fortitude to reflect first on yourself.

1. What are some examples of well-intentioned attempts at relevance that ended up eclipsing the Gospel message?

2. What are some successful strategies to draw people in to hear the Gospel?

3. What primary goal has been communicated through attempts at relevance? While gaining a hearing was the intended goal, what was communicated instead (e.g., entertainment, the "cool kids" go here, affirmation)?

4. Complacency was given as one example of resignation. What are other examples of the church's resignation to decline, distrust, or seeing a lack of cultural relevance?

5. With religion and politics intermingled, what does winning look like? In what ways has "winning" caused distrust toward the church? In what ways, if at all, do political wins equal a win for the kingdom of God?

6. Take a moment to recognize the ways in which you or your church have participated in the three Rs of this chapter (relevance, resignation, resistance). Reflect on the outcomes. Ask the Lord for forgiveness when these things have been detrimental to the church's mission. What are some current practices you could change moving forward?

CHAPTER 2

Telling Time

What It Means to Live in a Secular Age

In almost any episode of the various versions of *Star Trek*, someone is teleporting somewhere. Often, they end up in a place that's unfamiliar. They must figure out where they are and adapt to their circumstances. Time-travel movies and TV shows have similar features. Imagine simply dropping into a new place and time, whether historical or futuristic, and having to figure out where you are, what time it is, and how to fit in.

Travel to a foreign country where you don't speak the language, and you'll have some sense of what this might be like. But at least you'd know when and where you are. With teleporting and time-traveling, adjusting would be that much more difficult. Thankfully, science fiction benefits from our willingness to suspend disbelief. We can watch or read science fiction and simply enjoy the story without asking questions like "How?" or "What if?" because it is expected that we bracket those questions out.

For followers of Jesus in our radically unfamiliar times, there is no suspending of disbelief. We're constantly asking, "How?" "What happened?" If you grew up in the church, it might seem like the world around you is convulsing and you don't know how to relate to it anymore according to the faith you were taught. If you are a trained church worker, you might think that your training hasn't served you all that well, feeling rather like it prepared you for ministry in a time that no longer exists.

This chapter seeks, in a basic way, to help you discern what time it is and where you are. No, we didn't teleport or time travel. But things are without a doubt much different than they were just three or four decades ago. There are a lot of questions and much adjusting to do. This chapter will tell the story of how we got here and what happened to bring about this new world and all its circumstances that affect our journey of faith and service in the church. The specific and practical discussions in the rest of the book will build on the foundation we lay in this chapter.

In particular, we will discern what it means to live in a secular age. It's probably not what you think. Let's begin with a metaphor.

WEATHER AND CLIMATE

In a report on the state of American democracy published late in 2020, esteemed sociologist (and one of our recurring thinkers) James Davison Hunter described how he and the other authors of the report were interested in the "climatological" changes happening in our culture, rather than the everyday occurrence of the "weather."[1] In other words, Hunter was most keen to report on the underlying cultural conditions and context—the climate—that give way to and make possible the weather, the day-to-day conditions and events. While Hunter's research mostly paid attention to issues affecting the political landscape of America, I want to apply this metaphor to the religious landscape.

---

1   James Davison Hunter, Carl Desportes Bowman, and Kyle Puetz, *Democracy in Dark Times* (New York: Finstock and Tew, 2020), iv.

Much research and reporting has been done in recent years on the changing religious landscape of our society. Perhaps nothing has been more significantly reported than news of the decline of Christianity and the growth of the so-called nones, or religiously unaffiliated people. A few times each year, trusted polling organizations such as Gallup, Pew, and the Public Religion Research Institute publish new survey results demonstrating that fewer people are identifying as Christian or participating regularly in worship. The reports also show corresponding growth among those who identify as having no religious affiliation, thus ticking the box "none" or "no religion" on social surveys.[2]

Following these reports, journalists and pundits begin feverishly parsing the data and publishing articles reflecting on the latest trends. Those who include themselves among the nonreligious tend to laud the increase of their ranks. But those who are experiencing the loss and decline tend to respond with hand-wringing and despair. Their gloomy reflections often signal that the two phenomena highlighted by the survey reports—the declining number of people who identify as Christians and the decrease in regular participation in worship—are the most essential issues for the Christian Church to focus on. They argue that we're in a crisis. Somehow the loss must be mitigated, they suggest. The bleeding needs to be stanched. Because these problems are given such significant attention in the media, church leaders naturally believe that decline and lack of

---

2   See, for example, "In U.S., Decline of Christianity Continues at Rapid Pace," Pew Research Center, October 17, 2019, https://www.pewresearch.org/religion/2019/10/17/in-u-s-decline-of-christianity-continues-at-rapid-pace/ (accessed April 16, 2024); "The 2020 Census of American Religion," Public Religion Research Institute, July 8, 2021, https://www.prri.org/research/2020-census-of-american-religion/ (accessed April 16, 2024); "How Religious Are Americans?" Gallup, March 29, 2024, https://news.gallup.com/poll/358364/religious-americans.aspx (accessed April 22, 2024).

participation should be some of their most important ministry concerns, if not the primary ones.

It's easy to catastrophize in these situations. The apparent magnitude of the problem and the sense of responsibility church leaders feel—especially as it affects the perception of their ability to lead faithfully and well—can make these declines seem truly catastrophic. Undoing the catastrophe becomes urgent.

This is no surprise. The numbers and reports reflect real consequences. From a ministry perspective, it means that fewer people know Jesus as the only way to salvation. In a practical sense, fewer people in our congregations means less financial support and therefore increased risk for pastors and other church professionals whose livelihoods (not to mention church programming and building maintenance) rely on congregational giving. It also means fewer volunteers to help with programs and fewer disciple-makers participating in faith-formation activities, such as teaching Sunday School, leading mission trips or Vacation Bible School, or even teaching the faith to children in households.

It's entirely reasonable, then, that church leaders view decline and lack of participation as a problem. As a result, we see conferences, workshops, books, and other resources that are advertised as offering the most effective and innovative solutions for getting people back in church, and even more, growing our congregations. This collective sense of urgency—both ministerial and practical—drives church leaders to concentrate on overcoming the crisis of decline. The crisis of decline is the problem of our moment, perhaps the biggest ministry challenge our generation will face.

Or is it?

What if these reports are just telling us about the weather? The data on shrinking participation and the ongoing increase of

those leaving religion or identifying as religiously unaffiliated—
the so-called crisis of decline—simply tells us what is happening
now. It's empirically verifiable and even observable in some of our
Sunday experiences; we see fewer people around us in the pews.
To say this data is more like a weather report is not to deny that
the data is true. It is true. It's true in the same way that whatever
the weather outside is, well, that's what the weather outside is. But
should we really be so concerned about the "weather"? What if we
should be more concerned about the climate, the very conditions
that make the weather as we experience it possible? Rather than
attending to decline and lack of participation, might we not ask
what has caused these precipitous concerns in order to address the
underlying issues of our times?

What would it mean to be more concerned about our climate?
For one, it would mean asking deep and probing questions about the
cultural context in which we live. We would seek to take notice of
the underlying, subtle, and often taken-for-granted conditions that
create the possibility for the "weather." That is, I want to argue that
there are underlying "climatological" conditions that have created
the possibility for the current crisis of decline. Only by attempting
to understand those conditions can we truly influence the "weather"
we're experiencing. Concerning ourselves with the climate instead
of the weather will help alleviate the pressure and urgency we feel
to do anything we possibly can to get people back into church and,
even more, to grow it. After all, many of these efforts are exhausting
us. And because it's not producing the fruit we hope for, we are
often left feeling like failures, like we're spinning our wheels and
wasting precious time. In fact, many have left church leadership,
or at least considered doing so, because of this.[3]

---

3   "Pastors Share Top Reasons They've Considered Quitting Ministry in the Past

In the real-world discipline of climatology, scholars are used to thinking about how weather patterns develop. Climate conditions develop over a long period of time, giving way to the weather we experience on a day-to-day basis. So in our climate-weather metaphor, we want to move our attention away from recent trends and even recent cultural events and changes; instead, we will look much further back to track the long tail of historical developments that have given way to how we experience the world today, especially as it concerns the role and influence of religion and what it feels like to believe.[4]

So, what is our cultural climate? What are the conditions that have developed over time to produce the phenomena of decline? To answer this, I want to draw on the work of Canadian philosopher Charles Taylor, another of our recurring thinkers. Taylor's book *A Secular Age*, written in 2007, has been critically acclaimed and serves as a constant point of reference in conversations among people like us who are trying to wrestle with what's happening to the church and why. In fact, some scholars believe *A Secular Age* might be one of the first books written in the twenty-first century that people will still be reading in the twenty-second. Yes, it's *that* important.

Year," The Barna Group, April 27, 2022, https://www.barna.com/research/pastors
-quitting-ministry/ (accessed April 16, 2024).

4   While I argue here that historical developments have given way to the cultural conditions as we experience them and the weather they produce, neither I nor astute historians would argue it was an inevitable development. History is complex. And while ideas have consequences, the complexity of history prevents us from trying to tell a basic causation story. Rather, we're trying to tell a correlation story in which a whole constellation of ideas, social developments, and cultural innovations all came together in a way that produced the cultural conditions we live in. But it did not *have* to be this way; it could have been otherwise. Still, we have what we have in terms of the current cultural conditions. So it is to our experience, and not what could have been, that we give our attention.

As we proceed, the discussion below might feel strange, even uncomfortable. It should. Paying attention to our cultural climate instead of the weather amounts to a paradigm shift, and that will require us to see through different eyes. I will be presenting our world and experiences in ways that open our eyes to its strangeness, to the underlying conditions that have formed our moment.

COMPLICATING THE SECULAR

For the last few decades, the prevailing story to explain our current cultural climate has been that science and rationalism discredited religion and thus religion was marginalized and stigmatized. Taylor finds this explanation too simplistic. In *A Secular Age*, he proposes a much more complicated and compelling story than our usual account of how we came to live in a secular age and why we are experiencing religious decline.

Taylor locates his starting point about five hundred years ago, roughly at the time of the Protestant Reformation, when people such as Martin Luther and John Calvin changed the shape of Christianity irrevocably. At that time, Christianity was the sole religion for just about everybody in Western Europe. Atheism as we know it today simply didn't exist.[5] And while Islamic imperialism was making itself known on the far eastern borders of Europe, there really wasn't any other religion or set of religious influences to speak of.

In brief, their times were very different from those we experience. And that's precisely what interests Taylor—the startling contrast between society five hundred years ago and what we experience today. That starting point generates the animating question of his

---

5 For an insightful and challenging account of modern atheism, see Gavin Hyman, *A Short History of Atheism* (London: I. B. Tauris, 2010).

book, which he then explores over some eight hundred pages. He asks, "Why was it virtually impossible not to believe in God in, say, 1500 in our Western society, while in 2000 many of us find this not only easy, but even inescapable?"[6]

In 1500, Taylor argues, belief in God (not God in general theistic terms, but more specifically, God according to orthodox Christian doctrine) was not only the default for the population but in fact the only option; there were no alternatives whatsoever. Even more, the way people *felt* the world was different. They experienced reality in a way scholars describe as "enchanted." The world had its own agency—its own independent will, manifesting in all things—to which people were subject. Some forces could be harnessed toward good outcomes for humans, but others, such as disease or famine, brought chaos from which humans sought to protect themselves.

This posture of defense and protection shaped all human action and life. This is why cities feature so prominently in ancient literature, from creation myths like the *Enuma Elish* (the Babylonian creation story) to Scripture, where we encounter the language of "fortress" and "refuge."[7] The existence of walled cities represented in an architectural way humans' need to hold back the chaos, primitive as it might sound to modern ears. The walls were a boundary of protection, holding back the outside forces. More than just protection against thieves and rival enemies, they were seen as a bastion against the evil and danger that took magical, mystical, and embodied forms in the darkness beyond the walls.

Human life during this time was understood as porous and vulnerable. The enchanted world could affect us. Angels and demons

---

6   Charles Taylor, *A Secular Age* (Cambridge, MA: Belknap/Harvard University Press, 2007), 25.

7   See Joseph Minich, *Bulwarks of Unbelief: Atheism and Divine Absence in a Secular Age* (Bellingham, WA: Lexham Academic, 2023), 130.

were not imaginary but rather quite real to those who lived just a few centuries ago. Moods and dispositions were caused by physical elements affecting your body from the inside. For example, feeling melancholy was a direct result of black bile in your body; black bile *was* melancholy.[8] There was little talk of psychological disorders and much more talk of demonic possession, magical curses, and the like.

Following the Industrial Revolution in the 1800s and the magnitude of progress brought about by science and technology that led to our modern age, things have been remarkably different. The world *feels* much more under our control. In contrast to how people *felt* the world in early modern Europe, we tend to think of moods in entirely psychological terms, related to chemical imbalances. We consider this a more advanced and progressive perspective, as opposed to the "primitive" idea that one could be possessed by or subject to evil forces. Today, if your child is depressed, your first thought will not be that they are under some kind of demonic attack or that a witch has cursed your family. Rather, we tend to think of ourselves as buffered against outside agency, including the will of other humans. We think of ourselves as free individuals who can do what we want. We no longer feel ourselves to be subject to powers outside of us.

Five hundred years ago, believing in God was taken for granted—everyone around you was also a Christian and shared the same beliefs as you. Today, believing in God (whatever a person might mean by that) is an option. In fact, it's difficult for any of us to escape from the fact that myriad belief options are available to us at any given moment. Unbelief is also possible and not entirely uncommon. These attitudes toward religion are made possible because of how the world *feels* to us. We feel like we're in control of the world around

8   See Taylor, *A Secular Age*, 37.

us, and that control squeezes out the space that triggers our religious impulses. The experiences of life don't often prompt us to think of God. We don't *feel* like we need Him. The more pervasively we experience the world as under our control, the less room we have in our imagination to understand what role religion serves.

GETTING CLEAR ABOUT WHAT *SECULAR* MEANS

Before Taylor dives into his story about our secular age, he points out that we need some clarity on just what we mean by the word *secular*. It's commonly deployed by Christians, and most of us simply assume that we mean the same thing as everyone else does when we say or hear *secular*. But Taylor, as a philosopher, is careful not to allow us to carry on with this assumption. And in doing so, he does us an incredible service.

Taylor thinks that we use the word *secular* in at least three different ways. The first two are familiar.

In the first instance, Taylor suggests that we often use *secular* to refer to public spaces, those arenas empty of specific religious influence. We might think of most courtrooms, libraries, town squares, laboratories, or public schools as secular. We might think of activities like parades or harvest festivals or people who hold positions such as judge, teacher, or researcher as secular. The sense that religion is not present in these examples probably seems rather normal to us. In fact, many of us might believe that religion doesn't belong in these spaces. Since they are public and therefore shared by everyone, the challenge of allowing each religious or spiritual identity to have presence in such spaces is settled by allowing no religious or spiritual influence whatsoever. Furthermore, we believe some of these spaces require setting aside any sort of bias in order to advance knowledge or perform legal decision-making in as objective a manner as possible. Again, this feels normal to us. It seems to align in our imaginations with the American commitment to having no state-sanctioned religion and the so-called separation of church (or any religion or spirituality) and state.

Yet however normal all of this might seem, not so long ago, things were different. Many readers might recall the blue laws that restricted various activities on Sundays. These laws came to America with European settlers and were enacted to keep the Sabbath and reserve a day of rest. Most often, people remember the restriction on the purchase of alcohol on Sundays, either making Sundays completely dry or not allowing sales until after a particular time. While you might still encounter them in some parts of the United States, those laws no longer exist in many of the places they once did. Blue laws are an example of how Sundays were maintained as a sacred day of the week. Without them, the public sphere has become further emptied of religious influence.

Sundays have also been desacralized by the increasing treatment of Sundays as a day like any other. Thus, the sons and daughters of families in our churches increasingly have sports or other activities on Sundays. The commitments to such activities compete with the religious commitments of these families, often directly conflicting with worship times. This is another case of less and less religious visibility in the public sphere.

What do these examples reveal? It's not so much that we were previously less concerned with the separation of church and state or with objectivity in courtrooms and laboratories. Rather, they illustrate that cultural inheritances—like the European settlers' belief that Sunday was a sacred day—take time to fade from our social arrangements.

A second sense of how we use the word *secular* has to do with much of what we've already discussed in this chapter. This sense of *secular* refers to the idea that religion is in decline and connects to the ideology of secularism—the view that religion will continue to decline and that this progressive reduction is good for the future of human society. When we discuss the decline of those who identify as Christians, the decline of church membership, or the increase of those who identify as nonreligious or as religiously unaffiliated, we often think of them as secularizing phenomena. That is, they seem to indicate that our society is becoming less religious.

One way to distinguish our uses of the term *secular* is to use subscripts: secular$_1$ and secular$_2$.[9] Secular$_1$ refers to spaces where religion was once visible and normative but no longer has an influence. Secular$_2$ has to do more with social practices, how people understand themselves with respect to religion, and how we discuss the nature of our society (whether we're religious or not, and how much).

For readers of this book, when we are talking about secular$_1$ or secular$_2$, we're likely using the word to signal some kind of problematic concern. For us, less religious visibility in the public square and the decline of religious identification and participation are not viewed as positive developments. We're worried about them. And when we talk about them, we're often lamenting these realities or stirring one another up to do something about them. In other words, we tend to use *secular* only with a negative connotation.

But Taylor suggests yet another meaning of *secular*. If we listen closely, this third definition will be helpful as we consider

---

9   See James K. A. Smith, *How (Not) to Be Secular: Reading Charles Taylor* (Grand Rapids, MI: Eerdmans, 2014), 21.

our weather-climate metaphor. Taylor's third sense of *secular* is the hinge upon which our paradigm for thinking about our times will shift. To help us imagine what that shift will feel like, let me tell a brief story.

SEEING EVERYWHERE
WHAT WE NEVER NOTICED BEFORE

A friend of mine recently bought a car. She needed something small to get around town for picking up groceries or transporting her young kids but also fuel efficient and easy to park in her family's tiny garage. Before making her purchase, she asked around to see if anyone had good recommendations. Finally, she bought a small hatchback that several people had suggested. It had a good reputation and met all her criteria. However, she had never heard of the car beforehand and couldn't recall seeing others drive the same make and model. Yet soon after she bought the car, she began to see it everywhere. It was as if that car was only visible once she was looking for it.

A paradigm shift is like looking through a new lens that brings into view something that had previously been obscured. Through the new lenses, we see a rather different world than what we previously perceived. And what tends to stand out is not the familiar but the strange. Yet, as we move through the world wearing our new lenses, we realize just how common the strange actually is, to the extent that if we keep wearing the lens, the strange quickly becomes common. With a paradigm shift, what used to appear strange slowly becomes the preferred way to see and understand the world. Eventually, we wonder how we ever navigated the world properly before we had the new lenses.

Understanding Taylor's third sense of *secular* will be a bit like my friend's experience with her new car—a paradigm shift, a new way of seeing things. This third sense is an innovative understanding of what it means to live in a secular age. It refers more to the climatological conditions than to the weather we're reacting to in any given moment. Taylor spends the majority of his book discussing *secular* in this sense. Making this third use of the word more central to our thinking will require repeated engagement with it, especially when it comes to our ministerial work of responding faithfully and appropriately to the times in which we live and helping others do so too.

Secular$_3$, to follow the pattern we've been using, refers to implausibility, or the fact that it's difficult to believe.[10] To say that it's difficult to believe is not to say that Christianity is difficult or that the Scriptures are wrong to describe true faith as childlike (Matthew 18:2–4; Mark 10:14). Rather, we are acknowledging the complicated reality that believing is fragile for almost everyone living in the West. This is especially true in the twenty-first century, when we encounter a plurality of ways of belief around every corner, particularly online.

Another way to describe Taylor's sense of implausibility returns to the idea of how we *feel* the world today. Because we feel like we're in control, functionally, it's rather easy to believe more strongly in God's absence. [11] While the intellectual part of us might think believing in God makes good sense and even seems logically necessary, it has little effect on how we experience the world. It is easy to live without reference to God, the divine, or any sense of a

---

10   See Smith, *How (Not) to Be Secular*, 21–22.

11   See Joseph Minich, *Enduring Divine Absence: The Challenge of Modern Atheism* (Lincoln, NE: The Davenant Institute, 2018).

transcendent realm beyond our physical reality. We tend to think of belief from a purely intellectual perspective. But if we begin to consider belief as something people *do*, not just think, we can explore what believing *feels* like. And what believing *feels* like in a secular age is fraught.

Taylor's description of implausibility, of belief being difficult, names the climate—the conditions—of our secular age. More simply, we live in a time when objections and contestations can be mounted against any belief. Objections come from many angles: alternative belief systems (say, competing religious traditions), scientific questions that seek evidence for belief, philosophical questions that raise concerns that might lead to skepticism. Whatever the means of objection, it's fair to recognize that beliefs are contestable. And since they can be contested, they will be. We are immersed in an environment where almost everything that might be understood as a form of ultimate or religious conviction will be contested. That experience makes us hesitant to believe much of anything, and our grasp on those beliefs we do hold can feel tenuous.

DIFFICULT AND EASY BELIEF

Let's take this conversation a bit further by comparing the idea of implausibility with plausibility. What makes something difficult to believe (implausible) as opposed to easy (plausible)?

The concept of plausibility has been a part of the study of religion since the latter half of the twentieth century. The late sociologist Peter Berger discussed it significantly in his classic book *The Sacred Canopy*. There Berger described in a rather technical way something he called plausibility structures.[12] Rather than give a

---

12   Peter Berger, *The Sacred Canopy: Elements of a Sociological Theory of Religion* (New

technical description, let me use a pop culture reference to help us make sense of it.

In the film *The Matrix*, the main character (played by Keanu Reeves) is first introduced to us as Thomas Anderson, whom we know later and primarily as Neo. The early part of the film shows Anderson living a rather normal day-to-day existence. He has a job as a computer programmer and works quietly for his respectable public company. On the side, he also works privately as an illegal computer hacker. All this is a simulated reality generated by the Matrix. But he experiences it as if it's normal—it's just the way things are.

The viewers are privy to the fact that he's living in a simulated reality, but we have to imagine that to him, such an idea would be absurd, a fantasy. Were we to argue the point with him, he would think we were crazy. This is because his experience of reality provided him with a plausibility structure: a set of boundaries concerning what's possible to reasonably believe, a sense of how one's beliefs about reality hold together in a coherent way, and an equally strong sense of what would be incoherent or just plain wrong. To propose to him that he's living in a simulation would be received as incoherent, and thus very difficult to believe with any kind of seriousness.

The world as Anderson knows and experiences it, his reality as he bumps up against it, and the way he interprets all these things collectively with other people in his society—all this constitutes Anderson's plausibility structure. That structure is how things hold together as meaningful for him, such as doing his job to get paid and hacking to have fun or cause trouble. In other words, the reality that Anderson experiences in his day-to-day work as both computer

York: Anchor, 1967). See also Berger, *A Rumor of Angels: Modern Society and the Rediscovery of the Supernatural* (New York: Anchor, 1970).

programmer and hacker constitutes for him the limits of what is plausible or believable. To propose that he's living in a simulation would be, for him, implausible.

Part of Anderson's interest in hacking involves finding out more about the so-called Matrix—an obscure rumor he's stumbled upon in the world of illegal hacking. Eventually, he makes contact with those who can tell him the truth about the Matrix. To learn that truth, he makes a choice to take the red pill, which disrupts his connection to the Matrix and his simulated reality.

Shortly afterward, and now referred to as Neo, he is presented with the truth about the Matrix from Morpheus. The world as he knew it from within the Matrix became suddenly and demonstrably false. Yet, mentally and emotionally, Neo was still interpreting his experience from within the frames of reference and meaning provided by the plausibility structure he had always known, despite realizing that it was a simulation. Struggling to adapt and adjust his perspective to take in this new reality without having yet established a new structure of plausibility, Neo is overwhelmed. Not only is he confused, but he experiences something like a crisis, an irruption within his consciousness. He reacts viscerally from the shock. As the film carries on and Neo continues to experience the new reality and learns his role in it, he slowly begins to adjust and add frames of reference to create a new plausibility structure.

HOW ALL BELIEF BECOMES IMPLAUSIBLE

We live in a world where myriad possible ways of believing exist—from traditional religions such as Christianity or Buddhism to alternatives like Wicca or Scientology to hybridizations of various belief systems and even pseudoreligions like SoulCycle.[13] Because of this, Taylor describes us as living under a constant experience of cross pressure. What he means by this is relatively simple. It captures our daily experience of encountering people who believe something different from us, especially when it comes to things like religion.

Most of the time, religious belief systems are comprehensive. That is, our religion tells us the way things are, the story of everything. When we encounter someone whose convictions about the way things are happen to be totally different than ours, who have a different story of everything, several responses are possible. On the one hand, we might avoid them because, at the very least, they seem strange or, worse, scary. On the other hand, we might get to know them and realize that, other than our religious beliefs, we have a lot in common. What happens then?

Those are the situations in which we begin to feel what Taylor calls cross pressure. He describes it this way:

> This kind of multiplicity of faiths has little effect as long as it is neutralized by the sense that being like them is not really an option for me. As long as the alternative is strange and other, perhaps despised, but perhaps just too different, too weird, too incomprehensible, so that becoming *that* isn't really conceivable for me, so long will their difference not undermine my embedding in my own faith. This changes when through increased contact, interchange, even perhaps inter-marriage, the other becomes more and more like me, in everything else but faith: same activities, professions, opinions, tastes, etc. Then the issue

---

13   See Tara Isabella Burton, *Strange Rites: New Religions for a Godless World* (New York: Public Affairs, 2020), chap. 5.

> posed by difference becomes more insistent: why my
> way and not hers? There is no other difference left
> to make the shift preposterous or unimaginable.[14]

When we get to know another person well and perhaps even care deeply about them, we might begin to wonder why our convictions are right as opposed to theirs. And perhaps the other person is experiencing the same thing as they get to know and care about us. Cross pressure is what we experience when we responsibly recognize that the other person is not simply a fool for believing as they do, yet at the same time, we have no method for adjudicating between the opposing views to which we are each committed. At best, we're only able to ask, "Why my way and not theirs?" The unsettledness of that question is what we mean when we say that believing is difficult, and that the beliefs we do adhere to feel fragile.

In other words, Taylor's sense of secular$_3$, the sense of implausibility, has much more to do with our experience in everyday life than it has to do with merely adhering to a set of propositions that constitute a religious belief system, like Christianity, Bahá'i, or Taoism. We're not speaking of a rational deliberation between competing beliefs, as if we can just follow where the evidence leads. No one becomes a follower of Jesus like that, just as no one comes to believe other things in that way.

A simple way to understand how we come to have beliefs is that beliefs actually have *us*. We are captive to them. Consider an ailment like the common cold or a headache. We would usually say, "I have a headache" or, "I have a cold." But it's more accurate to say that they have us. We are in their grip until they relent. The role of

---

14   Taylor, *A Secular Age*, 304. Emphasis in original. To be clear, while Taylor claims situations like these make changing belief *possible*, he does not go on to suggest such change is inevitable.

beliefs in our lives is similar. Beliefs *have* us, and to the extent that this is true, Taylor's reflection on implausibility, cross pressure, and the fragility of belief demands our sustained attention.

If we are to do ministry in a secular age, proclaiming the Good News of God's saving grace in Jesus Christ, we must reckon with the fact that the Gospel is not just a set of propositions that a person adheres to or can rationally defend. Yes, they are believable in a rational way, that is, Christian doctrine has internal coherence—it all hangs together in a way that makes sense. It is a story of everything, after all. But there is more to it than that. The believability (or plausibility) of the Good News also comes from the fact that the people who believe it live their lives in a way that reflects that they take Christian claims to be the truth about the way things are. To the extent that one claims to be a Christian but lives otherwise, to observers this makes Christian belief implausible.

Now, of course, Christians argue that none of us rationally deliberate to choose our beliefs when it comes to faith in Jesus. Belief is not a choice. As we have said, belief has us. This is quite fitting with Christian teaching, since we confess that faith is a gift given by the Holy Spirit. Yet Scripture and the history of the early church strongly testify to the fact that the Holy Spirit uses the living witness of believers to bring others to faith. The holiness codes of the Old Testament that set God's people apart, the instructions for households in talking about the faith, the exhortations of the New Testament that focus on faithful living in the midst of persecution—these all point to our living witness as a powerful tool in the hands of God to generate faith and nurture it throughout life.

A secular age, Taylor argues, means an age of implausibility. Christians must recognize the critical importance of our witness—of how we live among outsiders—in such an age. Implausibility is our cultural climate, the conditions that produce the weather that is the crisis of decline (secular$_2$) and the disappearance of religion from the public sphere (secular$_1$). These two things are not possible without the background conditions of secular$_3$.

OVERCOMING IMPLAUSIBILITY

Chapter 1 discussed how the church often acts in ways that unintentionally undercut its own efforts to expand the kingdom of God. We noticed that this is true especially when we seek to be relevant or when we resist cultural influences in aggressive, antagonistic ways that attempt to use political power to force others to live in Christian ways (even if they don't believe as we do). As we move forward in hope, we are now prepared to ask how Taylor's account of our secular age might help us in terms of our witness. For as we have just said, the way outsiders perceive the church matters immensely for the sake of plausibility.

So, how does the church overcome the challenge that our own public witness contributes, often unwittingly, to the difficulties people have in believing the promises of God, trusting Jesus, and following Him? The clearest and most basic answer is simple: when we live in a manner that aligns with what we say is important, only then will the world see a compelling public witness. Otherwise, we're not much different from anyone else. Our evangelistic efforts and overtures to outsiders that they should join the church will sound like nothing more than clanging cymbals in the noise of everyday life in which we all find ourselves as objects of myriad efforts to command our attention and devotion. The rest of this book will take up various ways in which we can do just that. Jesus will be our model for how we engage with others in the world, those outsiders who are looking for a genuine Christ-shaped and winsome engagement that, over time, the Holy Spirit might use to generate faith and bring more people to trust in Christ and benefit from His promises.

REFLECTION QUESTIONS

1. Where in life do you notice the reality that we are not in control? How can we meet people in their space of need in those moments?

2. Give some examples of how the beliefs of the institution of the church have been contested. How has the church's response, locally or as a whole, acted as a witness? Was that witness winsome for the Gospel or counterproductive?

3. How does considering the long view of climate versus weather affect your thoughts about the church and its witness? Does the length of time that contributed to decline make you feel uncomfortable and discouraged or hopeful and encouraged? What about the length of time it might take to see the fruit of your witness—do you feel discouraged or encouraged?

PART 2

Ministry and Social Challenges in a Secular Age

CHAPTER 3

How Not to Let Issues Prevent Relationships

DIVISION BY IMITATION

It's long been common advice that if you want to learn a new language, the best thing you can do is move to a place where you'll be immersed in that language as it's spoken by those who are fluent. In that environment, you are under significant pressure to use the language to do basic things like get directions, order food, buy goods, and so on. Travelers often get a sense of what this is like, but only for a brief time.

Immersion experiences are recommended because they most strongly support the conditions necessary to learn a language. There are other methods, of course, like ones that train learners in vocabulary, grammar, and other elements of a language. But immersion is the best because it works fastest. Even more, a person begins to pick up on the nuances of speaking, reading, and writing the language in everyday settings. In immersion situations, we put to work our God-given capacities to mimic others. We used these same capacities early in life as we learned to walk, talk, and function in our society.

Discipleship is another example of an immersion experience. Learning to follow Jesus has its own kind of training, but so much of it is learned by being around others, immersed in community with those who also follow Jesus. We learn to pray, understand Scripture, and talk to others about Jesus by watching and listening to how others do so. That's what the word *disciple* means, after all—"to follow," or better, "to follow after," since some person, group, or set of ideas is usually leading the way. We could say that we are disciples of whatever we're immersed in, whatever it is that we're following after.

For example, the people who raised us likely discipled us in the basic ways to get along with others. We were probably taught to be kind to one another or wary of strangers. We've undoubtedly been taught to share with others and that staring at other people is awkward. These are social rules that have been made explicit. They've become habitual for most of us because when we were very young, we were immersed in environments that forced us to practice these rules until they became automatic. Now, as we live in our social world with others who have learned the same rules, we consider violations of these rules to be inappropriate. Those who violate these rules have a more difficult time making their way through our social world.

But discipleship is not static. We're always following after. A good example of this is when new situations cause us to adjust social behaviors. Perhaps you're in a place where others speak a different language or have different habits for mealtimes. In those circumstances, we're forced to adjust. If we stay in that environment long enough, we tend to adopt similar behaviors—ones that help us to better fit in and make it easier for us to navigate a different social world.

One of the newest social worlds we've all had to adjust to is the digital one, and it has shaped us immensely. Because of widespread internet access, most of us have come to spend significant portions of our time in a digital environment, whether for learning, work, entertainment, or social connection. As we adapt to new technology that fosters our ability to participate in digital spaces, we've developed all kinds of habits and behaviors that people like psychologists, sociologists, economists, and political scientists find fascinating. Some developments are interesting and positive. Our ability to share information has vastly sped up innovation in certain sectors, such as medicine. New economic experiments—cryptocurrency, for example—are emerging.

Other developments have raised concern. Our constant immersion in these media environments has discipled us about how we should interact with others, affecting our behaviors and perception of what is considered the norm. Consider how we conduct social discussions and debate in our time. Perhaps you've noticed how much basic civility seems to have declined. In fact, in 2018, a survey from the More in Common organization found that 93 percent of us are frustrated and exhausted by how divided we are, yet at the same time, we are unsure what to do about it.[1]

These digital spaces have shaped our habits. We are being discipled in and by them. They invite us to render our thoughts and opinions concerning just about everything. The systems reward us with likes, followers, and the possibility of going viral. Targeting other people with our thoughts and opinions has become common, especially when we do so negatively, as the algorithms amplify voices and comments that consistently express outrage, anger, and contempt.

---

1   Cited in Arthur Brooks, *Love Your Enemies: How Decent People Can Save America from the Culture of Contempt* (New York: Broadside, 2019), 26

Slowly, we have been encouraged to attack without thinking about the people with whom we disagree.[2] We have been discipled online, and we are relearning how to live in the world as we mimic the models we see there. And we tend not to think about the consequences when it comes to imitation on a mass scale. That's what everyone else is doing, we think, so why not give it a try?

FRACTURED, SPLINTERED, BROKEN

Our social world is highly polarized. There is vast and strong disagreement among almost all of us about things that we consider critically important. Yet 93 percent of us ironically seem to agree on at least one thing—our dividedness is not good, and most of us dislike it. The More in Common report that discusses this ironic measure of agreement goes further and tries to make sense of what our divisions look like. The report suggests that our society is split into various "tribes" into which we all tend to fit. This tribalism doesn't always operate in visible and concrete ways. Many of us probably couldn't name our specific "tribe." But based on our social, political, and sometimes religious views, we're likely part of one.

An effect of this tribalism, especially in our nearly unavoidable media environment, is that we often end up in echo chambers, connecting only with people who are like us, with whom we agree. In part, the algorithms are responsible for this. But so are our choices, such that we might say the algorithms simply give us what we want anyway. Therefore, we are constantly confirmed and affirmed in the views we already have. Our rare exposure to people from other groups

---

2   See Jonathan Haidt, "Why the Past 10 Years of American Life Have Been Uniquely Stupid," *The Atlantic*, April 11, 2022, https://www.theatlantic.com/magazine/archive/2022/05/social-media-democracy-trust-babel/629369/ (accessed April 16, 2024).

and their ideas easily raises our hackles, and it's not uncommon for us to feel discomfort. We likely feel other things too, perhaps thinking, *How could they possibly think that?* or, *What's wrong with them?* or, *Those are the sort of people who are messing up everything.* We may even feel threatened by these others, as if their existence, much less their advocacy for ideas we disagree with or find offensive, endangers the things we support and believe are good, right, and true.

Notice how these "others" are characterized here. The language used above—"they," "them," or "others"—subtly shapes our imagination of them to be abstract, distant rather than personal. By means of the language we use to refer to them, we can maintain a distance; we don't need to know members of these alternative groups in any personal way. And that seems to be the preference. Lingering underneath all of this us-versus-them polarization is a powerful fearfulness that contributes to and is compounded by our ongoing characterization of them *as* a "them."

Where does this come from? It's not difficult to find a common response to this question. Within psychology, sociology, history, and anthropology, a mountain of research supports the idea that humans tend to divide themselves up into in-groups and out-groups. Historically, we see this with kin-based relationships in people groups that existed long before humans organized villages, towns, and cities.[3] In modern times, nationalistic impulses are more common, playing out in real-world conflicts like struggles for economic or military dominance but also in more trivial ways, such as support for your own country in the Olympics or the soccer World Cup.

As Christians, we have a model for how to engage with anyone we might consider a "them" or an "other" in some way: the hospitality

---

3   See, for example, the sweeping discussion of kinship and tribalism in Joseph Henrich, *The WEIRDest People in the World: How the West Became Psychologically Peculiar and Particularly Prosperous* (New York: Farrar, Strauss, and Giroux, 2020).

of God the Father that He enacts through Jesus and the Spirit, which is then embodied in the early church. A later chapter will address this more fully, but know that this chapter functions with that mindset. For the remainder of this chapter, we'll explore four challenges Christians face as we seek to engage winsomely and well with people who believe differently about issues we hold dear—whether that's race, gender, guns, abortion, immigration, sexuality, vaccines, politics, ethnicity, religion, climate, poverty, or any other issue. We'll also consider four solutions to help us more faithfully live like Jesus in how we approach others, especially those with whom we disagree.

MUST WE CUT OTHERS OFF?

The first challenge stems from a common human reaction: the tendency to cut off relationship with anyone who doesn't share our perspective on a critical issue. To believe it's best to disassociate from those with whom we deeply disagree seems more common now than ever, as in the cartoon from *The New Yorker* that was mentioned in chapter 1. It's as if we assume the issue of our deep differences must be settled and agreed upon between us *before* a relationship is possible, either to begin or sustain.

Disassociating offers us an easy way out of deep disagreement. A more difficult path, but one that many try to follow, especially with close friends or family members, is to try to convince the person that they are wrong. However, when we present alternative views or counterevidence to the person with whom we disagree, their response is often to merely absorb the information without it affecting their opinion. This is troubling to us. We end up feeling like we're in a futile, uphill battle, as if nothing we present will convince the other person. This occurs most often when some-one is caught in an ideology. A good example of the prevalence of ideology in recent years is the conspiracy theories that have run rampant across our society. Most people know someone (who knows someone) who is caught up in a conspiracy theory and how those theories are seemingly able to make sense of just about everything in a comprehensive manner for that person (even if appearing to be complete nonsense to outsiders). To the point, even efforts to dissuade someone from their convictions about the truth of a con-spiracy theory can be interpreted according to the conspiracy itself: all efforts to convince a conspiracy believer otherwise are just vested interests of the enemy to lead a person astray.

Ideologies that operate this way are different from religious beliefs. For ideologies of this sort, a primary feature is that there seems to be no way out.[4] In other words, in contrast to religious viewpoints, there is no room for repentance in an ideology, no room for a person to admit they might be wrong. Religion, on the other hand, especially the Christian faith, is characterized by repen-tance. Faithful followers of Jesus simply assume they are wrong because they are fallible and finite and do not know everything. For Christians seeking to correct those caught up in an ideology, it's best to assume such efforts will be foolhardy, a spinning of one's wheels while getting nowhere. In fact, psychologists and sociologists have long advised against trying to dissuade those trapped in an ideology. This is because conversion away from ideology happens differently. I'll illustrate with a story.

---

4   I'm thankful to my former colleague Scott Yakimow for this insightful way of framing ideology.

Breaking Through an Ideology

Almost thirty years ago, Terry Gross of the National Public Radio show *Fresh Air* interviewed a man who had left a white supremacy group.[5] You might anticipate before listening to the man's story that you'd hear him telling the host of all the ways he rationally and deliberately worked his way through the arguments against white supremacy and thus chose to leave the cult. But you'd be wrong.

Rather, the interviewer hears an entirely different kind of story—one filled with lots of affective language. The interviewee offered primarily emotional reasons for leaving. As Floyd Cochran tells his story, you learn that he was at a gathering of the supremacists listening to a rallying speech by one of their leaders. Besides the obvious groups the members had to be against (nonwhites), the person giving the speech began to name other groups that were in some manner problematic, even corruptive of the white race.

He mentioned one such group of so-called "defectives." As the speaker began to describe this group, he listed a number of medical conditions that are (even now) referred to as "birth defects,"[6] thus the speaker's term for them: *defective*. One of the conditions he noted was that of cleft palette—a medical diagnosis for babies who are born without a fully formed roof of the mouth.

As the speaker named this condition among his list of defectives, a metaphorical light bulb turned on in Cochran's brain. He experienced an instantaneous conversion from white supremacy. But

---

5   See *Fresh Air*, "Former Member of the Aryan Nations Floyd Cochran," National Public Radio, March 21, 1994, https://freshairarchive.org/segments/former -member-aryan-nations-floyd-cochran (accessed April 16, 2024). I learned about this story from Stanley Fish, who cited it in his "Beliefs about Belief," in *The Trouble with Principle* (Cambridge, MA: Harvard, 1999), 279–84.

6   See the "Birth Defects" index at the Centers for Disease Control and Prevention webpage: https://www.cdc.gov/ncbddd/birthdefects/index.html.

it wasn't because Cochran adhered to some kind of alternative view about people born with birth defects, a view which suddenly came into competition with his allegiance to white supremacy. Rather, it was something deeper.

In fact, Cochran's own son had been born with the condition of cleft palette. Cochran's conversion came about because of competing allegiances. The demands of the supremacist movement to be against such "defectives" went up against the fact that his own son was counted among those "defectives." Unwittingly, Cochran's commitment to white supremacy made him unaware of how that commitment would call into question his other loyalties.

Ultimately, his love for his son and commitment as a father revealed to Cochran his true allegiance. He could not carry on as a white supremacist. In fact, he famously became an activist and teacher who has traveled widely and spoken to large audiences about the despicable nature of white supremacy as an ideology.

Cochran's story reveals that people really can move out of the traps and seemingly circular reasoning of ideologies. But it typically does not happen when another person mounts an argument against the ideology in an effort to convince the person who is trapped. Rather, it must happen in more of a surprising, irruptive manner. This is something like a Wile E. Coyote moment.

If you recall the classic Warner Bros. cartoons, among them is the famous chasing of the Road Runner by Wile E. Coyote. In all his antics to catch the Road Runner, Wile E. Coyote always fails. He's constantly outsmarted by the Road Runner. His plans are always foiled. On more than one occasion, we see Wile E. Coyote tricked by the Road Runner into running off the edge of a cliff. In that moment, the scene stops, with Wile E. Coyote suspended in midair. He first looks down at his impending doom, then up at the viewer with a look of frustration and despair that he's been tricked yet again, and finally back down before he disappears with a yowl and the scene ends.

Wile E. Coyote's reaction to his predicament is a good metaphor for what someone might experience when their commitment to an ideology is suddenly short-circuited. We can imagine through our God-given gifts of human empathy what Wile E. Coyote might be thinking as he hangs suspended above his impending doom, knowing he's been tricked once more by the Road Runner. It might be something like, "Oh no! What have I done?!"

Until these experiences occur, our best course of action is not to argue or present counterevidence to a person caught up in an ideology. Christians know a better way: we can simply be there as a friend.

In other words, as the legal scholar John Inazu puts it, we should not seek to deal primarily with the deep differences that characterize the gap between our most sacred convictions and the person with whom we disagree. Rather, despite these gaps, we should seek to bridge relationships anyway.[7] And that's always possible, despite the presence of ideological or any other differences. A person's adherence to an ideology does not make someone a person with whom we cannot have a relationship. Our culture suggests that disassociation is not just the best but the *only* course of action to deal with such differences. But as Christians, we can look to Jesus to see that something more, something better is possible.

The only person who could have maintained such a standard by which disassociation is justified is Jesus Christ, the very Son of God. He could have decided that none of us were worthy of a

---

7   See John Inazu, *Confident Pluralism: Surviving and Thriving through Deep Difference* (Chicago: University of Chicago Press, 2016), 121–24.

relationship because we're not holy, as He is. But He did the exact opposite. Jesus never let an issue prevent a relationship.[8] In fact, He came to us all while we were still His enemies (Romans 5:10–11). That's a dramatic difference from the us-versus-them polarization we've come to notice and find frustrating, even exhausting.

If you've never thought of it that way, take note: Jesus never let an issue prevent a relationship. To see what I mean, let's look at a retelling of the story of Jesus and the Samaritan woman at the well from John 4. I've taken elements of that story and put them into my own words so that we can try to get a better sense of the historical and social contexts that loom behind the scenes in John's Gospel.

JESUS AT THE WELL

Once upon a time there was a woman who came to draw water from a well. There at the well when she arrived was a man. The man and the woman had different ethnicities, and their peoples never associated with one another. It's as if they were sworn enemies by default, even though the two of them had never met and no personal conflict existed between them. The woman seemed to recognize this most clearly, knowing simply upon seeing the man that he was one of "them." The barrier of hostility between their peoples made her hesitant to engage.

Still, it came to be that the man received a drink of water from the woman, for he had been weary from

---

8   I want to thank my friend Paul Linnemann for this phrase and for helping me to succinctly capture the posture with which Jesus approaches us and by which He simultaneously empowers us to embody in our approach to others.

traveling and was thirsty. This simple act of kindness led to a conversation.

At one point, the man invited the woman to call for her husband. "I have no husband," she said. Surprisingly, the man acknowledged the truthfulness of the woman's statement, revealing by his unexplainable knowledge that he was no ordinary man. He continued, "The fact is, you have had five husbands. And the man you are with is indeed not your husband."

Stunned, the woman responded, "I can see that you are prophet." But the man was more than that.

Their conversation meandered back into the historical circumstances that engendered the differences and divisions between their peoples. All along the way, the woman silently struggled to discern who this man really was, for she knew she was engaged in conversation with someone very special.

Finally, the man described a future when the differences between their peoples wouldn't matter. In fact, the differences and the divisions between all peoples would be transcended by something that all people have in common.

Suddenly the woman felt that the conversation was becoming too esoteric, too complicated for someone like her and this man to discuss. The mysteries they were considering would, she proclaimed, eventually be explained when the Messiah came.

Now, the Messiah, her people believed, was God's chosen one, the one who would heal and save the world. Certainly, he would undo the effects of the differences and divisions between their peoples, and not only theirs but all people. Yet, the woman found it difficult to believe she could be talking to that very Messiah.

At that moment, the man said, "I who speak with you am he."

Before she could respond, their conversation was interrupted by the arrival of the man's friends, who had gone into the town where the woman lived to buy food. Upon their arrival, the woman left, returning to her town. Along the way she was deep in thought about what she had just experienced.

Overcome with a sense of urgency and awe from the experience, she began telling other townsfolk, "Come, see a man who told me everything I ever did. Could this man be the Messiah?" In fact, many of the townspeople went out to meet the man. They too were so moved by their engagements with him that they invited the man to stay in their town for a while, despite the differences between their peoples. And over time, they, too, came to believe he was the Messiah.

This account stands in contrast to our normal way of operating. In our day, no one would be surprised if someone chose not to associate with another person based on some difference that we've decided has to be a big deal. Because that's what we did—we *decided* those things. We didn't have to, but we did. We act as if we *must* divide ourselves over any number of issues, including ethnicity, religion, race, politics, gender, sexuality, and more. We have *chosen* to let these issues divide us and prevent relationships, and we often feel as if we *must* operate this way.

But the story of Jesus and the woman at the well reveals that it doesn't *have* to be this way. Jesus demonstrates a different form of engagement. He helps us to imagine other possibilities for how we might engage relationally across differences.

Despite what Jesus knew of the woman—despite the "issues" that might normally cause us not to associate with someone like her (replace her "issues" of adultery or ethnic difference with your issue *du jour* concerning people you avoid)—He did not let those issues prevent a relationship. In fact, the Bible suggests that Jesus specifically chose to pass by the well where He and the woman had the conversation; John 4:4 says that "He *had* to go through Samaria" (NIV, emphasis added). This incident then led to Jesus spending a few days with even more people like her in the town of Sychar. In other words, He sought them out for the sake of relationship despite the issues. Jesus' approach to engagement becomes a model for us. And He sends the Holy Spirit to empower us to do as we see Him doing. No longer must we disassociate because of disagreement. Rather, we can always seek a relationship despite our differences and meet others as Jesus meets us, no longer as enemies, but as friends.

LISTENING WELL

The second challenge we face is the way we listen. Listening is a difficult thing to do. In our time, listening tends to look more like "waiting for your turn to speak." Perhaps you listened to a podcast, watched an interview, or read a social media post on a topic you care deeply about, but you encountered something you disagreed with. Immediately, you find yourself thinking about all kinds of reasons why whatever you read or listened to was wrong. Maybe you even posted a comment online to that effect. Perhaps you interrupt others regularly, never allowing them to fully express a thought before you begin to react with your own counterpoint. We tend to listen in order to react or respond rather than to know or understand. Online spaces show us at our worst in this regard.

Alan Jacobs tells a story about a person who was in the audience listening to a speaker. The person felt a sense of disagreement and then irritation with the speaker. The audience member finally approached the speaker, seeking to lambast his argument. But the speaker reacted in a surprising way, telling the audience member to "give it five minutes." The audience member had entered what Jacobs calls "Refutation Mode."

Jacobs says that in "Refutation Mode there is no listening."[9] He goes on to reflect on his own habits of entering Refutation Mode, offering a very relatable picture:

> I too am regularly tempted to enter Refutation Mode—and the more passionate I feel about a topic, the more likely I am to succumb to that temptation. I know what it's like to become so angry at what someone has written online that my hands shake as they hover over the keyboard, ready to type my withering retort. Many are the tweets I wish I could take back; indeed, many are the tweets I have actually

9   Alan Jacobs, *How to Think: A Survival Guide for a World at Odds* (New York: Currency, 2017), 18. Capitalization in original and will be carried on here.

deleted, though not before they did damage either to someone else's feelings or to my reputation for calm good sense. I have said to myself, *If I had just thought about it I wouldn't have sent that*. But I was going with the flow, moving at the speed of social media traffic.[10]

We've already noted that the digital world disciples us in particular ways. We just go with that flow. Jacobs admits that his habits, like all of ours, have been shaped by his digital engagement. Yet, I want to focus on this observation: Jacobs says, "The more passionate I feel about a topic, the more likely I am to succumb" to the temptation of Refutation Mode. Here he opens a space for us to examine why listening is so difficult.

In our listening, thinking is also involved. As much as we like to imagine we are rational, objective, unbiased, and so on, we never think in a purely rational, objective, unbiased, or unemotional way. Our thinking cannot be extricated from emotional engagement, as Jacobs notes. Thinking—especially the kind Jacobs has in mind when it comes to listening—is only something we do when we care about the matter at hand. Otherwise, why else would we get so impassioned and opinionated?

That our emotions are inextricable from our thinking, and therefore from our listening to others, is both a strength and a weakness. On the one hand, listening well and reflecting thoughtfully helps us become wise, advance knowledge, and carry on with our lives in a way that helps us and those around us to live well. This can only happen when we're emotionally invested in what we're thinking about.

---

10   Jacobs, *How to Think*, 19. Emphasis in original.

On the other hand, as Jacobs admits, caring so deeply about something may mean that our emotions cloud our thoughts about it. We encountered this in Cochran's story. His thinking was merely in line with his group. It felt right to him because he was part of something bigger than himself. He got caught up in the affirmative emotional feedback he received in the feelings generated by his sense of a shared identity with his group. And this emotional connection blinded him to something that was, for him, of vastly greater importance. Until he really listened to what his group was about, who they were for and against, he was not able to be shaken from his position.

Keeping an Elephant under Control

Psychologist Jonathan Haidt offers a helpful metaphor for understanding how our emotions can have such a significant impact on our thinking and listening. Picture an elephant with a rider. The rider and the elephant represent two ways we operate in the world.[11] The rider is our rational brain, small as a mouse, while the elephant is our emotional side, a lumbering beast. Imagine trying to control the movement of a huge elephant with influence the size of a mouse. Suffice it to say, this is not an easy thing.

Now imagine the elephant walking along and seeing a suspicious-looking stick on the path ahead. On instinct, the elephant would likely rear up and almost throw the rider off. The reaction would happen so quickly that the rider would not know immediately what was going on. But then, after the initial moment of shock and surprise, after the instant of fight or flight has passed, the rider

---

11   See Haidt, *The Righteous Mind: Why Good People Are Divided by Politics and Religion* (New York: Random House, 2012), 61–66.

can get a look and realize that it's not a snake, as the elephant pre-rationally assumed, but really just a stick, and everything is okay.

Here's another example of this type of experience, where our reaction comes before our rational thought. If you type a lot, you might notice that your body seems to know when you've made a mistake before your mind does; your fingers reach almost instantaneously to delete the previous few letters and then immediately move to make corrections. (I probably did that twenty times writing or editing this sentence!)

We might like to think that our rational selves are always in control. We choose what we want to believe, how we want to think, what we want to do. We imagine ourselves as always deliberating to make the best choices. But this vision of ourselves is easily undone when we reflect on what we do when we're hungry, tired, stressed, under pressure, or anxious. Think about watching your favorite sports team or athlete compete, only to see them lose or suffer an injury in a critical moment. We're crushed. We throw our hands into the air and our head into our hands. And we did it all without thinking. It's as if those actions just happened.

When we're hungry, tired, stressed, or anxious, our social skills are limited. I remember when my mother first taught me the meaning of *hangry*, the portmanteau of *hungry* and *angry*. When she helped me see how my emotions were connected to my hunger, and then later, how much different I felt after a meal, it was a revelation. Again, it's as if this just happens to us.

That's the rider and the elephant.

Even though we tend to value the rational side of ourselves as we think and listen, we can struggle to control the lumbering beast that is our emotional side. We quickly become impassioned, opinionated, and perhaps angry or outraged when we encounter ideas we disagree with or find abhorrent. Perhaps we just plain don't like the person sharing the ideas, and so we think nothing they say can possibly be good. In all these cases, our emotions are in charge. We're in Refutation Mode. Our ears have been stopped up. Our thinking has taken on a posture of attack.

In Jacobs's story, when the listener finally confronted the speaker, what happened wasn't what we might expect. The speaker didn't immediately argue back. Nor did he concede to the criticism he had just received. Rather, he told the listener to "give it five minutes." While a little taken aback, the listener eventually perceived the value in the speaker's recommendation, realizing he hadn't listened as fully as he could have. Five or ten minutes to let the point settle is just enough time for any high-energy, overly emotional reaction to burn itself out. This is good advice. Once we've cooled off, we can better tend to the plain argument we've heard, approaching it with a little more intellectual distance. In a way, we're able to hold it up and look at it from different angles, to really consider whether we agree or disagree. And then we're able to respond more thoughtfully, if necessary.

Jacobs also suggests that we try, with all the fortitude we can muster, to listen fully. Rather than responding with either affirmation or counterpoint to what we hear, we would do better to ask questions, invite the speaker to go deeper into a particular point they are making, or at the very least admit we've been given something worth thinking about.

I will add yet one more piece of advice. Acknowledging that we are not always the best listeners and that our emotions can get the best of us, consider asking yourself three specific questions before you respond. Comedian Craig Ferguson has noted these questions in the context of marriage, but they're good for almost every situation, whether you are listening to a speaker, reading social media posts, sitting in a work meeting, or talking with a close friend. Ferguson says, "There are three things you must always ask yourself before you say anything: Does this need to be said? Does this need to be said by me? Does this need to be said by me now?"[12]

INTELLECTUAL HUMILITY

Hopefully, all of this advice rings as both true and genuinely helpful. If it does, perhaps that's because it's really not new advice at all. It echoes the ancient wisdom of the Christian tradition of practicing intellectual humility. Intellectual humility is nothing more than recognizing the biblical truth that all of us human creatures are fallen and therefore fallible—that is, we don't know everything and are prone to error. Despite whatever intellectual talents, gifts, and abilities we might have, all of us are likely to change our minds many times during our lives. Our thinking will evolve and hopefully improve. And as we tend to the Scriptures, prayer, congregational worship, and the various ways we can study and learn about the grandeur of the world God created, we can rely on the promised Holy Spirit to lead us into all truth (John 16:13).

Christians have long practiced a sense of intellectual humility. Perhaps most famously, Augustine quoted Isaiah in saying, "Unless you believe, you shall not understand."[13] Seven hundred years later, Anselm of Canterbury continued this thinking, saying, "*Credo ut*

---

12 Ferguson's 2011 comedy special, *Craig Ferguson: Does This Need to Be Said?*, was based on these questions. See, for example, this clip from the special: MGM+, "Ask Yourself 3 Things," January 14, 2011, YouTube video, https://www.youtube .com/watch?v=baExtaIhP8g (accessed April 16, 2024).

13 These words are found in the title of Augustine's "Sermon 43, On What Is Written in Isaiah: Unless You Believe, You Shall Not Understand," in *Sermons, Volume II (20–50)*, trans. Edmund Hill, O.P., ed. John E. Rotelle, O.S.A. (Brooklyn, NY: New City, 1990), 238–43.

intelligam" (I believe in order to understand), and describing faith as *fides quarens intellectam* (faith seeking understanding). Both thinkers—along with many in between and many since—presuppose something a bit counterintuitive to our ears. For them, knowledge of any sort always rests on a bedrock of faith. Let's briefly try to make sense of this.

There are countless things we simply believe without the ability to intellectually support them with logical arguments or empirical data. Take just one example: we simply believe that gravity is always going to make things fall down and hold fast to the ground. Many of us cannot explain gravity, but we're nevertheless immersed in its effects. It's always worked upon and for us in the same way. It's extremely reliable. It's normal to assume it will continue working in the same way in the future. But there is no way we can know for sure that it will. While this may seem a little silly, the more we consider it, the more we realize the truth of it. We proceed *believing* something about gravity without knowing much about it or having the ability to justify our belief. Much of our "knowledge" about objects, experiences, and observations that we take for granted in daily life is held in the same way.

For Augustine, Anselm, and many other faithful Christians, the practice of intellectual humility opens a space to be drawn deeper into the truths about the world and our Christian faith. Starting with this perspective—that we have limited ability to know anything at all—turns out to be very helpful in reflecting on what we can and do know. We remain open to learning, perhaps developing curiousness about all kinds of subjects.

In our time, especially amid the deeper differences and disagreements that tend to divide us in our society, the practice of intellectual humility allows faithful Christians to fearlessly engage with people who think and believe differently. And we can do so winsomely because such humility embodies an openness and curiosity that allows other people to be heard and understood. When we listen to people and seek to understand their perspectives—rather than listening simply to react or respond—a space is opened in which they might just reciprocate.

This was the experience of Darryl Davis, a Black musician and writer who surprisingly made friends with members of the Ku Klux Klan and other white supremacists. He simply sought to listen to and understand those who would see him as an enemy. That was his only intention. He asked them a simple question: "How can you hate me when you don't even know me?" As he listened to their answers and probed with questions to learn more, his conversation partners began to do the same, asking Davis questions and listening to him. Over time, friendships developed, and some of the people he had gotten to know began to change their minds. Still, reflecting on his experience, Davis said, "I never set out to convert anyone. But in the process, they ended up converting themselves." (We will encounter Davis's story again in a later chapter.)[14]

Like Davis, we never know exactly where God might be at work allowing the light of our Christian witness to shine through, whether in words or deeds. We are, however, called to be faithful in how we engage with others. Listening and engaging well is a form of doing that. When we live fearlessly and faithfully across the boundaries of our deep differences, God is undoubtedly at work revealing His love to others through us because what we're describing here is simply a way of loving our neighbor.

14   *Accidental Courtesy: Darryl Davis, Race, and America*, directed by Matthew Ornstein (Sound & Vision, 2016), premiered February 13, 2017, on PBS.

ASSUMING MOTIVES

All of this leads to the third challenge we face. Whenever we think we're right in an argument, we tend to overemphasize the wrongness of others and exaggerate the rightness of ourselves or our group. Psychologists call this "motivation attribution asymmetry."[15] That is, we imagine that those who disagree with us are worse sorts of people than we are—less intelligent, vile, and not to be associated with. We, on the other hand, are well intentioned, rational, and on the side of righteousness.

In other words, we designate others according to a moral standard, which is usually our own position. When we elevate ourselves to be the criterion for what counts as exemplary, the only place for those who disagree is somewhere lower and less than. We make assumptions about their motivations from this same position. Using ourselves as the positive and excellent standard, we consider anything other than our own motivations to be evil, sinful, and abhorrent.

This framing of our differences amounts to a form of judgment. That is, we reduce what it means to be a person down to the ideas, opinions, or positions they hold, and then we decide whether the person is bound for heaven or hell on the basis of whether they agree with us. (We'll discuss this point more in a later chapter.) We feel unable to interact with others because we consider our differences too significant, as if those differences can be overcome only in a zero-sum game. Either a person fully comes around to our position and agrees with us, thus enabling interaction and perhaps even cooperation, or they are always untrustworthy, and thus worthy of our enmity.

---

15 See Brooks, *Love Your Enemies*, 21–22.

The trouble here is obvious. It's probably safe to say we all know the problem with making assumptions. They make us look bad, and when we make assumptions, we often end up thinking poorly of others too. Making assumptions is a habit of laziness. Rather than asking questions, digging deeper, and believing from the start that we don't know the whole story, we assign categories and labels, imprisoning the other person or group within the boundaries of our assumptions.

In the end, our assumptions about others and their motivations are likely to be wrong. Simultaneously, we remain oblivious not just to the possibility of our being wrong but also to the *fact* of our being wrong when it happens. And this can be deeply embarrassing. So embarrassing, in fact, that we are liable to protect our own sense of ourselves and our rightness by closing ourselves off to the possibility that we could even be wrong.

To avoid this kind of situation, we are again thrown back to the ancient wisdom of intellectual humility. We must recognize our own weakness of not knowing everything, of how often we do not have all the information, and certainly of our inability to know other people's hearts. Rather, it's likely that most of the people we disagree with are not nefarious at all. They are probably quite similar to us—motivated by good intentions for the sake of good outcomes for everyone. The difference between us is not motivation but rather our sense of what counts as a good outcome and how to achieve it.[16]

This space of disagreement does not warrant disassociation from the other. Rather, it warrants the long, hard work of discussion. Yet there are many who silently harbor the belief that openness to discussion about our differences is a weakness. For too many, openness to discussion signals openness to compromise, and to give

---

16   See Inazu, *Confident Pluralism*, 86.

even an inch, they believe, is to give a mile. This kind of "slippery slope" mentality betrays a deep insecurity in those who harbor it. Whether it is a position, belief, or idea they want to prevent from being challenged, or their own position of power, the end result of this approach is captivity to ideology, not truth. A willingness to discuss differences, then, especially from a posture of intellectual humility, is critical. But that's only possible when everyone comes to the table with an assumption that we can all agree is a good one: only together can we come up with the best possible plans for achieving good outcomes for all, rather than working singularly and without input from others. One person's blind spot is mitigated by another person's insight. Intellectual humility is a practice that opens space for this kind of collaboration.

Added to this must be the advice we receive from Paul, which tends to speak not just to our intellectual capacities or those of others, but to the whole person. Preceding his presentation of Christ as the most exemplary model of this, he says, "Do nothing from selfish ambition or conceit, but in humility count others more significant than yourselves. Let each of you look not only to his own interests, but also to the interests of others" (Philippians 2:3–4).

Paul's exhortation destabilizes us from the bad habit of considering ourselves and our motivations as the measure according to which we evaluate others, especially those with whom we have differences. Rather, seeing one another through the lens of and treating one another as if we were in the position of Christ upends the whole dynamic of antagonism that can result from assuming the worst about others that think, believe, or maintain positions different from ourselves.

REPUTATION:
WE ARE WHO WE HAVE BEEN

Joshua Harris is well known for his 1997 book *I Kissed Dating Goodbye*, in which he strongly discouraged dating with the argument that it led to premarital sex. The primary goal was to save sex for marriage. Many who have read the book or come under the influence of its ideas have confessed that, as they moved into married life, it was difficult to leave behind the rules that were in place before marriage. The anticipated freedom to engage in sex after marriage didn't come as easily as they'd been told it would, thus making the new marriage a rather difficult situation. Harris later apologized for these and other unintentional consequences, ultimately coming to support dating, as he saw its importance in relational development and discernment in the lives of his three teenage children.[17]

Harris's story highlights something about the reputation of the church and Christians in the minds of many: we are known for what we are *against*. This is the fourth challenge we face. Despite the fact that God's rules, such as those against premarital sex, point followers of Jesus to His best for them, what often happens is that the church overemphasizes those prohibitions, the things we are against. Considering the various positions of churches across America, the public believes we're against sex outside of marriage, abortion, divorce, gambling, drinking, dancing, swearing, using drugs, science, liberals, and much more. But there is a deep lack of understanding and articulation about what Christians are *for*.

---

17   Joshua Bote, "He Wrote the Christian Case against Dating. Now He's Splitting from His Wife and Faith," *USA Today*, July 29, 2019, https://www.usatoday.com/story /news/nation/2019/07/29/joshua-harris-i-kissed-dating-goodbye-i-am-not -christian/1857934001/ (accessed April 16, 2024).

The public imagination concerning the church tends to picture a man standing on a street corner with a megaphone in one hand and a Bible in the other. As he shouts his warnings into the megaphone, he shakes the Bible at those who might make eye contact. Hardly anyone likes such confrontational interactions. We try to avoid confrontation most of the time since it elicits the anxious feelings associated with a fight-or-flight response. Unsurprisingly, then, when the church is perceived as primarily telling a story about how everyone who is not a member is somehow bad, evil, or going to hell, it is unlikely to gain much of a hearing in our time.

Such approaches may have worked in the past when life was often shorter and more difficult. From the Reformation up through early modern American history, there was a strong current of preaching the possibility of damnation to elicit a change in heart. But in our late modern era of comfort and distraction, confrontation is not an effective approach. It tends to turn people away.

Alternative tactics, however, such as those that focus on making the Christian life attractive, can quickly go awry. Following Jesus can easily be narrated as if it's a product that will always make your life better, much like the digital marketing we absorb daily or the pitch of a salesperson who immediately descends upon our arrival at a furniture store or car dealership.

A more faithful approach is one that is both winsome and honest. By the word *honest*, we might think of not neglecting the hard truth that we are all sinners in need of a Savior. Yet we arrive at telling that hard truth not from a megaphone on a street corner but as God allows over a period of time that produces a relationship built on trust. This is the way many of us came to be followers of Jesus. God used people in our lives whom we had come to trust to tell us the Good News of Jesus, of our need for a Savior because of the problem of sin.

We might have learned how Jesus worked positively in their lives, how they learned about the amazing gift of grace, how God worked to change them for the better through the humble and regular admission of their sinfulness. And after hearing about how life is different as a follower of Jesus—often more fulfilling, despite not always being sunshine and rainbows and still including suffering, failure, and disappointment—we might have begun to see that this is the kind of life that makes sense. Perhaps we've also felt drawn toward this Jesus, who, up until that point, we had merely heard about but didn't know.

This presentation of the Gospel is winsome and attractive in ways that remain faithful to the narrative of Scripture and the lives of many who follow Jesus. More important, this approach to introducing people to Jesus is rooted in the very person of Jesus Himself. While it's easy to point out all the moments when Jesus had negative things to say—correcting His disciples for their weak faith, cleansing the temple, or calling out the religious leaders for their hypocritical unfaithfulness—the Gospel narratives contain many more moments of Jesus revealing what He is *for*. And what we see is exactly how He describes Himself: "For the Son of Man came to seek and save the lost" (Luke 19:10).

In other words, Jesus reveals Himself as someone who is *for* others. Dietrich Bonhoeffer centers our attention on this fact when he describes Jesus as "the man for others."[18] As in my retelling of

18 See Dietrich Bonhoeffer, *Letters and Papers from Prison*, vol. 8 of *Dietrich Bonhoeffer Works*, ed. John de Gruchy (Minneapolis: Fortress, 2009), 501. This edition uses the more inclusive language of "human being for others" when translating Bonhoeffer's German. I have retained the classic and more well-known phrase "man for others." See, for example, the translation by Eberhard Bethge (New York: Touchstone, 1997), 382.

Jesus' encounter with the Samaritan woman earlier in this chapter, we can see Jesus as the man for others across so many different encounters throughout the Gospels, from His compassion for the widow at Nain (John 7:11–17) to His redeeming of Zacchaeus the tax collector (Luke 19:1–9), from the healing of Jairus's daughter (Mark 5:21–24, 35–43) to the quiet, yet serious engagement with Nicodemus the pharisee (John 3:1–21), and so many more.

Even when we see Jesus confronting others, it is often quite clear that His posture against a behavior, practice, or belief is because He is advocating *for* something better. For example, when Jesus cleanses the temple and throws out the money-changers, He is seeking to reestablish the role of the temple as a house of prayer in which God's faithful followers can worship and commune with God (Matthew 21:12–17).

Bonhoeffer said in another place that the church on earth is "Christ existing as church-community."[19] When the church faithfully follows after its Lord, it is living in a way that embodies His presence to the world. The incarnate Christ, the Gospels tell us, came to those who did not know Him in order to make the Father known (John 1:10; Matthew 11:27). The Gospel writers tell this story of Jesus so that we might believe and have life in His name (John 20:31; 21:24–25). If Christ came into the world as a stranger, and the church is His embodied presence in the world now, then our approach to the world continues His ministry, which was not to condemn the world but to save it (John 3:16–17). Rather than take on the persona of a street preacher wagging his finger and hollering angrily at passersby, the church will, like Jesus, engage every variety of person in such a manner that everyone a Christian

19   Dietrich Bonhoeffer, *Sanctorum Communio: A Theological Study of the Sociology of the Church*, vol. 1 of *Dietrich Bonhoeffer Works*, trans. Reinhard Krauss and Nancy Lukens (Minneapolis: Fortress, 1998), 121.

meets might also meet Jesus, since He is present and embodied in every Christian. For as Paul has said, "It is no longer I who live, but Christ who lives in me" (Galatians 2:20). Carrying on Paul's words into Bonhoeffer's description of Jesus, if Christ lives in us and He is the man for others, that makes every Christian a person *for* others.

More than being known for what we are against, the church can and should be known for what we are for. The church is *for* what Christ is *for*—that is, others. Not rules, not morals, not orthodoxy. At least not primarily. All those are means to the greater end of lost souls encountering the One who was sent to seek them.

Ultimately this is what we see in Jesus and what we, as the church, are empowered by the Holy Spirit to emulate: someone who never lets an issue prevent a relationship. Nothing stood in the way of Christ coming to any of us—not even the fact that we were still sinners and even enemies of God (Romans 5:11), and what greater divide could ever exist? This is exactly how the church is called to live before the world if we are indeed "Christ existing as church-community," as Bonhoeffer says. In us, the world can meet Jesus.

HOW *NOT* TO LET
ISSUES PREVENT RELATIONSHIPS

In later chapters, we'll explore how the earliest centuries of the Christian Church lived in just this manner and reflect on how the same impact is possible today. We'll articulate even more practical ways to engage winsomely with others for the sake of the Gospel. For now, it's helpful to sum up the four habits from this chapter that we can cultivate to help us live in such a way that issues no longer prevent relationships. The goal is to build relationships of trust, to the end that people might meet Jesus in us.

First, by countering our knee-jerk reaction of disassociating from others who hold different convictions, opinions, or preferences from us, we can seek to overcome relational gaps. It's likely that, despite our differences with others, we share many common interests, preferences, hobbies, and so on. Trying to overcome ideological differences as the means of deepening a relationship is often futile. Focusing on the things we have in common—which, when we look for them, are often numerous—leads to building foundations of trust. Only in solid relationships of trust is it possible to deal with any ideological differences. The relationship of trust provides a cushion for the fall the person might experience after their Wile E. Coyote moment.

Second, listening to understand will always be more relationally effective and winsome than listening to respond. Trying to understand another person's perspectives, opinions, or beliefs often leads to opportunities to share our own positions. When we listen to someone, they often reciprocate. Furthermore, listening well helps us embody a posture of intellectual humility; doing so reminds us and signals to others that we realize our own knowledge is limited and our own positions may not always be correct. Listening well helps us and others get closer to the truth, which is where God promises to lead us by the power of His Spirit.

Third, when we "in humility value others above ourselves" (Philippians 2:3, NIV), we can overcome our bad habit of motivation attribution asymmetry. By refusing to elevate ourselves as the standard for what is right, good, and proper, we see that those who disagree with us are not nefarious as we presumed; instead, they are likely just as well intentioned, just as concerned for the good of others, even if they approach from a different angle.

Finally, it should go without saying that a negative public reputation is undesirable for any church or group of Christians. Bring up the Westboro Baptist Church, and you'll likely see a bunch of eyes rolling. While we will never be able to fully eradicate negative perceptions of an institution that's full of sinners, we can mitigate against it both by owning our identity as people *for* others and by actively narrating and describing who we are in terms that reveal that's who we are. Indeed, it is who we are because it is who Jesus Christ is. The man for others has made the church to be people for others. Let us follow where He leads that the world might meet Him in us.

REFLECTION QUESTIONS

1. As you take a look at your own life, what or who has discipled you? What habits or ways of being can you clearly name as coming from being surrounded by others?

2. Think of a debate or conversation that included two or more parties on opposing sides. What were some of the characteristics of the discussion that seemed helpful or fruitful? What were some characteristics that seemed divisive and unhelpful?

3. What issues have prevented relationships in your country, town, or personal life? What might a relationship with someone "other" look like in day-to-day life? How easy or difficult would it be to set aside the impulse to convince them to believe as you do?

4. Think of a time in your life or in the life of someone you know when a major belief was changed. What caused that change? What environment or actions and words of others influenced the change? Was it gradual or was it like falling off a cliff?

5. How has your church or the church at large allowed what we are against to eclipse what we're for? How has this contributed to the decline of the church? How might a transition to emphasizing what we are *for* contribute to a winsome witness?

CHAPTER 4

Hospitality beyond Boundaries

How to Welcome Others and Enemies

ERECTING BARRIERS AND POLICING BOUNDARIES

Crime dramas are perpetually popular. Beyond television and streaming, they are easy to find on podcasts, books, video games, and more. We all seem to love a good detective story, and there is almost always a satisfying ending when the dramatic plot is finally resolved.

Crime dramas usually show the so-called good guys going after the bad guys to serve justice after a crime has been committed. Those who have committed crimes are often pictured as reprobates. There is nothing good about these people, viewers are led to believe. They are scum. We feel a sense of repugnance about such people, and the drama's storytelling purposefully tries to evoke these feelings and sensibilities in us.

But those feelings are not limited to our time spent watching crime dramas. In fact, feeling repulsed and labeling others as scum are regular features of our experience as fallen human beings. We regularly fail to see others—especially those who have done bad things—as made in the image of God and as people for whom Christ shed His blood. Instead, as we discussed in the previous chapter, we tend to disassociate from anyone we disagree with or label as repugnant, as if associating with them will somehow infect us with their "badness." Fear of this kind of "infection" drives much of our social interaction in our time.

In the Old Testament, God's people were commanded not to associate with other peoples (see, for example, Deuteronomy 7:1–5). God's people were set apart. This is what it meant in the Old Testament to be "holy." Still, rather than following such commands, God's people often associated with other peoples, even intermarrying and taking on their worship of false gods.

In our secular age, the church tends to operate with the same Old Testament sensibility concerning our associations. On some levels, this is appropriate, such as when seeking agreement in matters of doctrinal theology. But we are New Testament Christians. We live *after* God's ultimate act of sanctifying the unholy—Christ's suffering, death, and resurrection. Thus, on most levels, this tendency to separate and break relationships is not appropriate. Instead, we are free to treat others, especially outsiders, with Christlike hospitality, as we will explore below.

In our time, however, we find it easy to give reasons for why we should not or cannot associate with any variety of others. Whether it's because of race, gender, sexual orientation, political preferences, ethnicity, social values and ethics, socioeconomic status, religious difference, or more trivial things like how a person speaks, how they look, or how they smell—we are quite skilled at staying away from people who somehow make us feel uncomfortable or threatened.

The writer Alan Jacobs suggests that we all have someone who is, for us, repugnant, disgusting, or abhorrent in some way.[1] Our current cultural moment sees us sorting ourselves more and more into splintered and fragmented groups, associating ourselves only with those who seem to be like us. We draw a strong sense of identity and belonging from these groups. We feel like we're a part of something. Our membership makes us feel like our lives matter. Because of our deep connection and commitment to these groups, we have a sense of what we're for and what we're against. As it happens, what we're often against is, in the end, other groups—the people who belong to "them" as opposed to "us."

Jacobs is worried about this common phenomenon many of us both experience and perpetuate as members of society. When we label someone as repugnant, disgusting, or abhorrent, we might be doing so for rather narrow reasons. They believe something we don't agree with. They live in a way that we find unattractive. They support ideas or people that we cannot. And as we discussed in the previous chapter, those disagreements frequently result in fractured relationships.

Jacobs concentrates on the unhealthy narrowness of this kind of divisiveness. He points out that, because of our almost singular focus on issues over which we'll cut ties with someone, we end up missing so much about that person. We might enjoy the same books, music, movies, sports teams, and more. We might have similar backgrounds that have shaped our life experiences. We may in fact have quite a lot in common. But to the extent that we coldly

---

1   See Alan Jacobs, *How to Think: A Survival Guide for a World at Odds* (New York: Currency, 2017).

calculate whether we can maintain a relationship on the basis of agreement on solitary issues of deep concern, we end up reducing others to something less than full persons. We fall afoul of the category mistake of thinking people are equivalent to their ideas, beliefs, or positions. We miss a great deal of their full humanity.

So, who's the repugnant, disgusting, or abhorrent person in your life? That's a hard question to answer out loud; even privately, we may not want to admit to an answer. We all want to be seen as the kind of person who loves everyone (this is perhaps more an American attitude than a Christian one, but the ethical impulse behind it has roots in biblical morality). Even more, we don't want to imagine that it's remotely possible we could be the sort of person who sees others as disgusting or repugnant. It's easier just to deny it. Rather than face down this difficult question, we dismiss it out of hand to save face.

Perhaps it's in an effort to preserve our social standing, but we all know it's undesirable even to appear to be people who think of others as disgusting, abhorrent, or repugnant. Yet despite our efforts to appear loving and accepting of everyone, there are moments when our behaviors betray us and reveal who we really are.

UNEXPECTED OUTCOMES

Darryl Davis is a Black man who makes friends with members of the Ku Klux Klan and other white supremacists. Davis even keeps a large collection of memorabilia and garb associated with these groups. As he tells his story, he shares that many people in his life question how he could possibly engage in such relationships. They wonder why he would keep the memorabilia and other items rather than burn them. This kind of questioning displays the modern impulse I have been describing, the nearly immediate disgust and sense of repugnance when faced with a cultural other. While the motive might be laudable (for example, concern for Davis's well-being), their questioning indicates that they don't understand what Davis is up to.

"How can you hate me when you don't even know me?" That's what Davis wonders. It's also the question he puts to the white supremacists he befriends—the people whom many of us assume would be least likely to befriend a Black man. But Davis's work of friendship, while never meant to convert anyone from their views, actually causes some people to realize the error of their ideological viewpoint. The documentary *Accidental Courtesy*, which tells Davis's story, shows seemingly genuine friendships developing because of his endeavors.[2] One of the things he tells us there is, "You don't burn our history, regardless of the good, the bad, and the ugly." Despite how repugnant that history might be, and especially for someone like a Black man engaging with white supremacists, Davis suggests that we can do no better than retain that history, take it seriously in all its ugliness, and learn not to repeat the way things have gone wrong. Without our history, we do not know ourselves. We cannot know ourselves without our past, since our past experiences are fundamentally formative for who we are today, as much for individuals as for society. Davis clearly sees the ugliness of our history, but rather than turning away or seeking to do away with it, he presses further in. He ends up pleasantly surprised at the hope he finds as he witnesses people leaving behind their lives of hate.

The unexpected outcomes of Davis's actions stretch our imagination. If his story were not documented in both film and journalism,

---

2   *Accidental Courtesy: Darryl Davis, Race, and America*, directed by Matthew Ornstein (Sound & Vision, 2016), premiered February 13, 2017, on PBS.

it would be difficult in our time to believe it was anything other than fantasy. The outcomes he describes seem implausible. But that's just what makes his story so attractive. It's refreshing. It enlivens our imagination to believe that more stories like his could be possible. And I think, rooted as we are in the Christian tradition, that many more such stories are indeed possible by the power of the living God.

Let's consider a more familiar story, yet one with an even more unexpected outcome. Often we are the ones who feel repulsed by others, who erect barriers and stay comfortably on our own side of the divide. But the Gospel of John helps us picture what it is like to be on the other side—to be the repugnant one, the stranger who is abhorred and shunned.

John writes of Jesus, "He was in the world, and the world was made through Him, yet the world did not know Him. He came to His own, and His own people did not receive Him" (John 1:10–11). God Himself came into the world, becoming flesh, living as a human to speak to other humans with a human voice. But the world did not recognize Him. What's more, as He grew older and began His ministry, He was often rejected and treated as a blaspheming heretic. While His ministry was meant for the redemption of the world, the world sought to erase Him from itself.

While we don't always read the story of Jesus' life and ministry this way, there is a thematic through line in Scripture that allows us to consider Christ as a stranger coming into the world, treated by the world as an enemy, and dealt with likewise by being put to death. Theologians have long said that God works under the manner of opposites. Followers of Jesus know the unexpected end of the story: the world's rejection and murder of the divine Son of God paradoxically led to the world's redemption. In fact, since we are privy to the historical accounts, we learn from Jesus' conversation with the traveling companions on the road to Emmaus that not only did everything happen as it was supposed to but also that the Scriptures testify that the events were ordained by God to have happened that way (Luke 24:13–35).

ENEMIES WELCOMED TO THE TABLE

So, as followers of Jesus, how can we start to imagine a different outcome to our own stories of divide and enmity? I suggest a simple yet deeply Christian idea: hospitality. The word *hospitality* in English comes from a mishmash of Latin words for "host" and "hostile." Notice how two strongly opposing terms—*host* and *hostile*—come together to give us *hospitality*. I want to draw out this apparent opposition. For our purposes, we should think of hospitality as a form of hosting, welcoming even and most especially the stranger, the enemy (or hostile one).

We might apply this sensibility concerning hospitality by picturing Jesus' meal with Zacchaeus the tax collector (Luke 19:1–10). As Jesus made His way through a crowded Jericho, He met Zacchaeus perched in a tree. Zacchaeus was the chief tax collector of Jericho, sitting at the top of the hierarchy of publicans in a rather prosperous city (vv. 1–4). Jesus told Zacchaeus that He would dine at his home that day. Because Zacchaeus was a tax collector, Jesus' decision to dine in his home would have been a public scandal—after all, Jesus was eating with a sinner (v. 7). Even though the meal was in Zacchaeus's home, Jesus was the true host of the meal. And Zacchaeus, after having been in the presence of his very Creator and even dining with Him, was deeply moved.

In other words, like the parable of the great banquet in Luke 14 and the similar narratives that follow, Jesus the King dined in the home of a sinner, but He extended the invitation. Jesus was host, Zacchaeus the hostile one—but only for a while. In fact, the effect of dining with the King rendered a significant change in Zacchaeus. The swindling and greedy tax collector repented. He told Jesus that he would pay back each person with four times the amount he had cheated them of (Luke 19:8). Jesus then spoke to him a restorative word, saying, "Today salvation has come to this house, since he also is a son of Abraham" (v. 9). Jesus immediately followed this by describing the direction of His mission: He had been sent by the Father, going out into the world to "seek and to save the lost" (v. 10).

The restoration of Zacchaeus is like our own restoration. Meeting the King—whether through casual engagements, sharing a meal, or in some other way—can be a transformative experience. Jesus called each of us while we were still His enemies, the hostile ones (Romans 5:10). But now we are the redeemed who live and do as Jesus did and commands us. This is because, by faith, the Spirit has constituted us as God's people, the church. And that means people meet Jesus in us because we are the Body of Christ. Dietrich Bonhoeffer captures this well in his *Ethics*, saying, "The church is nothing but that piece of humanity where Christ really has taken form."[3] The shape of God's mission is always a form of going out. We see this throughout Scripture, from the incarnation of the Son of God sent to seek and save the lost, to the sending of His servants to call the unworthy ones and to invite them to the banquet, to the Great Commission (Matthew 28:18–20) and being sent to the ends of the earth (Acts 1:8). This is Kingdom hospitality, the inviting and welcoming of the unworthy and hostile ones, like Zacchaeus, those

---

3   Dietrich Bonhoeffer, *Ethics*, vol. 6 of *Dietrich Bonhoeffer Works*, ed. Clifford Green (Minneapolis: Fortress Press, 2005), 97.

in the story of the great banquet, and us. And so, as beneficiaries of God's hospitality, we are called to participate in His missional activity of seeking those who are outside the Kingdom, that they might become its members.

This ongoing dynamic of the hospitality of God reaching down from heaven and outward through the church into the world reflects the same dynamic as the incarnation of Christ. As the church—and like our Lord Jesus—we are a community of strangers in the world, sent to bring a message of hope and redemption that is not always welcome. We go to our own as the renewed and redeemed, and it is as if we are unrecognizable; the world seems not to know us. But this act of going out after having been pulled in, this contraction for the sake of expansion, is the movement of the Kingdom. Christian hospitality is a concrete form of making the Kingdom known by welcoming the stranger—those outside the Kingdom, for whom the church and its message is also strange—for it is the very power of God in us that empowers our welcoming of strangers, just as we were first welcomed by Christ.

HOSPITALITY AND THE TRANSFORMATION OF HOLINESS

Hospitality, then, in contrast to the set-apart-ness of the Old Testament, becomes the New Testament's characterization of holiness. Just as holiness in the Old Testament was not a passive way of being but rather something that was actively maintained, holiness in the form of hospitality in the New Testament doesn't neglect our passively received righteousness but reflects our active living in the freedom we have been given as God's redeemed. Rather than keeping distance or policing boundaries so that we are not "infected" by the unholy, it is distance and boundaries that become the marks of unholiness. Christ came to His *enemies*, let us never forget. He actively crossed the distance between unholy sinners and a holy God. That means that we were at one time counted among such enemies. But our enmity was not and never would be counted against us in an ultimate way, as if somehow rendering us beyond the pale of the redemptive work of God in Christ. Christ came because God "desires all to be saved and to come to the knowledge of the truth" (1 Timothy 2:4).

To reconsider hospitality in this sense is both deeply convicting and a high calling. We realize that we are incredibly weak to accomplish any of this on our own, failing more often than not. And we simultaneously grasp that carrying out the call of hospitality to those who are vastly different and strange from us, including our enemies and those we consider repugnant, disgusting, or abhorrent, is only something we can do with the help of God.

Luke Bretherton helps us make sense of this dynamic shift in concepts of holiness. First, he points out that in the Old Testament, God specifically commanded His people to show hospitality to strangers (as in Leviticus 19:33–34) and to ensure sojourners had something to eat (see Deuteronomy 24:19–22; Ruth 2:2). At the same time, the people of God also were given commands not to entertain foreign guests, to maintain purity rituals, and so on. The purpose of the Old Testament code of holiness was to avoid being contaminated or polluted, to stay clear of the influence of sin from foreign ways of life. Even more, holiness is meant to shape the lives of God's people entirely so that their very lives stand as a living witness to God and His kingdom. Still, this combination of imperatives—between hospitality to strangers and yet being set apart from them—presents a tension.

Bretherton notes that, as we move fully into the age of the New Testament,

> Jesus does not resolve the tension between hospitality and holiness present in the Old Testament, but he does relate these two imperatives in a particular way. Jesus relates hospitality and holiness by inverting their relations: *hospitality becomes the means of holiness.* Instead of having to be set apart from or exclude pagans in order to maintain holiness, it is in Jesus' hospitality of pagans, the unclean, and sinners that his own holiness is shown forth. Instead of sin and impurity infecting him, it seems Jesus' purity and righteousness somehow "infects" the impure, sinners and the Gentiles.[4]

The reversal of the metaphor concerning infection should capture our attention here. For the concern about infection—that we might become bad, evil, or sinful, that we might become like *them*—often creates fear. In our time, that fear is perhaps the most significant barrier keeping us from interacting with others based on the points of distinction highlighted above, such as race, politics, and class. And even though we might confess with the New Testament church that the hospitality of Jesus is demonstrative both for our salvation (He welcomed and died for us while we were still His enemies; Romans 5:1–11) and for how the church should live in the world (practicing the same kind of radical hospitality), in practice, the church tends to be no different from the rest of the

---

4   Luke Bretherton, *Hospitality as Holiness: Christian Witness amid Moral Diversity* (New York: Routledge, 2006), 130. Copyright © 2006 Luke Bretherton. Reproduced with permission of the Licensor through PLSclear. Emphasis mine.

world. We fear some kind of infection, so we police our boundaries and warn people away from contact with strangers rather than find ways to interact.

Jesus, however, empowers us to move in the opposite direction of where our fears would move us. God has made His church a unique people who live out of a unique power—a power made perfect in weakness (2 Corinthians 12:9). On our own, we are likely to be influenced substantially by the ways of the world, and even as members of the Body of Christ, we cannot prevent such influence entirely. Within our earthly existence, we still retain membership in various groups, whether as benign as a sports fandom or as significant as a vocational guild. We are also defined by other contingencies, such as race, gender, ethnicity, and political persuasion. And though we know that our ultimate allegiance should be to Christ as Lord, it is a lifelong formative process to subordinate every other form of group commitment beneath that primary allegiance.

JESUS AND THE CHURCH AS INFECTOR

Perhaps the most significant New Testament image that conveys the sense that we are empowered to "infect" others for the sake of the Kingdom occurs in Mark 5. There, surrounded by a great crowd, Jesus was engaged quietly and almost secretly by a woman who had suffered hemorrhaging for many years (vv. 25–26). According to purity standards, such a woman was perpetually unclean. Therefore, she was marginalized. She took a significant risk even joining the crowd. In humbleness of faith, she did not demand an audience with Jesus or make any requests of Him. She simply sought to touch the hem of His garment, believing that if she could manage to do that, she might be healed (vv. 27–28). And that is just what happened

(v. 29). But Jesus was not oblivious to her presence. He felt power go out of Him, He reported to His disciples. He knew someone had touched Him (vv. 30–31). When Jesus asked who had touched Him, the woman confessed with fear and trembling that it was she (v. 33). Jesus looked upon her with love, told her that it was her faith by which she was healed, and sent her on her way in peace (v. 34).

Jesus said to His disciples in the Gospel of John, "Truly, truly, I say to you, whoever believes in Me will also do the works that I do; and greater works than these will he do, because I am going to the Father" (John 14:12). We are as fearful and often as perplexed as the disciples were, but this promise extends also to us, the church. Do we believe that God will work through us such that His power will go out from us as we make contact with others who are not yet His followers? Do we believe that, rather than others infecting us, by the power of the Spirit, we might actually "infect" them as ambassadors of the King?

As the Body of Christ, we harbor the power of the Holy Spirit, sent from God the Father and our Lord Jesus Christ, and that power infects others who are outside the Kingdom. For it is the Spirit who, working through human endeavors and relationships, tills the soil of the human heart, allows the seeds of the Gospel that we cast to land on good soil, waters those seeds, and brings people to fruitful faith.

Bretherton again helps us picture this dynamic and infectious work as he reflects on the meaning of the parable of the great banquet (Luke 14:12–24; see also a parallel image in Isaiah 25:6–9). The king's servants are sent out to invite those who would expect to receive invitations—the elite—and then once again to those who would never expect to receive invitations—those who were marginalized and ostracized from the centers of society. The church,

Bretherton points out, serves as messengers of the King, sent out to invite those who are not worthy, which is exactly what each of us experienced when we were invited to meet Jesus. Our invitations reach those who sit on the margins of society, who don't believe they are worthy of invitations, and who haven't heard there is a banquet set for them.[5] Bretherton continues,

> Some will reject the invitation, others will accept, and some will need encouragement to believe that such an invitation includes them. The invitation is not to revelry or idolatry, but to the messianic feast that has *already* begun. Like Jesus, the speech and action of the church is simultaneously centrifugal—they go out into the world—and centripetal—the world is drawn into participating in the banquet. Thus, the church, like Jesus, neither separates itself from the world nor becomes assimilated to the world.[6]

PETER'S TRANSFORMATIVE EXAMPLE

Another example of this infection reversal can be found in Acts 10, which highlights a transformative story in the life of the apostle Peter. Peter struggled with God's call to share the Good News in Jerusalem, Judea, Samaria, and to the ends of the earth (Acts 1:8). Peter, like his Old Testament predecessor Jonah, seemed jealous that God's grace would be made available to those other than God's

---

5   See Bretherton, *Hospitality as Holiness*, 135.

6   Bretherton, *Hospitality as Holiness*, 135. Copyright © 2006 Luke Bretherton. Reproduced with permission of the Licensor through PLSclear. Emphasis in original.

chosen people. Let's take a moment to remember Jonah's story to see how closely it relates to Peter's.

In the book of Jonah, we encounter one of God's servants who didn't want to follow God's commands, particularly because he found those commands offensive (Jonah 1:3; 4:1). Do you recall what he was called to do? He was to preach repentance to the people of Nineveh (1:2). Now, the people of Nineveh were not a part of God's chosen people—that is, they were not a part of Israel. Some scholars suggest that Jonah didn't want to go to the people of Nineveh because he was envious that God would extend His mercy and grace to others beyond God's chosen people. And by the end of the brief four chapters that tell the story of Jonah, it's unclear whether he ever fully came around. Even after being swallowed by the great fish—and tormented by fear of his impending death, causing him to repent and promise to carry on with God's command—he still ended up hearing God's chastisement as he grumpily wallowed in envy, jealousy, and perhaps just a bit of self-pity after his proclamation produced the desired repentance of the people of Nineveh.

God moved in Peter's life to help him overcome his shared sentiment with Jonah. Peter experienced a vision in which a sheet came down from heaven filled with animals and a voice told him to kill and eat of the unclean animals he saw on that sheet. Peter was resistant and fearful of blasphemy. The voice of the Spirit insisted three times, finally telling Peter not to call unclean what God has made clean (Acts 10:15). Peter was perplexed by the vision and struggled to understand its meaning (v. 17).

Immediately he received an invitation from strangers to visit the house of Cornelius, followed by a prompt from the Spirit to rise and go to Cornelius's house. As the story progressed, Peter began to grasp the meaning of his vision, saying upon arrival at the house of Cornelius, "You yourselves know how unlawful it is for a Jew to associate with or to visit anyone of another nation, *but God has shown me that I should not call any person common or unclean.* So when I was sent for, I came without objection" (vv. 28–29, emphasis added).

The remainder of the story is Peter's proclamation of the Gospel to these Gentiles at Cornelius's home, who welcomed the message and received the Holy Spirit. Unlike Jonah, who remained angry with the Lord for blessing a people beyond those who were members of Israel, Peter went on to become the voice of authority in leading the early church to proclaim the Good News to the Gentiles (Acts 11:1–18).

The rest of the book of Acts captures this expansive growth of the kingdom of God through frail, fickle, feeble people like us, none of whom are much different from His first disciples or even from Jonah. As we noted above, the church is sent out just as Jesus was sent out, so that the world may know Him and all might be saved (see 1 Timothy 2:4). Bretherton succinctly highlights what we see throughout the whole Acts narrative, saying,

> The book of Acts proposes that by going out to the world, and actively participating in it, Peter was able to enjoy greater communion [that is, fellowship] with God. For a central dynamic of the church's neighbour relations, as articulated in this encounter, is that going out is the way of coming home. It is not just that Christians are to seek the welfare of the city, even though that city be Babylon (Jer. 27:9), but it is in the very act of going out to seek Babylon's welfare that they enjoy table fellowship with God: that is, holiness or purity is defined by [fellowship]

with God (and not by separation from sinners and pagans) and [fellowship] is enjoyed by seeking the welfare of the poor, the impure and pagans.[7]

A MODERN EXAMPLE: BONHOEFFER

One of my favorite theologians is Bonhoeffer, whom we have already heard from several times. He was a Lutheran pastor, theologian, and martyr who worked with the German resistance against the Nazi regime. He serves as a good example for us because he lived in the modern age. He grew up in a world that, while not as globally connected as our own, was still significantly pluralistic. He traveled substantially and was exposed to and reflected upon various cultural experiences and ways of life. Throughout his years of education and even within his own family, he encountered people different from himself. Bonhoeffer was exposed to many things that tend to divide us in our time—political assumptions, skin color, language, religious assumptions—but weren't quite so divisive in his own. Still, those experiences could have resulted in him developing a very different theology, that is, very different guiding principles for his life. But what we receive from him about our relationships with fellow human beings is critically applicable in our time.

Bonhoeffer looked to the Scriptures to get a sense of what it means for us to be human. In Genesis, he saw that humans are created in the image of God (1:26). Bonhoeffer rightly realized the significant impact this has for how humans relate to one another. Somehow, when we relate to another human being, we also seem to be relating to the divine in a particular way because every person is

---

7   Bretherton, *Hospitality as Holiness*, 137. Copyright © 2006 Luke Bretherton. Reproduced with permission of the Licensor through PLSclear.

made in God's image. Engaging human beings is equivalent to engaging God's handiwork and thus, by a short distance, God Himself.

Bonhoeffer went even further than this. Reading in Galatians, he saw that not only do we encounter the divine in others, but we also are able to encounter Jesus Christ in those who trust Him (2:20).

Those who trust Jesus have all encountered the divine in some way. In particular, we have encountered the divine through the people God used to bring us into citizenship in His kingdom. Someone introduced us to Jesus and the salvation He gives. Perhaps it was through our parents or other family members. It may have been through an ordinary relationship with a friend or coworker. Or it may have been through a pastor or church worker who ministered to us during a time of grief or personal crisis. Whoever it was and however it happened, we have encountered the divine, God coming to us through His presence in others. And through that encounter, God has done something; meeting Jesus in others changes us. We leave the encounter different than before.

What does this mean for us? What does this look like for our lives in the twenty-first-century West? We live in a time of great anxiety and precarity. Broken relationships and social division are all around us. Some days it feels like the world teeters on the edge of its own self-destruction. We feel backed into a corner of hopelessness, despair, and cynicism, feeling as if we can do nothing about it. Bonhoeffer lived during just such a time a little more than half a century ago.

THE CHALLENGE OF OPERATION 7

Bonhoeffer came of age in Germany during the rise of the Nazi regime, which was bent on taking over the world. One of the things he believed implicitly was that the world was not his to save. He was not responsible for carrying all the burdens or all the fears of Germany, nor solving all the problems of Adolf Hitler's totalitarianism. Bonhoeffer clung to the promise that Christ has already saved and overcome the world. Christ tells us this directly in John's Gospel, even as He simultaneously promises us that we will have trouble in this world (John 16:33). And it's true. We do experience trouble, and Bonhoeffer did as well—much more trouble than we may ever know.

Yet Bonhoeffer did not give up or cower in fear. He did not give in to pressures of conformity even when his life was under threat. Rather, he lived with Christ as his Lord and resisted the ways and powers of his world.

One of the great stories that demonstrates this is his involvement in Operation 7.[8] While the Nazis were in power, Bonhoeffer was part of the resistance against Hitler, serving as a double agent for the German secret service. Many of the leaders of this group were also secretly working against Hitler and trying to save Germany from self-destruction. Bonhoeffer was placed in charge of Operation 7, which was an effort to smuggle a small group of Jews out of Germany—first into Switzerland and then beyond to their freedom.

For Bonhoeffer, this was a moment of hesitation, a moment of decision. Participating in Operation 7 would mean risking his own safety for the sake of others—strangers to him, people who might even be considered his enemies. As Jews, they believed that Bonhoeffer, in his commitment to Jesus Christ, was fundamentally wrong. And not only that, but they rejected Christ as the Messiah. More than just disagreeing, the people whom Bonhoeffer was charged with helping believed that the very things upon which he staked his

---

8   See, for example, Charles Marsh, *Strange Glory: A Life of Dietrich Bonhoeffer* (New York: Alfred A. Knopf, 2014), 317–18.

life were wrong. So why would he help them? Or we might better ask, how could he bring himself to help them?

Here we return to Bonhoeffer's sense of what makes us human. Whether or not he found himself in agreement with the Jews, whether or not he believed they were wrong, whether or not he was hurt by their rejection of his most cherished beliefs, Bonhoeffer knew that in his encounter with these humans, he was also encountering the divine. And when we encounter the divine, we face a moment of responsibility. That is, Bonhoeffer needed to decide if he was going to reject or welcome the trace of the divine in these others, despite the fact that they did not share a common way of understanding things, even of the most sacred sort. These Jews were radically other to Bonhoeffer. But he saw past the surface and cared for them, successfully helping them to freedom because he knew that in one very specific way, he was responding to the divine image within them and thus also honoring God. By doing this, Bonhoeffer put others before himself, risking his own life for the sake of the lives of others. Furthermore, his care for the Jews in Operation 7 provided a living witness to them. Similarly, the story of his involvement in helping them escape to freedom stands as a living witness to us, a model for how we might proceed in relating to others across deep difference.

WELCOMING OTHERS AND ENEMIES

Who might be "others" to us in our present cultural moment? Most likely, they are people we disagree with or strangers whose lives we do not understand: the poor, the ill, those we perceive to be socially awkward, those who are ethnically different, racially different, or politically different, the elderly, children, those with different views on sexuality, and so on.

But we still *live in a world with* these others. We are still presented with opportunities to respond to them. We often have to work together with these others. And yet often, we intentionally seek to avoid any engagement with them.

As we noted earlier, our response in these situations must always consider that Christ came to our world as a man who was "other" to us. Yet He became one of us by willingly sacrificing all that was different about Him (see Philippians 2:5–11) in order to give Himself to us so that we might be united once again with God and be made His people. By His broken body, He became a curse for us sinners. We were the true others when we encountered Christ. But now, because of the redemption we have received in Him when He was broken, we have become Christ to the world, reconstituted as His Body. *We* are His Body. As Bonhoeffer says, the church is "Christ existing as church-community" (*Christus als Gemeinde existierend*).[9]

If we ask, "Where is God in the world?" we must answer that He is wherever the church is. Where is God working in the world? Wherever God's people are active in doing the things that Jesus is doing. That is, wherever you are. So, when we welcome others and enemies, we embody the very same hospitality with which God welcomed us into His kingdom. Having been welcomed by Him, we are empowered to do as He has done. As in the parable of the great banquet, God sends us out to call and invite others—those who are still far away from Him, perhaps believing themselves undeserving, unworthy—welcoming them into the Lord's house and offering a seat at the banquet table.

---

9   Dietrich Bonhoeffer, *Sanctorum Communio: A Theological Study of the Sociology of the Church*, vol. 1 of *Dietrich Bonhoeffer Works*, trans. Reinhard Krauss and Nancy Lukens (Minneapolis: Fortress, 1998), 121. Emphasis mine.

CLARITY FROM THE OUTSIDE

As we conclude this chapter on welcoming others who disagree with us, let's put that into practice by considering some observations from someone we might consider an outsider. It may seem unlikely and even feel uncomfortable that the church could come to understand its own calling better by listening to those outside the church, but that's just the case with someone like Jacques Derrida. The late French thinker is often misunderstood by the church, but his reflections offer us a renewed sense of what Christian hospitality means, especially in a secular age.

Derrida was an atheist, but his insights on language that the church regularly uses—such as "unconditional" when referring to God's love and forgiveness or even to hospitality—can benefit us. He thought of the church as the gold standard for understanding and experiencing such things as hospitality, acceptance, and forgiveness. Why? Because even as an atheist, he saw that in the church, hospitality is not just for the people we like or people like us but for everyone, since all people are made in God's image.[10] Hospitality means offering full welcome to any and every stranger as God brings them to us. This is because each person God brings into our orbit is someone whom God might serve through us. They are a neighbor,

---

10 See Jacques Derrida, *On Cosmopolitanism and Forgiveness*, trans. Mark Dooley and Michael Hughes (New York: Routledge, 2001). See also Derrida and Anne Dufourmantelle, *Of Hospitality*, trans. Rachel Bowlby (Stanford, CA: Stanford University Press, 2000). To be fair, Derrida stretches unconditionality to the breaking point—for example, always deferring a pure or truly unconditional hospitality to a messianic age to come that, as an atheist, he believes will never arrive. Still, the church's practice of hospitality is the closest earthly reference point to what he is trying to describe. For a discussion of Derrida's thinking in this regard, see John D. Caputo, *What Would Jesus Deconstruct? The Good News of Postmodernism for the Church* (Grand Rapids, MI: Baker Academic, 2007), chap. 2.

as it were, just like the Good Samaritan and the injured person he served (Luke 10:25–37).

Jesus' depiction of the Good Samaritan suggests that to encounter another person, whatever their need (and even if they do not have one), is to encounter the fingerprints of the divine. And every meeting of this sort demands something from us. When we encounter another, how will we respond if we see them as made in the image of God? Even more, Christ shed His blood to forgive all people. And while not everyone accepts this, it is still true that everyone we meet is someone for whom Christ died. How will we respond to these others when we see them in light of the gift that God offers them? For Derrida, the church ought to be setting the paradigm for true hospitality, establishing the criteria against which all other efforts at hospitality can be measured.

If Bonhoeffer is right when he says that the church is "Christ existing as church-community," then we shouldn't be surprised even when unbelieving outsiders like Derrida recognize something beautiful about the church. When we live as Christ—showing hospitality to strangers, forgiving our enemies, accepting one another's weaknesses—those whom we encounter in the world meet Jesus in us. Through us, every person in the world can experience God's love for them, whether they are anything like us or not.

No doubt our habits of focusing on differences and fomenting division because of them will be difficult to curb. And we know we cannot do this using our own will or strength. We need help. We are too weak.

Thankfully we can rely on God's promise that His power is made perfect in weakness. In our powerlessness, God's power truly shows up. Derrida understood that the church, a place that sets the standard for what hospitality looks like, calls its members to love even its enemies—and not only calls but empowers them to do so. This is exactly what has happened to each of us. We were once Christ's enemies. And He loved us in spite of our enmity. He showed that love by giving up His life. And then He rose again and sent the Holy Spirit into our lives, who enables us to welcome others and enemies, as He has done, bringing them into an encounter with Him.

One of Derrida's interpreters, the Catholic philosopher John Caputo, depicts this well when he says,

> Whenever one would expect an exercise of power from a classical hero, Jesus displays the stunning power of powerlessness—of nonviolence, nonresistance, forgiveness, mercy, compassion, generosity. The divinity that shows through Jesus consists not in a demonstration of might but in a complete reversal of our expectations culminating in the most stunning reversal of all. It is the centerpiece of all this madness, the one that makes as little sense as possible from the point of view of worldly common sense, the most divine madness of all: love your enemies. The key to the kingdom is to love those who do not love you, who hate you, and whom you, by worldly standards, should also hate. . . . Loving the lovable is entirely possible, but loving the unlovable, those who are impossible to love, that is when the kingdom reigns.[11]

Loving our enemies might be the highest and most difficult calling of any follower of Jesus. But it's possible because God empowers

11   Caputo, *What Would Jesus Deconstruct?*, 84.

us to do so. We know it's possible because we've experienced it in Jesus. As Jesus' Body in the world, the church will be where the world can look for unconditional welcome, because in Christ, that is truly what they receive. Like the king's ambassadors inviting the unwanted ones to the great banquet, we are inviting others to meet Jesus in the mundane activities of our lives. That is where they encounter Jesus as the other living in us.

For healing to come to the broken social experiment we call American society, and even more, for the church to contribute to the social flourishing of all, we have only to lean into the reality that the church already has all the tools it needs. When the church faithfully follows Jesus into the world of others and enemies, the ways of the Kingdom will be revealed to the world, beautiful (and indicting) as they may be.

As we live faithfully and fearlessly, empowered by the living God, our witness and way of life constitute a powerful alternative that God Himself will use to bring about both the conviction and the repentance He seeks. And as this happens, may the church practice the same hospitality they have received in Jesus so that the Kingdom might expand.

REFLECTION QUESTIONS

1. "At first I thought you were . . . but now that I've gotten to know you . . ." Have you ever said this or had it said to you? How can this experience help break past the barrier of someone's otherness? When a relationship seems undesirable or impossible, what could guide persistence?

2. How has the idea of infection as exerting positive, Kingdom influence changed your perspective of hospitality and engaging with nonbelievers? How does this concept exemplify our active living in the freedom we have been given as God's redeemed?

3. In what ways has the hospitality of others stood as a living witness to God and His kingdom in your life?

4. How have you seen fear impair the witness of the church?

5. How can you, like Bonhoeffer, cling to the promise that Christ has already saved the world and overcome fear as a barrier to hospitality and a winsome witness?

6. "Everyone we meet is someone for whom Christ died." Everyone! Who is someone for whom you struggle to acknowledge the truth of this statement? Take a moment to ask the Lord for forgiveness. Pray for opportunities for that person to meet Jesus in you.

CHAPTER 5

How to "Find Yourself" in the Age of Authenticity

DISAPPOINTED IN OURSELVES

Megan, 19, wants to stand out and be "the person," but she perceives herself to be falling short. The problem began in high school. She attended an elite academy, where she began "to feel like I was mediocre or below average." Earlier, at a regular school, she "was the smartest person in the class" and had been on the gifted and talented track since the fifth grade. This heady recognition made her feel special. But then came the academy, where she was surrounded by very bright, high-achieving kids. She began to "feel marginalized" and yearned to "feel special again." These feelings carried over into college.

Although she is now a scholarship student at a first-rate university, Megan is frustrated and despairing of herself. She explains that she is attending her "safety school" and wants to "show that I should be somewhere better by acing all my classes and being president of 40 organizations." But, she adds, "that is really not happening. I am, if anything, a mediocre student . . . and that just makes me so angry at the world and then me for not being the person." Although she wants "to impress someone," she says, "I end up being impressively unimpressive," and that "crushes me."[1]

Many of us either know a person like Megan or we can empathize with her experiences on a deep level. We live in a time when we feel like we're under pressure to be someone special and stand out from the crowd.

It wasn't always like this. The emphasis on identity that Megan's comments indicate is a recent one, something we'll discuss in different ways across this and the next chapter. In short, we've moved from a time in which identity was treated more as a given to a time when identity has become something of a task. The task is this: we're all supposed to figure out who we are, to "find ourselves," as it were, usually settling on an answer at some point within young adulthood.

But the pressure to somehow accomplish this task is, as Megan says, crushing. For one, it's hard to know when we've finally arrived, when we've finally and fully "found ourselves." At best, we end up announcing to the world, "Here I am, the real and authentic *me*,"

---

1 Joseph E. Davis, "The Deeper Roots of Youth Anxiety," Institute for Family Studies, February 18, 2020, https://ifstudies.org/blog/the-deeper-roots-of-youth-anxiety (accessed April 16, 2024).

without knowing for certain whether we're being real and authentic at all or if we even like what we've found.

This focus on identity is yet another feature of living in a secular age, in a time when we find it difficult to believe anything at all. In our age of implausibility, Christianity and all its associated beliefs are both contestable and contested, and so the very story that defines human existence and helps us each understand our identity ends up feeling implausible. We're tempted to look elsewhere for answers about who we are—hence the impulse to "find yourself" that we hear articulated all around us, especially by young people. So in addition to an age of implausibility, we're also living in an age concerned with authenticity.

This chapter will start by first examining what we mean by "authenticity" and why it seems so important in our time, especially as regards our sense of who we are. Then we'll explore why we're not just stuck with the task of "finding ourselves." While it's true that the commanding influence of the Christian story has been significantly weakened in the last few decades, it is not without power to capture our imagination once again. The Christian story offers a helpful and deeply plausible solution—in fact, the only solution—to the aimlessness of trying to find ourselves, and it grounds our sense of who we are in the authentic story of our roles, relationships, and responsibilities as people made in the image of God.

ARRIVING AT THE AGE OF AUTHENTICITY

In chapter 2, we engaged with Charles Taylor, who helped us understand what it means to say that we're living in a secular age and how the changes wrought over five hundred years affected religious belief in particular. Here, we will consider how those changes have also influenced the ways we understand ourselves—the stories that define who we are. Inevitably, religious stories impact the identity story, if only because religious stories provide the fodder for understanding identity. We look to these kinds of stories for answers about identity because they inevitably speak to our origins, discussing where we came from and why we are here. Without these background stories, we flounder when trying to understand who we are.

In his sweeping narrative of how we arrived in our secular age, Taylor discusses the shifts and differences in how people have understood themselves over the last five centuries. Perhaps the most important feature of these shifts is that, five hundred years ago, especially in the West, people's sense of how life in the world was organized existed primarily in the background. Their origin and identity story was taken for granted. As we've noted, almost everyone living in Western Europe at that time was a Christian, so there were no alternative origin stories. Rather than thinking *about* their story, people would simply think *with* it. What makes Taylor's work interesting for us is that he brings the background influence of origin and identity stories up to the level of our attention, where we can examine it, understand the ways it shapes our imagination, and, especially in our present time, try to respond with new awareness and, if necessary, resistance.

Taylor primarily wants us to recognize that most of us don't "theorize" about our existence. Rather, we tend to live in societies and communities that shape our sense of who we are through stories, images, and even legends. In the example above, we can easily see that a certain set of expectations functions as an imperative in Megan's life. She lives according to a story that operates in the background. If we were to ask her why she thought she needed to meet these expectations, she would most likely answer that they are normal, natural, just the way things are. But with a little effort, we can articulate how her assumptions about who she *should* be are captured in the form of a story. That story shows up every now and again in rather explicit ways in our lives if we have the eyes to see and hear it. In what follows, I'll try to help us hear and see it clearly.

YOU MUST BE INTERESTING

The beer brand Dos Equis and its character, the Most Interesting Man in the World, offer a picture of the expectations that Megan feels. Watch any of the commercials that feature this character, and you'll find them creative and humorous. You'll also notice that very little time and attention is given to the beer itself. Rather, the commercials cleverly subordinate the role of the beer into a bigger story. Ultimately, drinking Dos Equis—a rare experience for the Most Interesting Man in the World because he doesn't always drink beer—only serves to contribute to the great story of each commercial. We all feel the imperative of the commercials, which is not to drink Dos Equis but rather to be interesting. In other words, every Dos Equis commercial featuring that character tells this story: we should live lives like the Most Interesting Man in the World. Those are the only kinds of lives worth living, after all.

As for the beer, we should only drink it because the Most Interesting Man in the World does so. The commercials assume we will want to be like him because he is interesting; that is, they assume we want what everyone else also apparently wants: to be interesting. Drinking Dos Equis, then, is what interesting people do. It's a brilliant bit of advertising, in part because it's so entertaining and so subtle at the same time.

Those Dos Equis commercials make explicit what Taylor points out and what Megan feels. The Most Interesting Man in the World is presented as a model for us. Because of his stories and experiences in the commercials, we see him as a kind of legendary figure. We begin to compare our lives to his experiences, the access he has to such amazing opportunities and high-status people. When we do this, we quickly realize that our lives are not like his. Presumably, this is meant to feel a little disappointing, but in a light-hearted way. Still, we are also meant to be motivated—maybe we can be just a little more like the Most Interesting Man in the World by drinking Dos Equis.

The commercials and the character, while fictional and humorous, play on a subtle yet influential background story that tends to rule our lives. Like Megan, we all want to stand out, to be interesting, and thus to gain attention, receive affirmation, and feel good about ourselves.

FEELING GOOD AND BEING INTERESTING

Christian Smith, a sociologist of religion at the University of Notre Dame, helps us recognize the prevalence of Megan's story—that, really, this imperative to be interesting affects all of us, seeming to promise that becoming interesting will result in happiness and a good life. For more than two decades, Smith has conducted research on the lives of young people in the United States, especially looking at their interaction with religion and spirituality. More recently, he has also focused on their parents, who most strongly contribute to the religious or spiritual sensibilities of American teenagers.

Smith's research reveals that modern American teenagers share a widespread and homogeneous set of religious commitments that don't tend to differ, even if they officially adhere to different religions. In other words, while some participants identified as Roman Catholic and others as Mormon, Wiccan, Muslim, and so on, this set of commitments is shared despite the differences inherent in their belief systems.

Smith's findings are fascinating because they seem to point to something that lies beneath the surface of how the teenagers involved in his study identified themselves. There was something they all held in common that was supported not just by their religious commitments (whether Catholic, Muslim, Wiccan, and so on) but perhaps even more so by the cultural context within which each of them was growing up. In fact, the cultural context emerged as having more influence than did the specific religious group with which the teens claimed they were associated.

Smith articulated this common set of commitments by listing them as religious tenets and naming the set of commitments Moralistic Therapeutic Deism.[2] Smith explains each term and how they hang together. First, the set of commitments are "moralistic" because they are based on following specific rules to generate a

---

2   Christian Smith lays out the tenets as follows, referring to them as the "creed" of Moralistic Therapeutic Deism:
   1. A God exists who created and orders the world and watches over human life on earth.
   2. God wants people to be good, nice, and fair to each other, as taught in the Bible and by most world religions.
   3. The central goal of life is to be happy and to feel good about oneself.
   4. God does not need to be particularly involved in one's life except when God is needed to resolve a problem.
   5. Good people go to heaven when they die.

   Christian Smith, *Soul Searching: The Religious and Spiritual Lives of American Teenagers* (Oxford: Oxford University Press, 2005), 162–63. Copyright © 2005 Oxford University Press. Reproduced with the permission of The Licensor through PLSclear.

specific outcome. That is, people are supposed to be kind to one another, and if they are good people, their reward will be that they get to go to heaven when they die.

Second, the set of commitments are "therapeutic" in the sense that they function like a tool. Religion is not an end in itself but rather instrumental, useful toward a greater end—that of living a happy, enjoyable life. It is assumed that part of the moralism of being kind to one another is meant to help everyone achieve this good outcome of happiness. But when life doesn't seem to be going well, God is always there in the background, waiting to help out. And this is His primary function, it is assumed—He doesn't tend to meddle in human life otherwise.

Deism, then, is the final aspect of the set of commitments, drawing from the traditional sense of Deism, which holds that God created everything but then stands at a distance and does not intervene in human affairs. The classic metaphor for Deism is that God is a watchmaker who created a watch, wound it, and then set it to run on its own without interference. The difference in this modern version is that God is conceived of as wanting us all to be happy and will therefore intervene when we call upon Him to help us achieve happiness.

Smith captures the full sentiment of American teenagers' religious sensibility: "What appears to be the actual dominant religion among U.S. teenagers is centrally about feeling good, happy, secure, at peace. It is about attaining subjective well-being, being able to resolve problems, and getting along amiably with other people."[3] This same sensibility runs beneath the surface of Megan's story. She is frustrated because she is not experiencing a sense of "subjective

---

3   Smith, *Soul Searching*, 164. Copyright © 2005 Oxford University Press. Reproduced with the permission of The Licensor through PLSclear.

well-being" and is not "feeling good, happy, secure, at peace." That is, she seems to believe wholeheartedly that she *should* be experiencing life in this way and is frustrated and angry that she is not.

THE STORIES WE THINK *WITH*

These two examples—Moralistic Therapeutic Deism on the one hand and the Most Interesting Man in the World on the other—highlight what Taylor is getting at when he calls attention to the fact that stories, images, and even legends tend to lurk in the background of our lives. And these stories are not harmless or banal; rather, these stories shape how we understand ourselves, how we get along with others, how we make our way through life, what we should seek to attain and be during our lives, and which markers determine whether we have achieved our goal. In other words, the stories associated with these two examples are background stories that we often don't think *about*, but rather think *with*, as if they are simply normal, natural, just the way things are.

Taylor gives a name to this group of features that contribute to a person's sense of identity and which therefore help them make their way through life in whatever era or society they live in. He calls it the "social imaginary." He writes,

> Our social imaginary at any given time is complex. It incorporates a sense of the normal expectations we have of each other, the kind of common understanding that enables us to carry out the collective practices that make up our social life. This incorporates some sense of how we all fit together in carrying out the common practice. Such understanding is both factual and normative; that is, we have a sense

> of how things usually go, but this is interwoven with
> an idea of how they ought to go, of what missteps
> would invalidate the practice.[4]

In other words, each of us, whether or not we are aware of it, share with all other members of our society a sense of how life should be, what it means for life to be good, how human interactions should go, how to deal with trouble, how to get things done together, how to measure our status compared with others, and so on. None of this has been explicitly taught (usually). Rather, it has been *caught* as part of our formational experiences in institutions like schools, churches, the media, civic law, sports, the arts, and more. That is, we've absorbed it by being immersed in our culture.

To put it as simply as possible, the French thinker Rene Girard argued that our desires—our wanting of whatever it is we want—are not something we deliberatively choose with our free will. Rather, we learn to want things because we see others wanting them, like when a small child suddenly wants a toy only after seeing another child playing with it. We all retain something of that child within us. This is how Apple got us to buy iPhones and how Nike made us want Air Jordan shoes. We saw others who had them (usually in an advertisement), and those people looked genuinely happy. We wanted that same feeling, and it clearly seemed like that thing (whatever it might be) promised that we would feel the same happiness if we had it. So we bought it. When it comes to wanting, we have all learned to want by watching others. Free will had nothing to do with it.[5]

---

4   Charles Taylor, *Modern Social Imaginaries* (Durham, NC: Duke University Press, 2004), 24. Copyright © 2004 Duke University Press. All rights reserved. Reprinted by permission of the rights holder and the publisher.

5   For a helpful engagement on this, see Luke Burgis, *Wanting: The Power of Mimetic Desire in Everyday Life* (New York: St. Martin's, 2021). For an entertaining example of

INHERITING WHAT HAS BEEN PASSED DOWN

How did we come to have these shared sensibilities—in Taylor's terms, the social imaginary—that so powerfully determine much of what we expect from life and how we attempt to fulfill those expectations and desires?

One way to think about it is to return to the idea of immersion as a kind of discipleship mechanism, as discussed in chapter 3. Remember, we don't have to be talking about the Christian faith to use the language of discipleship. Discipleship is simply formation into a particular way of being in the world according to a particular story. The stories we are immersed in become the stories we live by. We inherit these sensibilities from all of the social settings that influence our formation—households, classrooms, entertainment media, even civic events that inculcate a kind of patriotism. Seen in this way, it's easy to recognize how we are discipled and learn to live according to similar stories or to have a shared social imaginary.

For most of us, it was from our parents (or at least those who played the most significant roles in raising us from small children into adulthood) that we learned or, better, *absorbed* our social imaginary. Returning to Smith's work, the shared religious sensibilities he found among modern American teenagers were, in fact, handed down by their parents. As Smith puts it,

> Contrary to many popular assumptions and stereotypes, the character of teenage religiosity in the United States is extraordinarily conventional. The

---

Girard's argument, see Jerry Seinfeld's acceptance speech for a Lifetime Achievement Award at the advertising industry's 2014 Clio Awards: https://vimeo.com/108370993.

vast majority of U.S. teens are not alienated or rebellious when it comes to religious involvement. *Most are quite content to follow in their parents' footsteps.* Most feel quite positive about religion, pointing out many advantages and benefits they see religion offering individuals, society, or both. When it comes to practicing religion, most U.S. teens appear happy to go along and get along.[6]

Kenda Creasy Dean, one of Smith's co-researchers who published a separate book aimed at a predominantly Christian audience, rightly sees Moralistic Therapeutic Deism as a problem. She repeats Smith's point in a different way: "We have successfully convinced teenagers that religious participation is important for moral formation and making nice people, which may explain why American adolescents harbor no ill will toward religion."[7] Dean goes on to describe that, in addition to parents, religious communities like the church are also significantly responsible for forming the background assumptions that we use to negotiate our way through life. But troublingly, sometimes churches inculcate background assumptions that work against the very mission of the church.

---

6   Christian Smith, *Soul Searching*, 260. Copyright © 2005 Oxford University Press. Reproduced with the permission of The Licensor through PLSclear. Emphasis mine. For further research on the influence of parents on the religiosity or spirituality of young people, see Vern Bengston, *Families and Faith: How Religion Is Passed Down Across Generations* (Oxford: Oxford University Press, 2013); Christian Smith, Bridget Ritz, and Michael Rotolo, *Religious Parenting: Transmitting Faith and Values in Contemporary America* (Princeton: Princeton University Press, 2020); Christian Smith and Amy Adamczyk, *Handing Down the Faith: How Parents Pass Their Religion on to the Next Generation* (Oxford: Oxford University Press, 2021).

7   Kenda Creasy Dean, *Almost Christian: What the Faith of Our Teenagers Is Telling the American Church* (Oxford: Oxford University Press, 2010), 6. Copyright © 2010 Oxford University Press, Inc. Reproduced with permission of The Licensor through PLSclear.

The problem does not seem to be that churches are teaching young people badly, but that we are doing an exceedingly good job of teaching youth what we really believe: namely, that Christianity is not a big deal, that God requires little, and the church is a helpful social institution filled with nice people focused primarily on "folks like us"—which, of course, begs the question of whether we are really the church at all.[8]

THE CULTURAL MANTRAS WE'VE INHERITED

To press further into this elaboration on the stories we tend to live by, we need to widen the scope and consider other ways that the cultural environment in which we're immersed tends to shape the shared social imaginary that makes us all more or less someone like Megan. To do that, let's spend some time reflecting on other cultural "mantras," as I'll call them—that is, phrases and sensibilities that we've often heard and even said throughout our lives that function as the refrain of our modern social imaginary in the age of authenticity.

The fast-food chain Burger King has long used the invitational but also semi-imperative phrase "Have It Your Way" in its advertising. The sense of this marketing effort is simple. Whether by drive-through or counter service, you can order what you want exactly how you want it. But something else subtly underlies this message. It's the sense that not only *can* you order what you want and have it served to you exactly as you asked for it but that this is

8   Dean, *Almost Christian*, 11–12. Copyright © 2010 Oxford University Press, Inc. Reproduced with permission of The Licensor through PLSclear.

how it *should* be, as if it's your right for things to happen this way for you.

In a 2006 ad that is part of the "Have It Your Way" theme, we're given even more explicit guidance for how we should understand the message. Against a classic red background that is part of their usual advertising color palette, Burger King adds these words in smaller print under the headlining "Have It Your Way" phrase:

> You have the right to have what you want, exactly when you want it. Because on the menu of life, you are "Today's Special." And tomorrow's. And the day after that. And . . . well, you get the drift. Yes, that's right. We may be the King, but you my friend, are the almighty ruler.[9]

Burger King's example plays directly into the social imaginary that flies under the radar of most of our day-to-day life. It names explicitly a general expectation that we hold—one that hasn't necessarily been taught but which we have nevertheless caught due to the formative power of modern cultural values. Those same values come at us in a variety of other mantras that make up the refrain of our modern narrative.

David Brooks, a columnist at the *New York Times* and best-selling author, highlights other such phrases in his book *The Road to Character*. The mantra of Burger King's advertisement tends to center us as individuals and especially our happiness as the most important concern we could have. Brooks argues that this and other similar mantras signal that we live in the time of what he calls "the

---

9   Examples of this ad are easy to find online. For a sample of the image within a brief history of Burger King's "Have It Your Way" marketing campaign, see https://hookagency.com/blog/have-it-your-way/.

Big Me."[10] In the era of the Big Me, Brooks suggests that we tend to live by mantras that center our well-being and happiness as the highest good in life. Hearing and using phrases like those that follow reveal what we believe it means to live in this era of the Big Me.

"Follow your heart."

"Find your passion."

"March to the beat of your own drum."

"Be true to yourself."

"You do you."[11]

It's likely that we've all heard, been encouraged by, and even used those phrases to encourage others at some point in the past. Such phrases are peppered through commencement speeches for high school and university graduates. There's no reason to believe that anyone using the phrases is doing so for anything other than well-intentioned reasons.

Despite that, however, the power of these mantras in helping to articulate and shape a self-centered, personal-happiness-oriented social imaginary is undeniable. These mantras have become so normal that they seem natural and banal to us now. Yet in becoming normal, they've also become normative. That is, we don't tend to question them. Or if we experience someone questioning them, our knee-jerk reaction is likely to be defensive. *What's wrong with these mantras?* we wonder. *Aren't they positive and encouraging, and don't we need more of that in our lives?*

---

10   David Brooks, *The Road to Character* (New York: Random House, 2014), 6.

11   Brooks explicitly names some of these in *The Road to Character* and others in a brief presentation. David Brooks, "Humility in the Time of Me," Q Ideas, April 19, 2019, video, https://vimeo.com/329660091 (accessed April 16, 2024). Others in this list are familiar to us all, and I've added them to expand on his point.

CAN WE REALLY
TRUST OUR OWN HEARTS?

Fifteen hundred years ago, the African Bishop Augustine of Hippo wrote about an incident in his life that occurred when he was a young teenager. Out and about, he and some of his peers found themselves in an orchard. Whether they had permission to be in this orchard is not clear, but the way he tells the story makes it clear that it did not belong to any of their families. Augustine describes the incident, saying,

> We carried off a huge load of pears. But they were not
> for our feasts but merely to throw to the pigs. Even
> if we ate a few, nevertheless our pleasure lay in doing
> what was not allowed. Such was my heart, O God,
> such was my heart. . . . It was foul, and I loved it.[12]

To Augustine's insightful yet convicting realization, we can add another one, this time from twentieth-century Russian dissident Aleksandr Solzhenitsyn. Solzhenitsyn had been imprisoned for his resistance against the government, and his experience in the gulags offered him an opportunity to focus on where the fault for his situation really rested. However much he could legitimately point the finger away from himself, he realized he could not escape his own complicity in the evil of the world. His own deviance, regardless of whether it was a reasonable response to the mistreatment he experienced from his country's government, nevertheless only added more evil to the world rather than eliminating it.

---

12 Augustine, *Confessions*, trans. Henry Chadwick (Oxford: Oxford University Press, 1991), 29. Copyright © 1991 Henry Chadwick. Reproduced with permission of the Licensor through PLSclear.

In the end, he famously observed that evil is a part of every human heart. Solzhenitsyn concluded that there is no way to fully rid ourselves—much less the world—of evil because it is a surgical impossibility.[13]

Indeed, the Scriptures lend their own wisdom here, such as when the prophet Jeremiah cautions us about our hearts, saying, "The heart is deceitful above all things, and desperately sick; who can understand it?" (Jeremiah 17:9).

The writer of Proverbs redirects our attention from looking inward to a place of wisdom we can trust, saying,

> Trust in the LORD with all your heart, and do not lean on your own understanding. In all your ways acknowledge Him, and He will make straight your paths. Be not wise in your own eyes; fear the LORD, and turn away from evil. It will be healing to your flesh and refreshment to your bones. (Proverbs 3:5–8)

The era of the Big Me is part of the social imaginary we've been discussing. We tend to ignore criticism of the above phrases and the counterwisdom of Augustine, Solzhenitsyn, or the Scriptures because we take it for granted that advice that points us inward to find truth is not problematic but rather good and wholesome. The modern mantras seem natural, while the ancient and less recent exhortations seem antiquated and out of style.

We are better able to see the problem with the modern mantras, then, when we look at their consequences. Consider the struggles

---

13   See Aleksandr Solzhenitsyn, *The Gulag Archipelago: An Experiment in Literary Investigations*, vol. 1, Harper and Row Perennial Classics Edition (New York: Harper and Row, 2007), 168.

Megan faces with her own sense of self and the standards by which she tries to measure her sense of success. She feels she is failing at life according to how she imagines it should be. She is frustrated and depressed. Drowning in these feelings, she aims these emotions first at herself and then at the world. But who can do anything about it? Who can solve the problems that Megan sees for herself? Most likely, the challenge falls back on Megan. She's going to have to find her way out of this. Maybe it'll be counseling that aims to help her have a more reasonable set of expectations—but she'll be the one who must do the work. Or maybe it'll be another mantra: this too shall pass, and Megan will just have to endure.

Many of us have been influenced as Megan has by the now clichéd phrases that focus us inward to consult our hearts for truth and wisdom. Perhaps you, like many others in our time, have heard this kind of encouragement in a commencement speech, where such "inspiration" is common. Yet as we move from our days as students into the long seasons of adulthood, we experience changing responsibilities, work, bills, and eventually things like a marriage, a family to care for, investments, retirement, and concern for legacies.

As these new experiences take shape in our lives, perhaps we begin to wonder about what we've been taught and what we've taken for granted. It seems that all the advice to look inside ourselves and to follow our hearts doesn't actually tell a person how to live very well. So, while all those clichés sound lovely and seem to promise a lot of freedom and opportunity, they don't offer much real guidance. In particular, they don't say much about what a human life should look like or what it's for. In other words, while we've all been encouraged to embrace our unique individuality, we were taught very poorly about how to be a part of something bigger than ourselves, or what something of that sort would even look like.

SEEING OUR LIVES
THROUGH A DIFFERENT FRAME

The great scholar of human suffering Viktor Frankl had a life-changing experience not long after he began his career. He was a Jew living at the time when the Nazi regime rose to power in Germany and began to systematically eliminate the Jews of Europe. He was interned at a concentration camp and watched many of his own people give up and take their own lives before the Nazis could do it for them in the gas chambers.

Frankl noticed, however, that those who survived were those who had something to live for. What they were living for was usually some person or some task they could not bear to abandon. Frankl himself was one of these people.

Reflecting on his experience later, Frankl said that he had not imagined that his own life would take the path it did. It was not what he asked for nor what he intended. Becoming a scholar of suffering was nowhere on his radar prior to his time in a concentration camp. But it became something upon which he could not turn his back. "It did not really matter what we expected from life," he concluded, "but rather what life expected from us." In other words, as David Brooks puts it, Frankl felt summoned.[14]

What would it mean for each of us to sense that life was somehow summoning us? What if we had a story that made sense of the experiences we have that call us to something greater, similarly to Frankl? We might start by noting how different our approach to living would be. Rather than reflecting the approach we see in

---

14 Victor Frankl, *Man's Search for Meaning* (Boston: Beacon Press, 1992), 85. Copyright © 1992 Victor Frankl. Used with permission of Victor Frankl; permission conveyed through Copyright Clearance Center, Inc. David Brooks also tells this story and comments on it in chapter 2 of *The Road to Character*.

Megan or in the common cultural encouragements of the Big Me era, our approach might look like answering a call.

The language of being called is familiar to us. We hear it almost as often as the inwardly directed cultural mantras above. A calling is attractive in part because there is a sense that it aims us outward, pointing us toward and catching us up in something bigger than ourselves. Still, some care has to be taken with the term. For it's easy to romanticize the idea of a calling. We can quickly turn it into something we have to figure out, as if it's just one more thing to be found, yet another task. We also risk thinking of a calling as if it's something singular, as if we each have only one calling, and if we don't figure out what it is, we'll have somehow "wasted" our life.[15]

We can also be quick to idealize the concept of calling by getting caught back up in platitudes like those that tell us to follow our heart or find our passion. Theologian and author Frederick Buechner conceives of our calling in that way, describing it as the intersection of the world's deep need with our deep gladness.[16] This description appeals to our modern cultural sensibilities because it promises to help us make a difference while also making sure we're happy doing so—feeding back into our inward-facing mantras. But author Lori Brandt Hale points out what makes this definition "profoundly problematic": "What if the world's deep need requires me, bids me, to act against my own best interest? What if I am called, say, to participate in a conspiracy to take down a tyrant? My own deep gladness seems a problematic criterion for serving the world."[17]

---

15   On the idea of a wasted life, see Andrew Root, *The End of Youth Ministry? Why Parents Don't Really Care about Youth Groups and What Youth Workers Should Do about It* (Grand Rapids, MI: Baker Academic, 2020), chap. 2.

16   See Frederick Buechner, *Wishful Thinking: A Seeker's ABC*, revised and expanded edition (New York: HarperOne, 1993), 118–19.

17   Lori Brandt Hale, "Bonhoeffer's Christological Take on Vocation," in *Bonhoeffer, Christ, and Culture*, ed. Keith L. Johnson and Timothy Larsen (Downers Grove, IL:

FINDING YOURSELF SUMMONED

Were we to imagine ourselves as summoned, called, that would change everything for what we might mean when we use the language of "finding myself." As we proceed, I'll make the case for how much more fulfilling it is to find ourselves summoned or called and how we can envision our lives according to a story that offers us the possibility of understanding our identity, the roles and relationships of our lives, and even what our lives are for in a comprehensive way, catching us up in something bigger than ourselves.

The language of "finding myself" is common among young people as they move into young adulthood. The college years and those immediately following are often thought of as a time during which a person settles into themselves. Progressively, however, as we've moved into a secular age, one of the major contributors to this season of finding oneself is the sense that it is less discovery of an identity that is given. Rather, identity has become something more like a task for a person to complete.[18] And a major part of that task has been an effort to distinguish ourselves from others as unique in some way. The late sociologist of modernity Zygmunt Bauman captures this well when he describes how people are left with only one option for distinguishing themselves in our time: we must fabricate a community by making choices to associate with others who share certain idiosyncratic traits, interests, or some other unique way of demonstrating alignment. A person might

InterVarsity, 2013), 178. Hale's question about one's calling having to do with taking down a tyrant is a reference to Bonhoeffer's involvement with the German Resistance during WWII, which led to his martyrdom.

18 I have discussed this more at length in the chapter "Identity: A Task or Given?" in Scott Ashmon, ed., *Who Am I? Exploring Your Identity through Your Vocations* (Irvine, CA: 1517 Publishing, 2020), 1–21.

decide to associate with these others only temporarily, loosely, or on a trial basis as part of the process of distinction. Still, these decisions about distinctiveness and connectedness aim to settle the question "Who am I?" more fully.[19]

In the days of the Protestant Reformation and following, the questions of identity we experience in our time did not exist. People did not need to work at distinguishing themselves as unique individuals because their roles in society already provided that distinction. That is, there was almost no conscious concern for identity or uniqueness because this baked-in sense meant their understanding of these things was taken for granted.

Individual identity in those days often came from your family of origin—a person was the son or daughter of so and so. Or it could be from your region of birth or primary residence. For example, Martin Luther called his friend John Bugenhagen warmly by the simple moniker "Pom," in reference to his birthplace in the region of Pomerania. Similarly, we are familiar with others who carry this kind of identity in their names, like the inventor Leonardo da Vinci, whose name signals his town of origin, Vinci, Italy. The course of a person's life usually happened in the same place, from birth to marriage to burial. Their work was either in the home or following in the same trade or career as their father.

In other words, identity in those days was best understood as given, like an inheritance, and thus a calling to grow into and live out. It may not have been the most fulfilling identity in the sense we have when we use the phrase "Follow your heart," but we've already noted the problematic fact that such an imperative is oriented only toward ourselves. Instead, people's identities were

19 See Ricardo de Querol, "Zygmunt Bauman: 'Social Media Are a Trap,'" *El País*, January 25, 2016, https://english.elpais.com/elpais/2016/01/19/inenglish/1453208692_424660.html (accessed April 17, 2024).

formed by the distinct roles they played in the world—that is, through the contributions they made in their social relationships. Every town needed a butcher, a baker, a candlestick maker, a beer brewer, a cobbler, farmers, merchants, and so on. Similar to what we see in the Body of Christ, each person was part of something much bigger than themselves, and their lives contributed to it (see 1 Corinthians 12:12–31).

VOCATION AND IDENTITY AS *GIVEN*

Luther emphasized this when he articulated his doctrine of vocation. Vocation comes to us from the Latin word for "calling." Luther's doctrine was a radical innovation in his time built on the comprehensive story found in the Christian Scriptures. It was innovative because Luther was pushing against the sense of "calling" as it was traditionally used in his time. Then, only priests, monks, nuns, and others who held an official role in the church were considered "called," but Luther didn't find support for this position in the Bible. Rather, he saw that the roles each person plays are given by God according to the relationships we have and the ways each relationship provides opportunities to serve and love our neighbor.

In fact, Luther went so far as to say that every role we occupy, when carried out faithfully in service to others, is one in which God Himself is at work through us, reaching down from heaven to use our abilities to care for His creation. We are, as Luther would famously put it, "masks of God" in our multiple vocations. God's activity in the lives of others is hidden in, with, and behind our activity in their lives, which is more immediately detectable and tangible.[20] And because God has chosen to use us in this way, we are

---

20 Gustaf Wingren cites Luther's "Exposition of Psalm 147" from 1532, saying, "All our work in the field, in the garden, in the city, in the home, in struggle, in government—

caught up in something much bigger than ourselves, where even our most mundane and ordinary activities have an eternal significance.

It's important to briefly note that a proper understanding of vocation recognizes that we each have multiple callings at any given time. We don't have one singular calling that we must somehow discover or else be resigned to a wasted and unhappy life. (We are motivated to think this way by other cultural imperatives, such as YOLO, or "You only live once," so don't waste that one life.)

The idea that we have a singular, unique calling comes from two simple misunderstandings. First is the romanticized view from our cultural context that there is a calling for which we are destined. From our earliest days, we feel the pressure of the quest to figure it out. Similar to how we search for "the one" when we approach the usual age of marriage, so we search for "the one" calling meant for us. Many people in the church have absorbed this view and become convinced that there is only one person whom God has chosen for them to marry or one calling meant for them to live out. (Theoretically, there are many people we could marry; yet once we are married, our spouse is indeed the only "one" for us until death do us part.)

The second mistake is to think of our calling as singular—that there is only *one* special thing that God made me or you to do. We have inherited this severely impoverished sense of vocation from the modern impulse to equate the word *vocation* with the word *job*. *Job* in this sense reflects how we make our livelihood and support

---

to what does it all amount before God except child's play, by means of which God is pleased to give his gifts in the field, at home, and everywhere? These are the masks of our Lord God, behind which he wants to be hidden and to do all things. . . . God bestows all that is good on us, but you must stretch out your hands and lay hold of the horns of the bull, i.e., you must work and lend yourself as a means and mask to God." Wingren, *Luther on Vocation* (Eugene, OR: Wipf and Stock, 2004), 137–38. Used by permission of Wipf and Stock Publishers, wipfandstock.com.

our families, if we have them. While all jobs are vocations, not all vocations are jobs.

Vocations, or callings, range across several different domains of our relationships to others in the world and the responsibilities we have toward them. Luther used the fancy word *estates*, which doesn't ring in our ears quite the same way as *domains* or, more simply yet, *categories*. Vocations are also often simultaneous, meaning that we have many more than one at any given time.

Our relationships within the family provide the setting for one category of our multiple callings. We are all sons and daughters. Many of us are brothers and sisters. Some of us are parents, grandparents, even great-grandparents. Among us are spouses. We may have step-relationships. And many of us also are aunts, uncles, cousins, and so on. In each of these familial roles, we care for one another in different ways over time. Similar things could be said about other categories of vocation, such as our roles in the church or workplace, our responsibilities in our places of citizenship (e.g., nation, state, city), and in our relationship to anyone who could be considered a neighbor (that is, someone in our orbit who has a need we are capable of meeting—see Luke 10:25–37).

AUTHENTIC IDENTITY IN OUR CALLINGS

Luther's doctrine of vocation helpfully establishes a sense of identity for us in that, similar to people like Leonardo da Vinci or Luther's nickname for his friend John Bugenhagen, there is no effort that needs to be undertaken to "find oneself." Rather, we can discover our identity by reflecting on the roles we are given. Vocations are, more often than not, given. We don't choose our parents. We don't choose our siblings or extended family members. We don't choose our citizenship of birth. We don't choose whether we are a layperson in the church. We don't choose who is our neighbor in the biblical sense. Still, there are some vocations that we can and do choose. We choose whom we marry. We choose where we work (but not that we require a livelihood). If we choose to attend college, we choose where we want to study, provided our application is accepted. We play a partial role in choosing whether to become parents (it is God who knits us together in our mother's womb, as Psalm 139:13 says). As we age, we can choose where we want to live, thus affecting our roles as citizens.

This sense of our identity as given, stemming as it does from our various simultaneous callings, places us in a position of incredible freedom. Furthermore, it helps us understand exactly what we ought to mean when we use the language of authenticity. Let me try to explain these two things.

The Gift of Freedom

First, the freedom we experience when we do not have to treat identity as a task, as something we must do or figure out, releases us to simply live out the callings we have. God has, after all, caught us up in something bigger than ourselves. And not only that, but the work we carry out in our various callings fulfills the very human desire to make a difference in this world because God Himself is using us to meet perennially important human needs. The work we do in service to and love for all the people with whom we have relationships is not just fulfilling in a personal way (though it truly is that also, which is itself a gift from God); it also situates our sense of who we are within an eternal and transcendent framework.

Here is where the Christian story helps us envision who we are in the most authentic sense because it uses the terms provided by our Creator Himself. That the God who created all things has chosen to reach down from heaven and use each of us to accomplish His work of caring for all creation—most especially the crown of His creation, our fellow humans—is perhaps one of the most rewarding truths of all Christian teaching beyond the forgiveness of sins and promised eternal life won for us by Jesus. God did not have to choose to use us this way. After all, He created human beings from the dust of the ground in the beginning. He fed His children with manna in the desert while they wandered in the wilderness. Yet God has chosen to use us in the miraculous processes of bringing about new life and providing daily bread for those in our care. Even those tasks that we might consider the worst, the ugliest, or disgusting—for example, changing a small child's diapers—become something of eternal significance when viewed through the lens of the doctrine of vocation.

We experience freedom in seeing our sense of identity through the lens of the doctrine of vocation because it liberates us from the heavy weight of having to figure out our identity for ourselves on our own. When we are told to follow our heart to figure out who we are, we cannot but turn inward on ourselves constantly, for there are no external points of reference to determine when we have finally "found" ourselves. The task exhausts us. This doesn't change even if we try to find anchors in the cultural imperatives and orthodoxies of the world around us, for these are always moving targets, blown here and there by the winds of fashion and fickle attention.

Most important, there is freedom when we see our identity through the lens of vocation because we are no longer treating identity as if it were a means of salvation. That is, in the romanticized view that requires us to find the "one thing" God made us to do, successfully finding that "one thing" is like winning the big prize, proving we haven't wasted our lives. In this sense, we're "saved," at least from an unfulfilling existence. Yet we know that salvation cannot be earned by any sort of work. It is a gift, as is our identity. And our new identity, extending back into the waters of our Baptism (see Romans 6:3–11), is simply elaborated on and further revealed as we live out our various callings throughout our lives.

A Better Standard for Authenticity

Second, through the lens of vocation, we can finally discover our authentic selves. Authenticity is always an evaluative term. We judge things to be authentic or not. Paper money is scrutinized by the Secret Service to determine whether it's authentic or counterfeit. Experts exhaustively analyze works of art or literature attributed to great artists of the past to determine whether they are authentic or a forgery. Teachers and professors seek to determine whether their students are plagiarizing. In each of these cases, they evaluate against a background standard to decide whether the claim to authenticity is legitimate.

Think of it like relief sculpture. In the highest quality versions of relief, often called alto-relievo, a seemingly three-dimensional image emerges from a stable, flat background (often some kind of stone). The flat background is critical for this type of artwork. Without it, we might see the image in a partial manner, but with it, the full sense of the image comes forth due to the use of shadow. The play of light against the image and the background provides depth. Similarly, we need some kind of background against which to determine authenticity. If we do not have this background, our talk of authenticity becomes unintelligible. Sadly, this consideration is often missing from our conversations about authenticity.

Charles Taylor helpfully takes this point a step further by highlighting how our talk of authenticity can go wrong when we have no basis against which to judge it. Taylor discusses how we have privileged choice-making as something that should be absolutely free in our society.[21] That is, I am not to interfere with your choice-making, nor are you to interfere with mine—it is forbidden to forbid. Our very ability to choose matters much more than which choices are made. All this becomes troubling when people make choices as if they live in a vacuum, as if they are the only ones affected by their own choices. This kind of choice-making ignores the shared world we inhabit with others. But there is no escape from our shared world or the consequences our choices have for others, however much we might try to deny it. Authenticity, then, does have to do with choice-making, yet it also accounts for the boundaries within which we make choices. Taking stock of how our choices affect others reveals the interconnectedness of our lives and the inevitability of solidarity as the background against which we evaluate all claims to authenticity.

A simple example can make a bit more sense of this. If "You do you" is true and we are all allowed to make our own choices without limits or with respect to the web of relationships that constitute our lives, we run into a dilemma. For if I follow the "You do you" mantra in choosing what I believe is best for myself, and you do the same, yet our two choices are in conflict, there is no external authority by which to decide who gets to have what we want and who does not. In other words, if I want to order the chicken wings and you want to order the chicken wings, but then we're alerted that there is only one order of chicken wings left, there is no way

---

21   See Taylor, *The Ethics of Authenticity* (Cambridge, MA: Harvard University Press, 1991), 37–40.

to rationally decide which of us gets what we want. One of us will have to sacrifice our desires for the other. But there is no external set of rules to help us determine how to do this in a "You do you" world. In this way, "You do you" will always fail us because it causes us to forget that we live in a world with others and that our choices have consequences for others as much as they do for us. We simply cannot always have or do what we want.

TRUE AUTHENTICITY

Taylor's complicated philosophical argument simply brings us to a position to better champion authenticity as best understood through the lens of the doctrine of vocation. Through this lens, we come to discover who we are within the story that says we are people made in the image of God, called to care for our neighbors and advance the flourishing of those around us. When the people around us are not burdened by having to care strictly for themselves—or struggling through a crisis of some sort with no support—they are able to flourish and join in caring for others. When this kind of social solidarity becomes visible in the world as the Body of Christ lives it out, the Gospel might better gain a foothold among people in our society. In other words, as Christians display the fruit of the freedom and authenticity that comes with living according to the doctrine of vocation, our life together becomes attractive in a way that might cause people in the world to wonder about us and perhaps ask what makes us different. Christians can easily answer (as we are encouraged in 1 Peter 3:15) by talking about the sense of identity and fulfillment we have from understanding our roles and relationships according to God's gifts in our various callings.

Vocation helps us see our most authentic identity and live it out because it is an identity given by God with exhortations and patterns of life that are modeled for us in the Scriptures and in the Christian community. To understand that our roles come out of our relationships with others is fundamentally to recognize that we are connected to others via a web of relationships in some kind of community of solidarity. Already, then, there is a background against which we can evaluate whether we are living authentically. Luther's Table of Duties in his Small Catechism offers a helpful way for us to evaluate how we're doing in this regard. We can ask ourselves about the ways that we have loved and served our neighbor, be reminded that we should be doing so, and then, based on our assessment, endeavor to do better.

Of course, Christians also recognize our reliance on God to enable us to live in such a way that we fulfill our callings as "masks of God" in the lives of others in the world, as well as the importance of repentance. However, I want to point out an important opening in how the doctrine of vocation so intricately dovetails with the cultural imperative of authenticity: vocation provides a grand story within which even those who do not yet know Jesus might make sense of their lives in a comprehensive way. As we've noted, the doctrine of vocation helps us see ourselves as part of something greater and speaks to the desire many people have to make a difference in the world. In this manner, the doctrine of vocation can also serve as a bridge for those outside the Kingdom to engage more deeply with the ways of the Kingdom and, perhaps, through the work of the Holy Spirit, to step fully across and be added to its membership.

FINDING YOURSELF FOUND

Joining others who follow Jesus in the way described above—through the lens of vocation that helps us envision our place in a web of relationships of responsibility—outstrips any sense of religion as a kind of "personal identity accessory." This is how Christian Smith, whom we heard from above, describes the role of religion in the lives of people who are trying to "find" themselves in our age of authenticity.[22] Rather, the comprehensive vision of our lives as defined by the various callings and responsibilities we have, coupled with the transcendent sense that our labor with and care for others has eternal import, enjoins us to see ourselves in a more traditionally religious way, as part of what Smith calls a "community solidarity project."[23] Smith's purely sociological definition of how religion ought to function simply describes what can be observed in the lives of a faithful community of Jesus followers. They walk together as one, with Christ as their Head, each part of the Body joined in unity, recognizing the critical role each other part plays as they carry out their collective role in the mission of God in the world.

I believe that someone like Megan, with whom we started, would find an entirely different sense of self as a member of a faithful Christian community. There, she would learn to see and evaluate her own life through the lens of her various roles and callings instead of through the self-referential and community-resistant lens of secular authenticity. She would be less exhausted with chasing after being the best at everything because, in God's kingdom, she

---

22   Smith and Adamczyk, *Handing Down the Faith*, 226. Copyright © 2021 Oxford University Press. Reproduced with permission of The Licensor through PLSclear.

23   Smith and Adamczyk, *Handing Down the Faith*, 226. Copyright © 2021 Oxford University Press. Reproduced with permission of The Licensor through PLSclear.

would recognize her inherent value through the important roles she has already been given in her community. She would be less frustrated with herself because she would encounter the peace that comes when one knows their own place of belonging, in which they experience love and care, rather than trying to achieve everything they think they should be on their own. Ultimately, she would find herself by having been found by Jesus, who confers on her not only an identity as a child of the King in her Baptism but also many eternally important roles to play each day in her relationships with those around her.

Megan is living under the paradigm of identity as task. Identity as a task, however, offers no redemption, no sense of arrival at having truly found one's authentic self; it offers nothing but perpetual exhaustion and a looming existential crisis of always wondering "Who am I?" with nowhere but inward to turn for guidance. In the Kingdom, we live with a sense of identity as given. A given identity is always already authentic, for even when we fail to live as we are called, the identity we are given as "follower of Jesus with many callings" includes redemption. May we help all the Megans we know to discover who they truly are by introducing them to the better way of Jesus, His kingdom, and His callings for our lives.

REFLECTION QUESTIONS

1. Have you, like Megan, ever made life choices guided by an effort to feel a certain kind of way—smarter than others, at peace, happy? Were you aware of the motivation for your choice at the time? Did you achieve what you were after?

2. Take a moment to think about what contributed to the social imaginary you think *with*. What did you come up with? Were there any specific people, laws, social moments, or cultures (whether current or ones inherited from your ancestors), for example?

3. As you read this chapter, did you have any aha moments when you realized or identified a guiding principle you have lived *with* but never thought *about*? What is it? In what ways has it guided your decisions?

4. The chapter said, "We have all learned to want by watching others. Free will had nothing to do with it." What was your initial reaction to this idea? Upon close reflection, who has influenced the "wants" in your life? If who you watch affects your "wants," who would be beneficial to watch?

5. What are some examples of people fighting for the "right" cause while being complicit in the problem (evil in the world)?

6. What are some communities that you connected yourself with in an attempt to define yourself?

7. Thinking of vocation as described in this chapter, what are some of your current vocations? Have you always had them? Or have they changed over time?

8. Describe a situation (family, work, church, community) where you could clearly see the various callings of multiple people coming together to serve the whole. Were you able to see this "greater story" view while it was happening or only in hindsight?

CHAPTER 6

Identity through a Different Lens

Concentrating on Sameness Rather Than Difference

CAUTION: HIGH CONFLICT AHEAD

The La Brea Tar Pits are a famous archaeological site and tourist attraction amid downtown Los Angeles. If you visit the museum there, you'll see many kinds of fossils, including plants, insects, rodents, and large animals. What is interesting about the Tar Pits is the explanation given for why we find so many different kinds of animal fossils there, especially the large fossils of dire wolves, coyotes, saber-toothed cats, and mammoths.

As it's told, it probably all started with one single creature getting stuck in the tar. Struggling to free itself, it would probably cry out, signaling its distress to other creatures. If that creature were a young mammoth, we can imagine that, like modern-day elephants, older mammoths would have heard the cry and sought to intervene. Unwittingly, these efforts to help would have resulted in additional animals getting stuck in the viscous liquid. They, too, would have cried out in distress as they sought to escape the tar that gripped them. As their collective cries grew louder, other creatures would have been drawn to the pits. This time, however, they weren't the kind of creatures looking to help but rather predatory animals responding to what was seemingly their lucky day. The wolves, coyotes, and cats would have gathered to prey on the pitiful, stuck creatures, only to find themselves also caught in the mire.

The grim end of the story is that all these creatures would have died, and while their flesh decomposed, their bones sank into the pits, preserved for future discovery because of the nature of the tar. As gravel excavations struck oil near the surface in the 1800s, people discovered the remains of the animals locked away in the sediment. Hundreds of creatures and millions of plant, animal, and insect specimens have been found over more than a century.

The journalist Amanda Ripley uses a similar description of the La Brea Tar Pits to develop a discussion of what she calls high conflict.[1] Ripley argues that we should not understand conflict as singular; instead, it takes a variety of forms and sometimes evolves. The Tar Pits are an analogy for high conflict, something that emerges when a conflict attracts attention, pulling other people in like an irresistible vortex, until, like the animals who died in the pits, many more people are embroiled in a seemingly irresolvable situation.

In our present moment, the conditions for this kind of conflict are just right, to the extent that tar pits seem to appear around every corner, both in daily life and online. Indeed, conflicts do not just exist but are even stoked, encouraged, exacerbated, and exploited all around us, engendering the anxious feeling that we're trapped and any move we make will only get us further stuck. As we saw

---

1   See Amanda Ripley, *High Conflict: Why We Get Trapped and How We Get Out* (New York: Simon and Schuster, 2021).

in chapter 3, the myriad perspectives and opinions on important issues—from guns, climate change, poverty, immigration, and abortion to differences of education, politics, age, ethnicity, race, religion, gender, sexuality, and more—generate conflict. On its face, we ought to acknowledge this phenomenon as normal. Differences between groups of humans have been generating conflict on a large scale at least since God confused human language at the tower of Babel (see Genesis 11:1–9).

As we noted in chapter 5, questions of identity and "finding ourselves" are important in our culture. We find them so important, in fact, that our national conversation is nearly always monopolized by discussions of identity. Why is that? Why has identity become such a commanding subject in our society?

My working assumption is that one overarching concern motivates our discussions, regardless of which identity category we're talking about. It's simply this: historically speaking, some aspects of human identity have predominantly been treated in some way as if they matter less than others. Thus, the goal behind the rise of identity discourse is often to give attention to that which is overlooked, ignored, or treated as insignificant.

There are good Christian reasons to lean into the conversation about identity. But there are also pitfalls that are difficult to see. And, like the animals stuck in the Tar Pits, it's difficult to extricate ourselves once we end up in such a conversational pitfall. This chapter will deal with one major idea that we as Christians can use to navigate and negotiate our engagement in identity conversations, such that we're less likely to be caught off guard and fall into one of these difficult places. Rather than get caught in the trap of concentrating solely on what makes all of us different, I will encourage us to focus on our sameness—on the image of

God that all humans share as their identity. It is only through first recognizing this sameness that we can move on to better discuss what might be different about us. By doing so, I hope we will less often find ourselves in conversations or reflections about identity that seem intractable or defined purely by conflict, as if there is no way out. Rather, our conversations and thoughts on this difficult but important topic will be productive and reflect the wisdom our Christian tradition offers us.

A DOMINATING DISCOURSE

Don't think of an elephant!

You did, didn't you? Don't worry. I knew you would. Let's see why that worked so well.

The cognitive linguist and philosopher George Lakoff is well known for helping us see that almost all of our conversations and thinking are anchored by metaphors. He also helpfully shows that our conversations and thinking are easily "framed," as he describes it. Framing, in essence, gets you to think in a certain way, and it's a helpful tactic in trying to make persuasive arguments. It can also shape a dominating form of discourse.

Lakoff uses the simple example of something we hear from politicians who are trying to get into office or establish policies once they are in office: tax relief. "Tax relief" is a frame, says Lakoff. He breaks down how this is a frame by saying,

> Think of the framing for *relief*. For there to be relief there must be an affliction, an afflicted party, and a reliever who removes the affliction and is therefore a

hero. And if people try to stop the hero, those people are villains for trying to prevent relief.

When the word *tax* is added to *relief*, the result is a metaphor: Taxation is an affliction. And the person who takes it away is a hero, and anyone who tries to stop him is a bad guy. This is a frame. It is made up of ideas, like *affliction* and *hero*.[2]

Lakoff's "framing" is helpful for understanding how we get caught up in situations of high conflict around the idea of identity. It's not just that the media environment in which we are immersed seems constantly focused on discussions about identity; it's also *how* those conversations are framed that ends up producing the conflict we find ourselves in. In other words, the rules of the game about identity are established before we enter the conversation. And it's difficult to refuse to play by the rules. Without the help of someone like Lakoff, we are unlikely to recognize there are rules in the first place. But indeed, there are.

Identity discourse is often framed in a certain way before we enter it. I want to help us recognize and understand that frame. The frame of identity discourse can be described similarly to Lakoff's frame of "tax relief." It, too, has heroes and afflictions. The affliction is marginalization and oppression. No one likes to be marginalized or oppressed. Heroes in this frame are those who properly address marginalization with equality and counter oppression with freedom. The ultimate desire is that all people would be treated with dignity and be able to flourish. This hero-affliction frame is most often leveraged when comparing people who are included in the

---

2   George Lakoff, *Don't Think of an Elephant! Know Your Values and Frame the Debate* (White River Junction, VT: Chelsea Green, 2004), 3–4. Emphasis in original.

majority group of our society with minorities, or those who are not included. The reasons for the differences are myriad, determined across a variety of identity markers such as race, sex, gender, religion, politics, ethnicity, socioeconomic status, and more. The primary goal of our modern identity discourse is to raise the status of all minorities, lifting them out of marginalization and oppression to a place of equality and freedom.

Using this frame of heroes and afflictions often causes us to give substantial attention to our differences. Those who seek to fulfill the role of hero contribute to our discourse on identity by drawing attention to the plight of those who are afflicted, often citing their differences from the majority as the primary reason for their affliction (regardless of the identity category used). In the end, we turn to politics—that is, the laws, policies, and arguments concerning how we've decided we will function and arrange ourselves as a society—as the primary means to achieve our goals of equality and freedom for those who are afflicted.

In what follows, we will reveal some of the weaknesses hidden in contemporary identity discourse, especially concerning the underlying goal that drives our significant focus on identity—that is, our desire to achieve equal and dignified recognition and flourishing for all people despite differences.

A POLITICS OF DIFFERENCE: THE WAY WE ARE NOW

Well-known political theorist Francis Fukuyama argues that the rise of identity discourse depends on two things: a shared sense of resentment among those groups who have historically been treated as outsiders within a society (the minority) and, following from that, a demand for dignity and respect equal to that received by the dominant social population (the majority).[3]

This makes sense at first glance. Among the myriad examples we could cite, two are well known and often taught in history classes that tell the story of our country. Women sought equality with men in the twentieth century because women had long been treated as second class. Blacks have sought equality with whites since the time of slavery. And even though we have enshrined both of these kinds of rights into the rule of law in America, the efforts to fully enact them are ongoing. Similar examples can be found when considering the so-called "culture wars" between conservatives and progressives.

In the 1990s, sociologist of culture James Davison Hunter proposed and popularized the idea of "culture wars," as we noted in an earlier chapter.[4] He was writing about the competing visions about what was best for America when it came to considering the family, art, education, the law, and politics. In the introduction to this book, we also noted Hunter's later work describing how people are easily unified around a common pain point and their shared motivations for trying to do something about it. The resentment and search for equal recognition that animates our society's identity discourse is just the sort of thing that Hunter was getting at. When people share resentment and a desire for greater dignity, they

---

3   See Francis Fukuyama, *Identity: The Demand for Dignity and the Politics of Resentment* (New York: Farrar, Strauss, and Giroux, 2018).

4   More than three decades ago, James Davison Hunter coined the phrase "culture wars" in his book *Culture Wars: The Struggle to Define America* (New York: Basic Books, 1991), a phrase which is now widely used, including in politics, the media, cultural critique, and more. He extended his argument from that book, applying it specifically to American Christians concerning their embeddedness within American political culture for the sake of leveraging its power to enshrine Christian morals and values since the latter decades of the twentieth century. See Hunter, *To Change the World: The Irony, Tragedy, and Possibility of Christianity in the Late Modern World* (Oxford: Oxford University Press, 2010).

coalesce around those feelings and desires, often distinguishing themselves as one group opposed to another that is the apparent cause of their affliction.

The group's sense of identity first comes together around a shared feeling of resentment. This resentment arises from their internal sense of being harmed (perhaps by being ignored or, worse, silenced). In addition to feeling resentment, they also feel a shared lack of recognition, whether that's from not being recognized as equal with others or from not feeling seen at all. To be recognized and affirmed with dignity and respect are basic human needs that contribute to flourishing. To some extent, such groups emerge and go on to attract members because they give members a sense of social affirmation. By virtue of their membership and inclusion in the group, members are respected and recognized as having dignity by the other members. Each member is a part of something bigger than themselves, fostering a sense of deep meaning in each person's life. These feelings extend further as they work collectively to achieve the broader recognition desired by the whole group.

So, membership entails both the experience of being included and the participation in the group's work to achieve recognition. In our current social climate, then, much of the conflict that exists between identity-based groups has emerged because each group's members hold a deep sense that they or their affliction have previously been unrecognized. As a result, they have also felt marginalized, ignored, or oppressed. In some cases, violence has been committed against them, often in ways that seem capricious, senseless, and tragic.

Again, we can review the history we were all taught about women's suffrage and then their increasing advocacy for rights in the workplace to see how Fukuyama's and Hunter's assessments are accurate. Likewise for Blacks and their ongoing endeavors toward equal rights in American society. But it is not only these populations. Many people in the categories we named earlier are also struggling with a diminished sense of recognition, and what they want is something every human wants: a sense of dignity and equality with others. Christians have good reasons to support this, yet we must do so without getting embroiled in the culture wars.

THE WEAKNESS OF FOCUSING STRICTLY ON DIFFERENCES

In a brilliant and probing essay about what it means to be an American today, historian Johann Neem recounts his experience as an immigrant to America.[5] Neem was educated in the United States after having grown up here from a very young age. His family came from India. The neighborhood they settled in was diverse. His early schooling took place in classrooms filled with people from a variety of ethnicities and backgrounds. Despite their differences, they believed it was what they *shared* that made them who they considered themselves to be, that is, Americans.

When Neem went off to study at a university, he began to notice that his experience was not like the experiences of other immigrants. There were clear lines within American society distinguishing between people by their skin color, gender, ethnicity, religion, and politics. But Neem could not understand why such differences were becoming the dominant framework for how people imagined themselves and others fitting into society.

As multiculturalism efforts took off and identity categories began to proliferate, Neem's sense of our unity, of what it meant to

---

5   See Johann Neem, "Unbecoming American," *The Hedgehog Review* 22, no. 1 (Spring 2020): 102–13.

be an American, was eroding. Neem began to detect the inherent contradiction in these efforts at inclusivity: the growing impulse to focus strictly on the identity categories that make us different—the identitarian impulse—was chipping away at an inclusive foundation. While these endeavors were aimed at greater recognition, equality, and inclusion for groups based on emerging categories of affinity and identity, they were breaking apart the sense that all of us together shared something in common. For the sake of some greater unity that would be achieved by means of greater inclusion, any prior categories of unity were disintegrating, offering us fewer ways to imagine how we shared something in common, how we were a people together despite our differences. Neem highlights how it was becoming easier to notice just how different we all are. And those differences were becoming the only thing that seemed to matter.

Neem's early life experience provided a foundation for him to understand the significance of others' experiences, especially those who told stories of their difficulties on the margins of American society. He came to realize that these stories needed to be told and heard, a process that generates empathy, opening the possibility that such tragedies might not be repeated.

Yet at the same time, his life experience also prompted him to recognize that making identity the primary category for imagining the structure of human social organization harbors inherent weaknesses that undermine the very purpose for which identitarian politics exists—equality, inclusion, and recognition. Neem began to call into question the identitarian framing. His assessment is important because, as an immigrant, he ostensibly should have benefited from the identitarian movement. We would imagine that he, as a minority, would be deeply committed to its mission. But instead, while he appreciates the attention given to people's stories and experiences, he fundamentally began to question the framing, the rules of the game around identity.

In other words, the efforts to bring attention to certain narrower identity groups tend not to account for the fact that people are part of more than one identity group. (This is often referred to as intersectionality; e.g., a Black woman is a member of the gender group female and the racial group Black.) One of the narrower identity groups becomes the primary focus of attention despite the larger goal of attention to and inclusion of all identities. This is called essentializing. The focus on one element of a person's identity as primary—whether race, gender, sexuality, and so on—eclipses the important roles other elements of identity play in a person's day-to-day existence. Ultimately, such a focus is reductionistic. This is the best reason for Christians to resist this kind of identitarian discourse, for as we'll see below, in the eyes of God, we share something in common that transcends any lesser identity category we may use to distinguish ourselves from others.

Another weakness is that there is often debate within identity groups about who *really* belongs. While Christians tend to have strong opinions on the topic of sexuality, let's set those aside for a moment to allow a specific example from that identity group to help us see how belonging is a troublesome experience, even when belonging and recognition are the primary motivations of the identitarian movement.

Consider how among LGBTQIA+ people those who identify as bisexual often don't feel like they belong or are wanted as part of the larger constellation of the group. Why is this? Well, on the one hand, those who are gay or lesbian claim bisexuals are not same-sex oriented enough and thus don't belong in the group; their sexuality is not alternative enough to warrant full inclusion. On the other hand, those who identify as heterosexual claim bisexuals are not heterosexual enough to warrant inclusion in the group. In the end, those who identify as bisexual tend to be rejected by both the former and the latter equally, despite the claims and efforts of each group to be working toward greater inclusion.

This phenomenon reveals an additional point: it is unwise to treat groups homogeneously. We often do this, thinking in generic and sweeping ways since talking about groups as if they are the same throughout is easier than to nuance or qualify what we say all the time. Yet, as we can see, there is often a significant amount of internal division and debate about who really belongs.

A POLITICS OF SAMENESS

We noted in an earlier chapter that a vast majority of us, roughly 93 percent, are frustrated and exhausted by how divided we are. Ironically, this seems to be one of the few things we agree on. Yet, despite unity in our frustration and exhaustion, we feel stuck about what to do about our social divisions and how to move forward.

So what can we do? Perhaps a good place to start, one that will help us see our neighbors and imagine our relationships with them differently, begins with a theological anthropology that high-lights something else we have in common. As we proceed, I want to elaborate on what I mean by this with the final aim of suggesting some practical approaches for engaging with others in such a way that greater peace, cooperation, and mutual respect might come to characterize our relationships. Even more, it is my hope that by reorienting our frame and thus engaging in identity discussions differently, people might meet Jesus in those of us who are His followers and simultaneously fellow citizens.

Civic Unity

In a practical sense, legal theorist John Inazu argues that despite the many differences and divisions in our society, Americans still experience a "modest unity" all the time.[6] Certainly, we might find part of that unity demonstrated in our shared frustration and exhaustion over our divides. Yet we also find unity in our shared interest in good infrastructure, clean water, access to education, access to health care, and more.

Beginning with this rather ordinary unity as a foundation on which to build, we can begin to explore ways to slowly overcome the differences and divisions that pull us apart. Across our society, we experience embodied and virtual spaces populated by a diverse swath of people who, on the basis of demographics, socioeconomics, commitments, and allegiances, could easily be placed into a variety of identity and affinity groups. Many define themselves, at least in part, over and against those who are outsiders to their group. A sense of unity can be extended using a theological anthropology that views all human beings as creatures created by the living God and made in His image. A theologically informed modest unity helps us imagine ways of interacting with the variety of people around us, allowing greater trust to emerge and thus for the witness of the Christian Church to bear greater fruit.

What can the church do to participate in and foster healing of the divisions in our larger society? Perhaps the best place any of us can focus is on where we are. Congregations dot the landscape of our country. While the media environment almost always concentrates our attention on what's happening at the federal level, especially regarding how to improve our society, thinking locally

---

6   John Inazu, *Confident Pluralism: Surviving and Thriving through Deep Difference* (Chicago: University of Chicago Press, 2016), 15.

is more fruitful for the church. We tend to know best the needs of those where we live. And we're likely able to relate better to the people near us than those farther away, if only because we share the same community and thus have a basic, even if not always well articulated, sense of unity.

"Neighbor" is a reliable biblical category to use when thinking about the people in the communities surrounding our churches. Christians have a long tradition of thinking about our "neighbor," reaching back to the Old Testament exhortations to hospitality. More famously, Jesus' parable of the Good Samaritan in Luke 10:25–37 prompts us to consider who our neighbor might be. As we saw in chapter 4, the parable answers, perhaps surprisingly, that our neighbor is anyone whom God brings to us and whom we have the capacity and capability of serving in some manner. In the communities where our congregations exist, relationally speaking, there are countless people who fit this description.

Our modest unity funds a shared way of imagining life together. It's something we've inherited from our communities themselves. Our imagination concerning our community's infrastructure is only possible because of the people who first gathered and began settling there together, as neighbors, united in a common purpose aimed toward mutual flourishing. Some of the earliest language from which we derive the word *city*, especially the Latin *civitas*, refers to a sense of citizenship and community membership. Our modest unity should mean we can rely on the fact that our neighbors share common endeavors, goals, and benefits together.

Yet, in our present moment, we tend to overlook these basic bonds of community, blinded by the abundance of conflict. We treat one another as enemies instead of neighbors. Even among fellow church members, the conflicts of the wider society make themselves known. So, first and foremost, it is our own preaching and teaching that can begin to heal the fractures that divide us, because our modest unity stems from the biblical story that grounds our identity in the image of God we all share.

THEOLOGICAL FOUNDATIONS

Let me build on this by extending some comments from an earlier chapter in which we engaged with Dietrich Bonhoeffer. There, we noted that every human being is made in the image of God (Genesis 1:26–27). That means that whenever human beings encounter one another, they are encountering someone who has been indelibly marked with the fingerprints of God's handiwork (Psalm 139:13–16). We are all creatures of the same Creator. Bonhoeffer famously concluded from this that, because of our shared identity as God's creatures who bear His image, followers of Jesus have an ethical responsibility to address and respond to other human beings as if we are addressing God Himself.[7] Bonhoeffer's theological discussion of human social relations requires careful articulation and thus is beyond the scope of this chapter. Suffice it to say, however, that this theological anthropology led Bonhoeffer to see that he had something in common with those who could reasonably be called his enemies: they, too, were made in God's image.

Bonhoeffer's involvement in Operation 7, which we discussed earlier, illustrates this. It was Bonhoeffer's sense of what we shared, what made us the same—our being made in the image of God—that motivated him to care for those Jews despite their differences

---

7   See Larry Rasmussen, "The Ethics of Responsible Action," in John W. de Gruchy, ed., *The Cambridge Companion to Dietrich Bonhoeffer* (Cambridge, UK: Cambridge University Press, 1999), 206–25. Dietrich Bonhoeffer's argument is uniquely applicable in a theological way only to followers of Jesus, the redeemed who have been given new eyes to see and ears to hear.

from him. He saw the similarities first, and in so doing, he related to them on account of their sameness rather than their difference.

When we possess an imagination with which we see others as made in the image of God, we have a renewed sense of how human social relations might be organized. Rather than a politics of difference, as highlighted above, we can operate with a politics of sameness. For Christians, who are made in the image of God and who know this claim to be true of all humans (regardless of whether they know or acknowledge it), this politics of sameness liberates us from the current social pressures of identitarianism. We are freed from the impulse to constantly cut up and reduce humans to singular identity categories, which in turn generate conflict as each group pursues its own recognition. We are liberated to see from an overarching perspective, one that is inclusive of all identity categories because one fundamental identity category transcends all others: our creatureliness—we are made in the image of our Creator.

Jesus Christ, in His saving work, demonstrated the validity of thinking from the perspective of sameness (while still acknowledging, respecting, and seeing differences as good—for they, too, are created) by giving His life for *all* people, winning redemption for all who look to Him for salvation, and drawing them into His resurrected life, first in Baptism yet also in anticipation of the new heavens and new earth. He did this while *all* were still His enemies (yet another sense of sameness!)—and not only for the sake of redeeming the relationship of humanity with God but also for the sake of reconciling humans one to another, toward the eschatological vision of the wolf laying down with the lamb in perfect peace and harmony (see Isaiah 11:6).

The church on earth cannot achieve such perfect peace and harmony—whether between parishioners who harbor divisions with one another or between members of our communities who see one another as enemies. But the church, more than any secular institution or earthly social order, can narrate and thus shape the imagination of those who hear our preaching and learn from our teaching that true peace *is* possible—not because of human efforts, but because of the reconciliation with God won for us in Christ, through which God empowers His people to live in peace and reconciliation with one another.

We can go even further if we draw out some of Bonhoeffer's Lutheran and Pauline thinking. If Christ is, as Bonhoeffer said, the quintessential "man for others,"[8] and as Paul said, "It is no longer I who live, but Christ who lives in me" (Galatians 2:20), then the church is a collective of people *for* others, "little Christs" in Luther's sense.[9] So the church is thus constituted by God as "nothing but that piece of humanity where Christ really has taken form."[10] The church in the world is Christ to and for the world. Yet, does the world know?

The people of the world do not often see or experience their relationship with the church as one in which they come to know Christ *for* them. This is not to denigrate the preaching of the Law, which confronts, afflicts, and kills the sinner. Rather, it is to say

8   See Dietrich Bonhoeffer, *Letters and Papers from Prison*, vol. 8 of *Dietrich Bonhoeffer Works*, ed. John de Gruchy (Minneapolis: Fortress, 2009), 501. The editors of this edition chose the more inclusive language "human being for others" when translating Bonhoeffer's German. I have retained the classic and more well-known phrase "man for others." See, for example, the translation by Eberhard Bethge (New York: Touchstone, 1997), 382.

9   Luther writes in "The Freedom of a Christian," "As our heavenly Father has in Christ freely come to our aid, we also ought freely to help our neighbor through our body and its works, and each one should become as it were a Christ to the other that we may be Christs to one another and Christ may be the same in all, that is, that we may be truly Christians" (*Luther's Works*, vol. 31, pp. 367–68).

10   Dietrich Bonhoeffer, *Ethics*, vol. 6 of *Dietrich Bonhoeffer Works*, ed. Clifford Green (Minneapolis: Fortress Press, 2005), 97.

that the part of humanity in which Christ has taken form still struggles with its old Adam. Whereas Christ never let an issue prevent a relationship, those of us who are part of the church allow differences to ravage our communities. Even worse, nonmembers experience the closed doors of the church community for any number of reasons. Each experience of this sort is an obstacle in the way of their reconciliation with God because God has chosen the church as His ambassadors of that reconciliation (2 Corinthians 5:18) and co-laborers (1 Corinthians 3:9), even as the church is enabled to do so because it has itself been reconciled.

Christ shows us how to do this, inviting us to come along and participate in the story of His visit to the Samaritan woman, as we've already seen. This is a story of God's lavish love for those who are His enemies. Despite the social norms and practices of Jews avoiding Samaria, and despite the likely protestations to that effect from His disciples, Jesus set out on a journey that took Him to a well and a conversation with a sinner like you or me (see John 4:1–42). His conversation with the Samaritan woman led to reconciliation, and not just between her and God. This woman had been ostracized from her community, which was why she was gathering water alone in the heat of the day. But Jesus' reconciliation with her led to her playing a vital role in the reconciliation experienced by her fellow townspeople as they, too, came to know Jesus, the Messiah.

We see Jesus doing this over and over with figures such as Zacchaeus, the various centurions, Mary Magdalene, and Nicodemus the pharisee, as well as with the Gentiles through the apostles. Jesus never let an issue prevent a relationship (and thank God for that, since we each, as sinners, have countless issues), and He reaches down from heaven through the church to engender the same kinds of practices. The more we come to embrace His radical love for us in the Gospels, the more we will be formed to offer the same radical love to others.

SEEING OTHERS THROUGH THE LENS OF JESUS

In part, this chapter provides some solutions to the reductionistic approach of the politics of difference that shapes identitarian discourse by rehearsing ideas we've already encountered in a slightly new key. We come to realize that our theology is not just abstraction but can be the sort of thing we see, experience, and live out in our own embodied lives, much as Bonhoeffer lived out his theology in Operation 7. As the story of his life shows, he lived with a concrete integrity to his theological commitments.

Examples like Bonhoeffer make a politics of sameness seem possible, and perhaps not even incredibly difficult, for followers of Jesus. Those of us who have been transformed and live now as new creatures are enabled by the Holy Spirit to live not just differently but in fact *as* Christ before the watching world. When we see others through the lens of Jesus, when we see them with His eyes (just as He sees us!), our responsibility toward them is one that joins with God in His redemptive work in the lives of people around us. Because we have been renewed, the world can meet Jesus in us in the manner that God intends for His kingdom to expand.

REFLECTION QUESTIONS

1. Do you have any experiences similar to Neem's, in which people with many differences found common ground and a shared sense of purpose? What makes these experiences different from those we have had with like-minded or like-identified people?

2. What do you have in common with the person in your life who is most different from you? How did you discover this? What were the barriers to uncovering this commonality?

3. Consider the people you regularly encounter. With sameness in mind rather than difference, what similarities can you readily identify? (For example, perhaps you each have children, enjoy coffee, work hard, and so on.)

4. The chapter stated, "The church in the world is Christ to and for the world. Yet, does the world know?" Wrestle with that idea for a moment. Ask the Holy Spirit to help you see and discern ways to make this known.

CHAPTER 7

Light between
the Cracks

How to Reach Out in a Secular Age

AWAKENING

Paul Kalanithi was entering the height of his career. A neurosurgeon at Stanford, he knew well how such things as brain cancer began—it often came from the lungs. He had seen and operated on brain cancer patients many times. He was one of the most respected surgeons of his time, often taking on the most difficult cases. He was expected to take on the leadership of the neurosurgery department at the University of Stanford Medical Center. He would have been the youngest person to helm the department.

One day, he noticed that he wasn't feeling like himself. After some routine exams, he was surprised to learn his diagnosis—lung cancer. He immediately sought care from one of his close friends who was also a doctor and treated the kind of cancer he had. He was afraid; he knew his cancer was the most likely form to metastasize to the brain. Indeed, cancer would eventually show up in his brain. He continued treatment, but eventually, he succumbed to the disease.

Kalanithi's story, captured in part autobiographically and finished by his wife after he passed away, is one of unexpected crisis that led to a new kind of awareness, an awakening.[1] As he went through treatment for something about which he knew nearly everything there was to know, he had to learn how to be on the other side of a doctor-patient relationship. As a patient, he started to notice things he hadn't considered while serving as a doctor.

As he underwent treatment, there were seasons when he was feeling better and healthier, and his test results were encouraging. During these times, he was less tired and able to resume his work as a surgeon. But his approach was different. He acknowledged that prior to his own crisis with cancer, he used to treat patients as paperwork rather than people. Now, as a patient himself, he began treating them like people. And not just the patients but the patients' loved ones and caregivers too. He remarked about how the experience opened him up to his dormant spirituality. He even thought to himself that if he had not become a doctor, he might have liked to become a pastor. He found that caring for others, treating them as people, emerged not just from his own experience of being a patient but from the renewal he experienced in his spiritual reawakening.

HOW WE USED TO REACH OUT

For at least a generation, evangelism, or what many Christians call "outreach," has often taken one of two forms. On the one hand, Christians learned from popular programs like Evangelism Explosion how to engage with others in a manner that can best be considered

---

1   See Paul Kalanithi, *When Breath Becomes Air* (New York: Random House, 2016).

as confrontational in some form. No, Christians weren't called to stand on street corners with megaphones telling everyone within earshot they were damned if they didn't repent and trust Jesus. But in a sense, the suggested approach wasn't far from that. There was a focus on making cold calls, knocking on doors, and starting a conversation about the person's eternal destiny. Christians were taught to ask a form of this question: "If you died tonight, do you know where you'd be?"

The question was meant to spark a kind of existential or spiritual crisis by confronting people with their mortality: Were they saved and thus going to heaven, or were they damned and thus going to hell? Depending on the answer—especially if someone responded that they did not know and, in addition, did not know Jesus either—a space was opened for the presentation of the Gospel. The hope was that the encounter would result in the person praying the so-called sinner's prayer, during which one repents and, by the power of the Holy Spirit, begins a new life of faith and trust in Jesus.

On the other hand, much attention has been paid to worldview studies and apologetics. Christian apologetics is the presentation of the faith in ways that make it plausible and thus defendable. The modern approach to Christian apologetics has placed heavy emphasis on anticipating what objections outsiders might have about Christianity, at times characterizing those outsiders as hostile. This approach also sought to make Christian belief appear rational and coherent, especially to those outsiders. Apologetics of this form harbored an underlying assumption that if someone would just set aside all biases and approach what we know about the world rationally, following where the evidence leads, then everyone would inevitably come to see that Christianity is simply the truth of the world. The emphasis on logic, rationality, evidence, and the cognitive nature of belief and doctrine produced a sense that Christianity was merely a set of beliefs to which someone gives intellectual assent. The goal of Christians learning apologetics, and hence finding themselves able to coherently understand as well as defend the Christian worldview, was ultimately based on a misuse of 1 Peter 3:15 and the impetus to be prepared to answer the questions of outsiders, who were considered skeptical, godless if they were atheistic, or heretical and therefore damned if they were committed to another religion.

HOW WE SHOULD REACH OUT NOW

In our age of implausibility, which is how we have thus far been describing the most important way to understand what it means to live in a secular age, neither of these two approaches is fitting for outreach. That is not to say that they are useless altogether. Christian apologetics is still helpful for Christians who are working their way through better understanding their faith. After all, while there is a coherence and rationality to Christian beliefs, such coherence and rationality are unique. Christian belief, as much as the Christian life, simply does not lend itself to making sense according to the rules of modern rationality or evidentiary argumentation. That is to say, one cannot use argumentation of any kind to come arrive at certainty about Christianity, and yet, Christian teaching makes enough sense to believe.

The nature of today's implausibility is such that one could say, following James K. A. Smith, that we are all (doubting) Thomas now. Living as we do in a secular age characterized by the fact that beliefs are contestable and therefore contested, we all doubt *while* believing.[2]

---

2   James K. A. Smith, *How (Not) to Be Secular: Reading Charles Taylor* (Grand Rapids, MI: Eerdmans, 2014), 4.

One way to picture the mindset of our secular age is to see ourselves as living inside the enclosed dome of the heavens, captive to immanence—that is, the near, the physical. Our imaginations have become so shaped by our secular age that the idea of something transcendent—the spiritual, anything beyond our material reality—is not just difficult but nearly impossible for us to believe.

Kalanithi's story illustrates this. During his early adult years, through his training and into his residency as a surgeon, his sense of the place and role of spirituality had diminished such that his life was absent any sort of spirituality at all. His was not a definitive rejection, but more that he had ignored his spiritual life for so long that he didn't notice it anymore. And further, as someone trained in the scientific art of medicine, his focus had been subtly reduced to a strict and minute attention to the physical world alone. He lived only in immanence, and his imagination had been so molded that the transcendent was squeezed out.

For many people in our society, the transcendent is utterly eclipsed, hidden by the concentration on the knowable world of immanence. Our secular age is framed in, the heavens enclosed. This is how we experience our lives in a secular age, and thus the possibility of belief in something greater, something beyond, something after or outside of what we can see and know is tragically reduced, making belief incredibly difficult for most of us.

The question for us today, especially as we harbor a sense of urgency to share the hope of the Gospel of Jesus Christ, is how to engage with those who, because of the age of implausibility in which we live, are closed off to spirituality or religion. In other words, how do we find the cracks in the enclosed heavens of the secular through which the light of the seemingly inaccessible transcendent is breaking through?

We will approach our search for these "cracks in the secular" using three kinds of human experiences.[3] The first is the experience of, as Smith has described it, being "haunted" by the questions that arise when we have to face our own mortality.[4] We are all going to die at some point, and this realization, especially for those who have no assurance of their eternal destiny, haunts us with concerns about what happens after we die. The second is the experience that some have called the "religious impulse," which might also be called "reaching up." That is, some people have the sense that there is a higher power that they must please, whether they call that power God or some other name. Here we'll discuss the impulse to please or to procure a sense of affirmation of one's existence, a sense of worthiness. The third is what I'll call the holy moments, or times when the transcendent seems to be "breaking in." These include the many kinds of experiences of pain. As C. S. Lewis has famously said, God "shouts in our pain: it is His megaphone to rouse a deaf world."[5] Moments of breaking in also include experiences of exceedingly great joy. While joy tends to raise existential feelings of awe and gratitude, pain often elicits the question "Why?" Each of these responses seem to be aimed at a recipient beyond the merely immanent, physical world.

---

3   I'm borrowing this idea from the Fall 2014 issue of *Comment* magazine, organized around the theme "Cracks in the Secular." James K. A. Smith, "Cracks in the Secular," *Comment*, 32, no. 3 (2014), https://comment.org/cracks-in-the-secular/ (accessed April 17, 2024).

4   Smith, *How (Not) to Be Secular*, 4.

5   C. S. Lewis, *The Problem of Pain* (New York: HarperCollins, 2001), 91. *The Problem of Pain* by C. S. Lewis copyright © 1940 CS Lewis Pte Ltd. Extract used with permission.

HAUNTED BY ETERNITY

The writer of Ecclesiastes has said that God has placed eternity in the hearts of human beings (Ecclesiastes 3:11). It's no wonder, then, that when we face the truth that our own life will someday come to an end, that we will die, we become anxious about what comes after. Stories like Kalanithi's reveal that when we are faced with our mortality, questions and concerns that had previously been virtually ignorable suddenly become pressing. Kalanithi was young, and he was anticipating much in the advancement of his career. He and his wife also had plans for a family. With all these future plans, he wasn't giving much attention to spiritual things. His mind was on the here and now. Yet, after receiving a terminal diagnosis, Kalanithi was suddenly awoken, as it were, to pressing existential anxiety about the future.

In a similar manner, Smith cites Julian Barnes as an exemplar. Barnes, a British novelist, begins his memoir *Nothing to Be Frightened Of* by admitting that he doesn't believe in God—has never even attended a church service, in fact—but nevertheless feels as if he misses God.[6] With a touch of humor, Barnes describes his sense of being haunted by the possibility of transcendence after an unexpected encounter with his own mortality, comparing it to the feeling you might get when, upon falling asleep in a hotel, you're suddenly pitched from sleep by the alarm clock going off. Rubbing the sleep and sudden disruption from your eyes, you recognize that the alarm was left on by the room's previous occupant. Awaking to the realization that we're all going to die is something like that, Barnes says. We realize our time here is short, and that prompts

---

6   See Julian Barnes, *Nothing to Be Frightened Of* (London: Jonathan Cape, 2008), 23, cited in Smith, *How (Not) to Be Secular*, 4.

questions about what might be next, whether there is anything like eternity.[7]

Smith is not surprised by Barnes's confession of his openness to spirituality, to God and the divine. Smith notes, as we've already observed, that "questions in the orbit of death and extinction inevitably raise questions about eternity and the afterlife, till pretty soon you find yourself bumping up against questions about God and divinity."[8]

However, being haunted by the possibility of transcendence and being open to embracing spirituality does not necessarily mean someone is open explicitly to Christian spirituality. Their openness might be to many different kinds of spirituality. What is important for us in this discussion is the *openness* itself, for in it, we (and perhaps they too) are offered an opportunity. When people experience this kind of disruptive openness, the Christians in their lives have an opportunity. By compassionately caring for someone living through such crisis, Christians can embody Christ and offer more than just a vague spirituality. We can give their openness something solid to clamp down on, as it were, by sharing with them the hope of the Gospel, the Good News that God Himself did something about the death they face when Jesus Christ put death to death by rising from the grave.

Another way of putting all of this—the sense of being haunted by transcendence, especially because of coming to grips with one's impending death, often sooner than expected—is that such experiences are in a category more generally called "religious experiences." This might include anything from epiphanies to visions, near-death

---

7   See Barnes, *Nothing to Be Frightened Of*, 15, cited in Smith, *How (Not) to Be Secular*, 5.

8   Smith, *How (Not) to Be Secular*, 5.

experiences, encounters with angels, and more. Dale C. Allison Jr. has spent a great deal of time researching a variety of religious experiences that are of particular concern for us here—those involving the prospect of death that open us up to the possibility of the transcendent. Borrowing from the work of ethnographer David Hufford, Allison points out that such experiences cultivate an openness in people because something fundamental about spiritual beliefs makes them difficult to resist or disregard, even in a secular age.[9] People tend to hide the fact that they have had such experiences for fear their claim will be misunderstood or denied. Yet the experiences are so indelibly real that they cannot deny them. Allison's research shows that people who have had such religious experiences often do seek to share it at some point with someone they trust as a way to validate an experience they simply can't let go of.

Allison writes that, as Christians engage with people we know who exhibit this kind of openness, it's important to remember that God has equipped us to help decipher the meaning of such life experiences. That is, we can give language to what people are experiencing. As Allison reports, the work of deciphering is exactly what the Christian Church was doing before we moved so significantly into a secular age of implausibility. And we retain the resources to do it even now within the deep historical wells of the Christian tradition. For example, if someone has heard a heavenly voice, Christians can assist in the discerning process by determining

---

9   See Dale C. Allison Jr., *Encountering Mystery: Religious Experience in a Secular Age* (Grand Rapids, MI: Eerdmans, 2022), 180, and David J. Hufford, "Beings without Bodies: An Experience-Centered Theory of Belief in Spirits," in *Out of the Ordinary: Folklore and the Supernatural*, ed. Barbara Walker (Logan, UT: Utah State University Press, 1995), 28. Of note, Allison's concern with "experience" joins with other scholars who exhibit a renewed focus on the legitimacy of experience in the Christian life, especially stemming from the magisterial Lutheran reformers and their confessional writings. For more on this, see especially Simeon Zahl, *The Holy Spirit and Christian Experience* (Oxford: Oxford University Press, 2020).

whether the message aligns with Scripture. If someone believes they have been miraculously healed or that angels were involved in protecting them from harm, what prevents us from joining them in giving thanks to God for the gift of life they continue to enjoy?

REACHING UPWARD

In 2022, Common Sense Media reported that American teenagers spent more than eight hours per day using screens, mostly for entertaining themselves. For adults, recreational screen time was reported in 2021 to be 28.5 hours per week.[10] When we think of screen time, one thing that is not often reflectively considered is what the habits of watching and entertaining ourselves so much are doing to us. In other words, since habits are always formative, how are these particular habits forming us?

In his creative engagements with the subtle commentary of the late David Foster Wallace on modern culture, philosopher Adam S. Miller observes that screen-based entertainment subtly critiques the experience of real life by presenting unachievable standards for what real life should be like, as if everything and everyone should always be amazing, beautiful, humorous, adventurous, and so on. By submitting ourselves passively to this kind of formative influence, Miller argues, we begin to develop a new sense of our own selves.[11] With the amount of time per day we passively engage in screen-driven entertainment, our imaginations undergo a change

10 Victoria Rideout, et al., *Common Sense Census: Media Use by Tweens and Teens, 2021* (San Francisco: Common Sense, 2022); Jamie Friedlander Serrano, "Experts Can't Agree on How Much Screen Time Is Too Much for Adults," *Time Magazine*, May 9, 2022, https://time.com/6174510/how-much-screen-time-is-too-much/ (accessed April 17, 2024).

11 See Adam S. Miller, *The Gospel According to David Foster Wallace: Boredom and Addiction in an Age of Distraction* (New York: Bloomsbury Academic, 2016), 32–34.

such that we start to believe that to be alive is to be like what's on our screens, to be someone who lives a life like the Most Interesting Man in the World.

All of this is a version of what Christians have long understood as a search for righteousness or the need for justification. Each of us wonders, ultimately, whether we are worthy. And if we feel like we are not worthy—most of us feel this at least some of the time—we wonder what might make us worthy, and thus we seek to find some way, some method, to achieve worthiness. To be considered interesting or, if reality were like TV, watchable is merely a secular or nonreligious method of meeting this standard. As Miller notes, it is as if the criterion by which we measure our worth is whether people consider us interesting or watchable.[12] And our ways of achieving that status—the way we pay attention to what we wear and what others are wearing, who we hashtag, retweet, vote for, how many grand and glorious experiences we're sharing (and comparing with those of others), and so on—generally leave us feeling unworthy, alone, and ashamed that our own lives are not as shiny and significant as others' lives appear to be.

How Much Is Enough?

What we are longing for here, deep down, is a sense of what David Zahl captures with tremendous simplicity when he calls it "enoughness." We all want to be enough, he argues. So, he suggests, we seek to be enough—to be, finally, righteous—by trying to procure it for ourselves. He pushes further on the fraught process of achievement that we've been discussing, saying,

---

12   See Miller, *The Gospel According to David Foster Wallace*, 34.

You'll hear about people scrambling to be successful enough, happy enough, thin enough, wealthy
enough, influential enough, desired enough, chari-
table enough, woke enough, *good* enough. We believe
instinctively that, were we to reach some benchmark
in our minds, then value, vindication, and love would
be ours—that if we got enough, we would *be* enough.[13]

And yet we end up living our lives with our inner accountant
constantly reminding us that we're coming up short.

These efforts we make to somehow arrive at "enoughness"
become what Zahl suggests are replacement religions. These could
be our jobs—are we more successful than others and increasing in
that success (often a moving target)? Or they could be the com-
petitive games we play in which we perform acts of worthiness for
others by trying to appear as if we have achieved what we're striving
for—just look at our lawns, our grown-up toys, or (vicariously)
the success of our children. Still, that accountant is haranguing
us—it's not enough.

Troublingly, while this sort of struggle affects all of us, we nevertheless tend to struggle through it alone. We experience the goal
to be "enough" like a small child trying to reach the sky. Reaching
upward, as I'm calling it, is an attempt to reach not the sky, however,
but rather what's beyond the sky, beyond the boundaries of our
physical reality all the way to the transcendent. It's as if we're trying
to get in touch with our very Creator, seeking to please Him. Yet
we treat all these earthly measures of "enoughness" like proxies for
divine acceptance—"See, God, all these people love me and think

---

13   David Zahl, *Seculosity: How Career, Parenting, Technology, Food, Politics, and Romance Became Our New Religion and What to Do about It* (Minneapolis: Fortress Press, 2019), xiv. Emphasis in original.

I'm great. How could You think otherwise?" Yet we know from Scripture that righteousness is not achieved by our own efforts (see Ephesians 2:8–10). We need something more than our own strength.

NEEDING TO CONFESS

As we struggle through this alone, always making sideways glances at that nagging accountant who keeps reminding us of what we still owe, we seek to achieve love and affirmation from people around us via other means. The silent sides of our lives tend to be hiding places full of deep—sometimes dark—secrets. In our secular age, we've moved away from the traditional religious attitudes of keeping such things private or at least for a very limited audience; instead, we have gone very, very public with our secrets. This, too, is an effort to find the kind of affirmation that makes us feel worthy and like we are enough. Elizabeth Bruenig captures this new impulse to "confess" when she writes,

> *Confession*, once rooted in religious practice, has assumed a secular importance that can be difficult to describe. Certainly, confessional literature is everywhere: in drive-by tweets hashtagged #confess-anunpopularopinion, therapeutic reality-television settings, tell-all celebrity memoirs, and blogs brimming with lurid detail set to endless scroll. Public confession has become both self-forming and culture-forming: Although in some sense we know less about each other than ever, almost every piece of information we do learn is an act of intentional or performative disclosure.[14]

---

14   Elizabeth Bruenig, "Why We Confess: From Augustine to Oprah," *The Hedgehog Review* 17, no. 1 (Spring 2015), https://hedgehogreview.com/issues/too-much

One might wonder, then, if what we're seeing here is the explosion of a latent impulse to confess, to be known authentically on very deep levels, and by being known in this way, to gain some sense of assurance that even when our deepest (and sometimes darkest) selves are revealed, even then we can find acceptance. To expose ourselves in this way is a move of great vulnerability. In finally letting others behind the curtain, we wonder: If you know *this* about me, will you still love me? If *this* is true about me, am I still acceptable? Am I *alone* here? Must I remain *alone* now that you know?

Again, it is as if our social tendencies of this sort in seeking to gain the affirmation, love, acceptance, and care of other human beings is a proxy for our reaching upward, seeking a sense of ultimate affirmation from the divine beyond, from our Maker. If so, then just as it is true that we cannot overcome our status anxiety through our efforts to procure a sense of "enoughness," it is also true that merely confessing to everyone (and possibly no one, at least on social media) will not get us what we're seeking. Rather, true confession requires forgiveness.

WORTHY AND RIGHTEOUS

Both phenomena should be understood as human efforts toward self-righteousness. We don't always notice when we're engaging in this kind of endeavor, but now that we've pointed it out, it won't be difficult to begin noticing it everywhere. This is because seeking after righteousness is a genuinely human activity. It is simply part of what it means to be human in a fallen world. The theologian Oswald Bayer captures this succinctly in the opening lines of his book *Living by Faith* when he says,

-information/articles/why-we-confess-from-augustine-to-oprah (accessed April 17, 2024). Emphasis in original. This essay originally appeared in the Spring 2015 issue of *The Hedgehog Review* and is excerpted here by permission.

> Those who justify themselves are under compulsion
> to do so. There is no escape. We cannot reject the
> question that others put to us: Why have you done
> this? What were you thinking about? Might you not
> have done something else? . . . Complaints are made
> against us. We are forced to justify ourselves, and as
> we do so, we usually want to be right.[15]

Bruenig is on to something when she suggests that there is a new, widespread impulse to confess in our society. It may be one of the newest forms of what Bayer describes. Humans want to be right, to be justified. But that is not something we can do for ourselves. Thankfully, however, God has already been at work on this predicament.

If we're going to confess, as we've said, what is required is something that comes from outside of us—forgiveness. What's fascinating here is that in the acts of confession and forgiveness, when conducted together in the traditional Christian manner, our earthly social realities are suddenly enchanted and imbued with a power from outside, from beyond, from the transcendent.

That is, as Dietrich Bonhoeffer has said in his classic book *Life Together*, "In confession the light of the gospel breaks into the darkness [through the cracks in the secular] and closed isolation of the heart." No longer are we alone when we truly confess. As Bonhoeffer suggests, "Since the confession of sin is made in the presence of another Christian, the last stronghold of self-justification is abandoned."[16] He goes on to add that one who confesses

---

15 Oswald Bayer, *Living by Faith: Justification and Sanctification* (Grand Rapids, MI: Eerdmans, 2003), 1.

16 Dietrich Bonhoeffer, *Life Together and Prayerbook of the Bible*, vol. 5 of *Dietrich Bonhoeffer Works*, ed. Geffrey B. Kelly (Minneapolis: Fortress Press, 1996), 110.

experiences the restoration of fellowship and true community with others once again because he or she has confessed not only to another person but also through that person to the whole of the church, and through the whole of the church to God Himself. Thus, in speaking the words of forgiveness to a fellow Christian, a single member of God's people speaks forgiveness as from God Himself. As Martin Luther wrote,

> Thus by divine ordinance Christ himself has placed absolution in the mouths of his Christian community and commanded us to absolve one another from sins. So if there is a heart that feels its sin and desires comfort, it has here a sure refuge where it finds and hears God's Word because through a human being God looses and absolves of sin.[17]

Reaching upward might be the kind of human experience that we exhibit when we don't already know that God Himself has reached down to earth to touch all of us. The very blood of the incarnate Son of God, Jesus Christ, was shed for us all. And not only does it heal us in our acts of confession, but it also deals with our other troubles of status anxiety.

John D. Rockefeller is known to have been asked, "How much money is enough?" He famously answered, "Just a little bit more." When we find ourselves living like Rockefeller, trying to secure enough status in our lives by whatever means just to be "enough," we finally have to ask ourselves when enough will be enough. We Christians have an answer to that for all who struggle with "enoughness." Jesus

---

17   Eds. Robert Kolb and Timothy J. Wengert, *The Book of Concord: The Confessions of the Evangelical Lutheran Church*, Large Catechism, "A Brief Exhortation to Confession" (Minneapolis: Fortress Press, 2000), 14.

Christ is more than enough for all of us, and even more, God has made Him enough for you and me all for free. In this truth, we find release, rest, and freedom from the grind of seeking to make ourselves righteous. For our righteousness comes from beyond, from outside ourselves, from the transcendent as a gift from the hand of God Himself because of Jesus.

When we're reaching out in a secular age, when we encounter people who struggle with being enough, struggling to know if they are pleasing before the eyes of their Maker, we can tell them that Jesus has already done enough so that they can be enough, that He has already pleased God immeasurably more than we can imagine. He did it for them and for us.

MOMENTS OF BREAKING IN

Times of suffering are common throughout life. Sometimes we use a word like *excruciating* to describe them. *Excruciating* literally means "out of the cross," from the Latin *ex cruce*. This is the word to describe Christ's suffering as He hung on the cross for the sins of humanity. Modern society has inherited this word, and much else, from a past influenced by Christianity. This inheritance is often oddly hidden from us. We don't realize just how much the West has been shaped and influenced by Christianity, even if today that influence seems to be severely waning. We use a word like *excruciating* or metaphors like "Turning swords into plowshares" in a manner that takes them for granted. But their provenance offers us something helpful when we're trying to assist others in making sense of the cracks in the secular that they experience.

Suffering is one of those cracks. As we've already observed, C. S. Lewis famously said, God "shouts in our pain," seeking to wake us up to His presence. Kalanithi's story, which opened this chapter, is a case when suffering brought about a spiritual awakening, an openness to God and transcendence. In these moments, Christians can walk alongside those who are suffering, carrying the burden with them (as in Galatians 6:2). Since suffering creates an openness, we should, with discernment and sensitivity, based on the trust built in the relationship, look for opportunities to offer words of hope and share the Good News of the Gospel (see Colossians 2:3–5).

Tragedy is a form of suffering that opens a crack. To lose someone we love is one of the most painful experiences of human life. Death is a tragedy because, while with our rational minds we can admit that it is a fact of life, we still seem to have a haunting sense that it should not happen. Perhaps this is because we were not made to die.

Experiencing the loss of another person can be a kind of existential crisis, prompting questions that weigh heavily on us. In fact, experiencing the death of another can make us wonder whether life has any meaning at all. Why would this be? Charles Taylor helpfully notes, "It's not just that they matter to us a lot, and hence there is a grievous hole in our lives when our partner dies. It's also because just because they are so significant, they seem to demand eternity."[18]

Writer Alan Noble reflects on Taylor's point, saying, "With death, something that seemed *infinitely* meaningful is cut short, however hard we may try to memorialize them." The ultimate trouble seems to be that death "defies our embodied sense that personhood ought not have an end. As a result, death feels incomprehensible."[19] Noble and Taylor capture well what we all might be feeling in our

18 Charles Taylor, *A Secular Age* (Cambridge, MA: Belknap/Harvard University Press, 2007), 720.

19 Alan Noble, *Disruptive Witness: Speaking Truth in a Distracted Age* (Downers Grove, IL: InterVarsity, 2018), 164. Emphasis in original.

grief: that death is a problem, an enemy, an experience that should not be. In experiencing the loss of another, our own feelings reveal that we and others are made for something more, that life was meant to be eternal. Regardless of whether a person recognizes the Christian claim of eternal life promised to those who trust Jesus, the words of the teacher in Ecclesiastes ring true when someone we love dies: "He has put eternity into man's heart" (Ecclesiastes 3:11). That sense that life was meant to be eternal comes to the fore in grief, opening a space for the light to shine through the cracks of the secular, making it possible for us to speak words of Good News and offer hope in what seems like a hopeless moment.

There is a remarkably helpful place we can turn to for help amid tragedy or any other kind of suffering: the Psalms. The Psalms have brought comfort to God's people for ages and are part of the provenance I mentioned above. This is why even outsiders are comforted by the famous words of Psalm 23, for example. Authors like Henri Nouwen, who wrote the book *The Wounded Healer*,[20] help us to see how our own experiences of enduring suffering tend to form and shape us such that they prepare us to help others through their times of pain. Sometimes the best advice for supporting others during their pain is the simplest: be present. Words aren't required, nor are flowers, cards, or other gifts. Just be present with them. Whatever the case, and whatever the approach, our goal is to compassionately help people discern how God might be shouting, calling them to wake up to His presence and promises.

Yet suffering is not the only crack through which the light of transcendence breaks in. We can also glimpse that light in the various unspeakable joys of life. They, like suffering, present opportunities

---

20   See Henri Nouwen, *The Wounded Healer: Ministry in Contemporary Society* (New York: Image, 1979).

to lean on our inheritance, to use the language of Scripture and the Christian tradition to help people name and describe what they are experiencing as unspeakable.

Joy Unspeakable

After a pregnancy with some rather difficult challenges, especially in the beginning, my wife went into labor with our first child. Labor was also difficult, eventually warranting a C-section. I had been by my wife's side, trying to balance supporting her in the ways she needed and keeping my own emotions in check. To prepare her for the C-section, we had to be separated for a short while (which seemed like a mini forever to me), but finally, they signaled that it was time for me to join the team in the operating room. Within minutes, I finally held my daughter in my arms, the glorious conclusion of one of the most challenging seasons of life my wife and I have endured together. The emotions of that moment reached an intensity I've only felt one other time: at the birth of my second daughter. I was called upon by the medical staff to name my child, and I could barely blubber forth her name and our desired spelling through tears of joy.

There are many times in life when you can only know what something is like after you have experienced it for yourself. While you've likely heard descriptions based on the accounts of others, you can never fully know in the same way until it's happened to you. Before my first child was born, I had heard people talk about how they never thought they could love another person as much as they love their spouse. It was likely they simply could not imagine a greater kind of love. But then they report that, upon having a child, they experience the scalability of love. When I held my daughter in my arms during those first few moments, it felt like the filling in of a space that had been created within me over the difficult preceding months. Like the excavation of new ground upon which to establish the foundations of a building that will reach toward the heavens, it was as if God had been preparing my heart to experience the expansiveness of love, only to have it filled in all at once when I held her against my chest for the first time.

As a Christian, the almost inarticulable joy I felt during all of this was something that I eventually had a word for: miracle. Part of our inheritance as Christians is this word *miracle*, which implies that the so-called natural order of things had been disrupted by a power that transcended it. We Christians are used to the idea of miracles. This kind of language is our provenance and a gift we can offer to others who experience similar things. As I held my newborn daughter, I knew that I had experienced one.

KINGDOM LANGUAGE

For those who are farther from the Kingdom than you or me, there may be times when the light of transcendence breaks in through the cracks in the enclosed heavens of the secular. These moments might be those of inexpressible joy, circumstances to which we can bring our words, our inheritance, and give the gift of naming and description to experiences beyond our ability to comprehend. We can talk of miracles when children are born. We can use God's own description of how each of us has come to be—that He has knit us together in our mother's womb and that we are fearfully and wonderfully made (Psalm 139:13–14). We can speak of new identities that emerge in such moments, when one becomes a mother or father, and in so doing, we can relate those roles to the Christian story.

Here is another application of Luther's doctrine of vocation as a means of giving witness to the reality of the Kingdom. On the one hand, God was not required to involve humans in the bringing forth of new human creatures. After all, in the beginning, He created the first human from the dust of the ground. He could have kept doing it that way. But He didn't. He chose to involve us. We are part of the grandeur of God's continuing creative activities; He has caught us up in the making of the pinnacle of all His creation. This truth is both a gift and a mystery for continued reflection and thanksgiving.

On the other hand, by involving us in the bringing forth of new human creatures, God has also given us roles and responsibilities as mothers and fathers. Each reflects God's careful, and perhaps even fussy, mindfulness over all of us (see Psalm 8:4), knowing each hair on our heads (see Matthew 10:30). As parents, we will surely fuss over the new creatures for whom God has made us responsible. He will work through us in our various tasks, almost all rather ordinary and mundane, to reach down from heaven to care for one of His creatures. And in this, we are once again caught up in the grandeur of God's work in the world.

These two truths are by no means the limit of what we could say following the miracle of childbirth. And certainly childbirth is not the only kind of moment of inarticulable joy that we might experience. Falling in love, miraculous healing, experiencing divine protection, and even simple moments when it feels as if everything is going your way in life—these are all gifts from God that Christians can name and for which we can give thanks with those who are experiencing them. Because the language of miracle and the language of the Kingdom are our provenance, we have concrete ways we can help others interpret the light that breaks in through the cracks as moments of inarticulable joy. And perhaps through these efforts at helping them interpret their experience, they might come to meet Jesus and follow Him.

ONLY THE BEGINNING

Reaching out in a secular age requires a kind of creativity that looks for new opportunities to share the Good News of the Gospel. While the news itself is ancient and timeless, the time in which we live is new and challenging. People are struggling with implausibility. Belief in just about anything is haunted by questions and doubts. Simultaneously, as each of us proceeds through our lives, various experiences produce new hauntings in us, making us ask, "Is this all there is?" By noticing cracks in the secular where the light of the transcendent is breaking through, we can leverage our relationships of trust with others who are experiencing these hauntings and, as the Spirit leads, tell them about the God who made them, who is with them in their suffering, who has a purpose for their life, and who loves them without end.

In this chapter, I have named just a few of these cracks. Perhaps as you read, you've thought of more ways God seems to be at work letting His light break through the enclosed heavens of our secular imagination. I pray this chapter is only a beginning, that by helping you see just a few cracks, God will open your eyes to more of them so that you can walk through the doors God has opened for the message of the Gospel and proclaim it clearly, trusting the Spirit to lead (see Colossians 4:3–5).

In the final section of this book, we'll further explore some practical ways our lives are used by God to let the light of the transcendent shine through. We'll consider some historical and modern examples of how the church's witness can be resilient in our dark times.

REFLECTION QUESTIONS

1. Have your own life experiences opened you up to be more understanding of others, as Kalanithi experienced? In what ways?

2. What are the similarities and key differences between outreach methods such as Evangelism Explosion and the sense of being haunted by eternity?

3. We likely don't have to look far into our memories to find a moment when we felt personal relief from knowing we are forgiven by God. However, can you describe an example when you witnessed the power of forgiveness in the life of another because you extended forgiveness, sharing a little of what God has already given you?

4. Where in your life (or the lives of those you know) can you readily see the light shine through? What were some moments when you only saw the light after the event? In what ways do you rehearse or retell those instances to others?

PART 3

A Resilient Witness in Dark Times

CHAPTER 8

How to Renew the Church's Social Trust

Here in part 3, we'll examine several practices of the ancient church that effectively grew its reputation through winsome engagement with the world around it. The way the early church lived is more than a historical artifact for us to examine and learn about. Rather, early Christians practiced a way of life we can adapt for our lives today. Their practices are not just ancient. Rather, they are the lifeblood of the church living as a unique community in the world. Their practices reflect the ways of Jesus as He is embodied in the life of the church—for as we've noted several times, following Dietrich Bonhoeffer, the church is nothing less than "Christ existing as church-community" in the world.

The ways of the early church reflected its very essence. This way of life helped set the church apart from the rest of society, and it was countercultural in such a way that the church grew in stature and reputation with the wider society.

Many of us are familiar with thinking of the early church as living through an age of persecution. It is surprising to learn that such suffering was also part of what contributed to the church's growth. How did that work? Well, since people could see Christians living for something that they considered so important that they would willingly give their lives for it rather than recant their beliefs, that willingness to become a martyr was ironically attractive. It's not that outsiders were interested in some macabre cult that would require them to give their lives. Rather, the Holy Spirit used what we might consider the mundane, ordinary practices of the early church—the very practices that, for them, might have resulted in a martyr's death—to bring about a positive reputation for the church. This reputation did not come from heroic feats of strength and growth in power but from humble care for others, merciful attention to the weak, and a devotion that aimed them toward something beyond the here and now, beyond the daily, nihilistic grind of "eat, drink, and be merry," or a stoic rejection of such things. All of this made for an attractive alternative—one that the Spirit would use to draw people to the One each of these new Christian communities were following. As the Spirit drew them, those communities came to embody the way of Christ in their local areas, slowly expanding the reach of the global church and the influence of the Kingdom in the world.

The ways of the early church are wisdom for us today. The practices of the early church still live within the memory of the modern church. We simply need to practice them again. Like a person who takes up bike-riding after years and years of never touching a bike, the church can remember how to work these old muscles and get them back into shape.

The call is simple: the church today must lean backward to the wisdom of the past to live forward into the modern future. Let us remember and apply to our modern situation what the church long ago learned so that our reputation would be such that people might see Jesus in our collective life, meet Him through us, and come to know Him and be saved. Let us concentrate on their ancient virtues, inculcating them through practice and habituating them in our gathering together. And in doing so, let us set aside the culture wars and antagonism that more often define the church's relation to the world today. In this way, the church might come to be trusted once again, for it is through relationships of trust that God has chosen to expand His kingdom, one person at a time.

Consider this final section a bit of a history lesson that draws on several voices and memories to remind us who we have been and, thus, who we can be again. In addition, we will learn in each chapter how to mimic the early church's practices in a modern context. We'll begin in this chapter by exploring the importance of vulnerability, drawing specifically on Bonhoeffer, who was himself drawing on older practices of the spiritual life; discussing how that applies to the church's reputation and social trust as an institution; and remembering forgiveness as a central practice in our life as the church. Then in chapter 9, we'll continue to use the example of the early church to explore the ways that our thinking and conversation concerning our differences in the modern world get unhelpfully caught up in what I'll call category mistakes. In the final chapter, with help from John Inazu, we'll examine three of what he calls civic practices, which he pulls from the deep wells of early Christian teaching for the sake of navigating our divided world.

THE VITALITY OF VULNERABILITY

When Bonhoeffer was called upon to train future pastors for the Confessing Church (those who were resisting the takeover of the church by the Third Reich in Nazi Germany), he faced a tall order. Such training was illegal, so it had to be clandestine, but the students also needed to develop comradery and fraternity so their ministry would be undergirded by mutual support from one another. Bonhoeffer studied the ancient practices of the church, along with some monastic practices, mining their wisdom to adapt and apply them in his time. His method of pastoral formation is captured most significantly in *Life Together*. This chapter draws on Bonhoeffer's ideas, especially concerning the critical roles that vulnerability and forgiveness play in the life of the church.

True Christians are always vulnerable. As we've already emphasized several times, Christ came and died for us while we were still His enemies (Romans 5:8–11). Said this way, Scripture tells us who we are and why we need Jesus. We are, in our old sinful selves, God's enemies who at our core want nothing more than to have things our way, to live as if we are in charge, as if we are God. This is a violation of the First Commandment. And our disordered desires lead to violation of all the rest of the Ten Commandments. If this is true, we cannot escape having to admit we are sinners. We are confronted by this truth about ourselves. It is painful. It causes a death experience, for seeing ourselves in the mirror of the Law that is the Ten Commandments causes us to see that we don't measure up. It reveals that we are vulnerable to the wrath of God.

But our enmity with God is not the last word. Paul's entire point in Romans 5 is that, despite our sinfulness and enmity, God has not actually dealt with us according to His wrath. We have received a gift that was completely undeserved. Instead of making us suffer the consequences of our own sin, God has visited His wrath upon His Son and treats us as if we are without sin, as if we have lived not as enemies but as holy and blameless, as Jesus did. This, too, breaks us open, for it is an encounter with a grace unearned, the depths of which come from a love that is before time, extending unimaginably through time and forward into eternity as we'll experience it, unplumbable to our finite hearts and minds. Nevertheless, we feel it and recognize ourselves as both broken and restored people who receive the unbelievable benefits of God's vicarious sacrifice of His Son in our place and His patient favor.

VULNERABILITY IN SCRIPTURE

In Matthew 18, Jesus taught His followers about this graceful approach from God in three lessons. Here we learn a practical application of God's gracious approach to us that we can embody with one another. The image of a child is central to this chapter in Matthew. Today we tend to think of children with sentimental feelings about their cuteness and an airy sense of their almost angelic innocence, but they were viewed quite differently in the ancient Near East. So to understand this image from Matthew 18:2–4 and the subsequent lessons correctly, we need to understand that historical context.

In New Testament times, children were understood in a manner that might seem offensive to us, even if on some level we can relate. To the people who would have heard Jesus' teaching, children were burdensomely needy. Life was challenging enough for most people, so adding children to that mix was just to bring about a greater burden. The wait for children to reach an age at which they could contribute to family and society was long and difficult.

From this angle, we can see why Jesus would use children as something of an object lesson to illustrate the ways of the Kingdom. Using the child as an image allowed Jesus to focus His listeners' attention on how God relates to us and how, as a result, we are empowered to relate to one another. Seeing that children were allowed to draw close to Jesus helped the listeners reframe their perspective about children and adults.

Children were revealed to be representative of all human beings before God—we all are the needy ones. And what we need is for the consequences of our sin to be dealt with, for we are lost in it. Jesus then drove this point home in the lesson about the lost sheep (Matthew 18:10–14). In Kingdom logic, we are lost sheep, needy ones whom Jesus, the Good Shepherd, pursues and adds to His flock.

Then Jesus moved to the sin-broken relationship between people, reframing common perceptions about our relationship to one another (Matthew 18:15–20). The sinner in our midst who hurt us or damaged our relationship is, simultaneously and paradoxically, the needy one. He or she is the very one we must go after (as the Good Shepherd pursued the lost sheep) with the goal of restoring the relationship. We do this just as God in Christ has sought out each of us, and in so doing, has gained each of us as a brother (Matthew 18:15). By restoring the sinner to fellowship with us and God, the relationship is healed.

Finally, because God knows that forgiveness is burdensome for us in that we struggle with forgiving others, Jesus taught another lesson about the ways of the Kingdom (Matthew 18:21–35). We sin in our relationships with others, and God knows that being vulnerable to confess those sins is difficult. Sometimes we must ask for forgiveness over and over for our bad habits and repeated mistreatment of others. In the same manner, we experience the effects of the repeated sins of others against us. When asked how often we must keep forgiving such sins, Jesus taught us to forgive as God does: to an endless degree—something we can only do as the Spirit empowers us.

THE VULNERABILITY OF CONFESSION

Later in the New Testament, James exhorts the members of the church to live in a manner that reflects Jesus' teaching in Matthew 18. He calls us to "confess your sins to one another" (James 5:16) so that we may be forgiven—and similarly, we may forgive others—by bearing one another's burdens in this way. Bonhoeffer took on this pattern of encouraging others to confess their sins to one another (following Luther's exhortation to confession in his Large Catechism) because he recognized what Scripture teaches us about our human relationships: we are like burdensomely needy children to one another.

There is a deep-seated part of us that desires to keep our sins a secret. Perhaps it's only to avoid revealing our burdensomely needy nature to others. This is likely based on fear that stems from our human pride. That is, we tend to believe that if others learn our deep, dark secrets, our faults, and failures, we will become a burden to them. We're afraid that the burden may become so significant, so *un*bearable, that they can no longer maintain a relationship with us. The cost of our confession will be our fellowship, we imagine. In chapter 7, we discussed a limited kind of confession that has become common with the rise of social media, often aimed at getting attention and seeking affirmation. But such confession never really gets to the deep, dark, embarrassing secrets we withhold from others. This is the kind of confession that Bonhoeffer and Luther are encouraging but which we tend to avoid. Instead, our social arrangements have become such that we tend to perform for one another, attempting to appear pious, holy, and affirmable. Our social expectations have been set such that we believe we are supposed to look good, pious, and strong all the time, otherwise we risk being cast out—excommunicated, as it were, exiled to the island of irredeemability—and this fear is often too strong for us to overcome.

Bonhoeffer knew this about us, having experienced it himself. But he also knew the value of the risk of vulnerability. Revealing our dark sides to others risks breaking our most important relationships. Yet in the logic of the Kingdom, vulnerability of this sort ironically makes possible a deep intimacy in our relationships that is not possible any other way. As Bonhoeffer described, when we confess our sins to one another, the very thing we want to keep secret is finally brought into the light. And when sin is brought into the light, its power over us in terms of guilt and shame is undone.[1]

In the forgiveness we receive from one another, we experience the concrete forgiveness of God Himself, for as Luther has helpfully noted, God has placed His forgiveness in the mouths of our fellow human beings.[2] Vulnerably confessing our sins, failures, struggles, difficulties, frustrations, and pains opens a space for us to experience God's forgiveness in the midst of an ordinary human relationship. The fear of a broken relationship, of being abandoned and left alone in our darkness, melts away, and the burden of guilt and shame disappears when we encounter a fellow Christian who forgives our sins, proclaims God's grace to us, and joins us in our burdensome struggle toward faithfulness. It's also incredibly powerful when they admit in solidarity with us that they, too, struggle in sin, shame, and guilt. In that moment, the darkness is replaced by light. And we in turn can come to that person's aid with the absolution that God has placed in our mouths.

---

1   See Dietrich Bonhoeffer, *Life Together and Prayerbook of the Bible*, vol. 5 of *Dietrich Bonhoeffer Works*, ed. Geffrey B. Kelly (Minneapolis: Fortress Press, 1996), chap. 5.

2   The Kolb-Wengert edition of *The Book of Concord* in particular translates it this way.

Putting It into Practice

Vulnerability of this sort—confessing our sins to one another—is not easy. Reading about it here is nothing like actually experiencing it. But it's more than an attractive idea on paper. Carrying it out is possible through practice. One of the best ways I've found to practice is using a prefabricated ritual in a communal setting that doesn't immediately demand that we tell our deepest and darkest secrets to one another during our first encounter (though the option does exist). For example, the Lutheran liturgical tradition contains a rite of individual confession and absolution that is often used between a pastor and one of his congregation members.[3] This rite is easily adapted for use between brothers and sisters in Christ as we practice what Luther had in mind when he exhorted Christians to confession in his Large Catechism. While the words may change slightly when adapted, the effect does not. Private confession and absolution are meant to be practiced by all Christians. And so, an old and underutilized practice can be renewed once again by trying it out regularly in community, whether in a congregational setting or within a household and amongst family.

Simpler forms are possible, too, such as making a habit of saying, "I forgive you," when someone apologizes, replacing more common phrases like "It's okay" or "No worries." Such responses don't perform forgiveness at all. Nor do they acknowledge the truthfulness of another's confession. Instead, they tend to erase or ignore the confession altogether, thus treating the person who confessed or apologized as if they somehow didn't truly understand or accurately describe their actions and the accompanying conse-quences. It's better to use faithful Christian language, saying, "I

---

3   See, for example, "Individual Confession and Absolution," in *Lutheran Service Book* (St. Louis: Concordia Publishing House, 2006), 292.

forgive you," for in this phrase, we both acknowledge the person's confession and apology and rightly respond by offering restoration of the relationship.

Vulnerability in this sense is integral to Christian community. We do not hold sins against one another. We bear the burden of one another's sinfulness because we are "members one of another" in Christ (Romans 12:5; Ephesians 4:25). As we again make a definitive practice in our communities of displaying our vulnerability through confession and forgiveness, that internal practice will bleed over into our interactions with people in the world who are not a part of the Kingdom.

THE CRITICAL IMPORTANCE OF REPUTATION

In AD 312, something happened that affected the Christian Church in a dramatic way. The Roman Emperor Constantine the Great became a follower of Jesus and started publicly promoting Christianity. It is said that he saw a vision of the cross in the clouds along with all his army. He took this sign as encouragement that he and his army would win in the coming battle, which they indeed did. He devoted himself to the God represented by the sign. He would eventually endorse Christianity, effectively making it an accepted faith among the plurality of religions and spiritualities that existed across the Roman Empire. His powerful endorsement as emperor was a turning point for the church in the world. From the time of Constantine the Great, the church enjoyed much more freedom. But if the church had not had its remarkable reputation, someone like the Roman emperor, much less anyone else, would have had no reason to sit up and pay attention.

This story prompts us to consider our reputation. God has chosen to grow His kingdom through the ordinary means of human relationships. Being in relationships with others requires trust, especially as we expose our vulnerabilities to one another. It's a necessity, then, that people outside the church can trust followers of Jesus. The church must be credible. Greater levels of trust translate into greater levels of plausibility. As outsiders encounter the ways of Jesus in us, they meet that same Jesus embodied in our actions. And the ways of Jesus are attractive when they are received as grace and love over and against antagonism, humiliation, oppressive demands, or moral grandstanding. Over time, God may use our relationships with outsiders to open the possibility of sharing about how the Jesus they meet in us has given Himself also for them, seeking yet another needy one to add to His flock.

The practice of vulnerability involves taking risks. Whether in human or divine relationships, each vulnerable moment presents an opportunity to build trust. God never fails us, but our relationships with other humans can cause pain. As we've discussed previously, the world is deeply suspicious of the institution of the church, particularly in our time. Social trust of the church is at an all-time low since surveys of institutional trust began in the 1970s.

As we've noted, God uses relationships of trust between individuals as a foundation upon which opportunities to share the Gospel might be built. Similarly, the institution of the church, when it is operating faithfully and engendering trust from outsiders, establishes a reputation that contributes to the possibilities for Kingdom growth. This is how it happened with Constantine the Great. Having come to know of the church's positive reputation, he was more than merely aware of Christians but actually open to their ways.

Several well-known accounts attest to the positive reputation of the early church. Tertullian, one of the leaders of the church in North Africa during the third century, famously recounted how outsiders spoke of the early Christians, saying, "See how they love one another." This kind of winsome reputation is possible in our time, but it will require the church to embody a posture toward the world that is more faithful than how we've been known in recent decades. We are who we've been, as we noted earlier. The church's typical posture of antagonism has generated a reputation for us among outsiders: we're better known for what we're against than what we're for.

Jesus' reputation, we've noted, was the opposite. What's more, everything that we know He was against was only intelligible and illuminated by His clear revelation of what He was for. Primarily, as Bonhoeffer described Him, Jesus is the "man for others."[4] And since the church is "Christ existing as church-community,"[5] we are people for others. But we have not been nearly as clear as we could be about *how* we are people for others. Our theological and doctrinal articulations concerning our relationship to the world and to one another are more often focused on maintaining rules and boundaries, as well as managing or condemning sin. It's no surprise that we're known more for what we're against than what we're for.

---

4   See Dietrich Bonhoeffer, *Letters and Papers from Prison*, vol. 8 of *Dietrich Bonhoeffer Works*, ed. John de Gruchy (Minneapolis: Fortress, 2009), 501. The editors of this edition chose the more inclusive language "human being for others" when translating Bonhoeffer's German. I have retained the classic and more well-known phrase "man for others." See Eberhard Bethge (New York: Touchstone, 1997), 382.

5   Dietrich Bonhoeffer, *Sanctorum Communio: A Theological Study of the Sociology of the Church*, vol. 1 of *Dietrich Bonhoeffer Works*, trans. Reinhard Krauss and Nancy Lukens (Minneapolis: Fortress, 1998), 121.

Institutional Vulnerability

Establishing a collective relationship of trust with outsiders—that is, establishing a trusted reputation as the institution of the church—will require its own kind of vulnerability. Constituted as they are by human beings, institutions also sin and make mistakes. The church is affected by and guilty of many of the same errors as other institutions in Western society. Racism and sexism are a part of our history and our present. But even more, gross abuses of power, financial and sexual improprieties, cover-ups and lack of accountability, and so many more instances of institutional sin have made local and national headlines, resulting in well-founded accusations of hypocrisy, betrayal, unfaithfulness, selfishness, and greed. All of this has cost the church unaccountable measures of social trust and thus undermines our public witness to the truth of God's reign and the presence of Christ's kingdom.

Christians and church leaders often bemoan that we are living in a time of hostility toward the church, but the church would be well off to recognize our own complicity in these experiences. Some of the hostile attitudes aimed in our direction are caused by our own errors and sins. Some outsiders are right to wonder whether the church even believes its own teachings. The church would benefit from examining the log in its own eye before pointing out the speck in the eyes of others.

There is no way to bring about correction and regenerate trust other than institutional vulnerability. The church must acknowledge its errors—the sins committed and allowed to go unaccounted. The church must also confess its omissions—the times when it has not shown up for the needy. Vulnerability in this manner will be only a beginning. But just as when individuals bring to light that which has been allowed to remain in the darkness, the church's vulnerability about its own failures can have a surprising effect on those outside the Kingdom. A generalized institutional distrust has festered in our society for decades. So, when an institution vulnerably confesses that it has been acting unfaithfully according to the expectations it has for itself, much less those that others have for it, people pay attention. They wonder if this kind of confession is real. They wonder if it will bring about sustained change. They wonder if they can trust again. They begin to watch and pay closer attention to what they have long ignored. And with sustained efforts aimed toward faithfulness and living in the light, the church may slowly regain a broader sense of social trust.

Contributing to the Trust Deficit

In our time, however, the church must do more than increase its own practice of vulnerability to address social distrust. There is a more insidious cause for the decline in social trust among our society's institutions—one affecting the church as much as many institutions.

Political thinker Yuval Levin (whom we engaged already in chapter 1) has helpfully begun to sound a kind of alarm about why social trust is in decline across many sectors of our society. He argues that a shift has occurred in what we imagine institutions to be. We no longer tend to imagine institutions as molds that shape people in terms of their habits, practices, or character. Rather, we see institutions today more in the sense of a platform used to amplify the voices of leaders associated with those institutions. When those leaders speak, they supposedly speak for the institution itself, all the while surreptitiously using the institution's social capital as if it were their own and for their own purposes. We end up confused about what the roles and responsibilities of those leaders really are, and we lose sight of what institutions are truly for.[6]

We live in a time of rising populism on the one hand and, on the other hand, a discourse on identity politics that seems to monopolize a great deal of political and institutional conversations and considerations (as we discussed in chapter 6). Given the trouble we have discussed throughout this book about how the church can live faithfully and resiliently in a secular age, Levin's concern for the strength of institutions and their influence in our lives is worth our attention. This is for no other reason than the fact that our most significant life experiences occur in institutions.[7] Yet, if we want to revive our institutions so that trust is regenerated in and for them, we'll have to consider some of the more challenging ways American culture insidiously influences our thinking about how we relate to institutions in our own lives. For example, we emphasize ideas like freedom and justice in individual ways in our society. These ideas are often discussed in terms of maximizing something about your and my experience of happiness and fulfillment in life. Discussing the renewal of institutions will require us to remember that our freedom to make choices must be constrained in light of the fact that we make our choices in a world shared with others, such that no choice we make will ever occur in a vacuum but will affect others

---

6   See Yuval Levin, *A Time to Build: From Family and Community to Congress and the Campus, How Recommitting to Our Institutions Can Revive the American Dream* (New York: Basic Books, 2020), 35.

7   I am borrowing this idea from Andy Crouch, who adds, "Institutions are at the heart of culture making, which means they are at the heart of human flourishing and the comprehensive flourishing of creation that we call *shalom*. Without institutions, in fact, human beings would be as feeble and futile as a flat football." *Playing God: Redeeming the Gift of Power* (Downers Grove, IL: InterVarsity Press, 2013), 170.

around us. Institutions form and mold us in ways that make us mindful of others and the effects our choices have on their lives.[8]

There is no better institution capable of leaning into Levin's suggestions about renewal than the church. This is because renewal is a characteristic of the church's life. The Holy Spirit is constantly at work in our lives, drawing us closer to Jesus and thus enabling and empowering us to live as He did and, even more, to do as we see Him doing in the lives of those around us.

This means that it is helpful for us to recognize the church as an institution—one of the many ordinary and mundane realities that God nevertheless uses to accomplish His work. The practices of the Christian Church aim us toward the goals that God has for us as we live faithfully under the reign of Jesus.

The fundamental goal here is for Christians to avoid the errors that Levin points out about institutions. Rather, when the church functions as a community in which followers of Jesus are faithfully formed and the ways of the Kingdom are inculcated, those outside the church encounter it as an institution operating with integrity, which builds trust. Levin's concern is thus also the church's concern. The church is not seeking to be a platform to make anyone a celebrity except Jesus. The church is never a platform for making ourselves known or leveraging our voices in a battle with those who think and believe differently. It is a mold within which God crushes and kills our old selves and raises us to new life through the Good News of the Gospel, encouraging us in our newfound freedom to live as we have been made to live—as people for others.

How do we do all this in a practical way? Levin suggests that we ask ourselves a simple question: Given my role here, what is it that I should be doing? Thinking about roles in this way orients

---

8   See Levin, *A Time to Build*, 23–24.

us toward thinking about the larger institutions of which we are a part. Drawing once again on Luther's doctrine of vocation, we made it clear above that we are all part of multiple institutions at once, from the church to the family to our places of employment, our citizenship, and even our neighborhood. The Table of Duties in Luther's Small Catechism helps us think through what is demanded of us in our roles when Luther asks us to reflect on whether we've fulfilled those responsibilities. While his purpose is meant to lead us to confess our sins in a concrete manner, the focus on the responsibilities inherent in our roles is appropriate for this discussion. Reflecting on Levin's question or thinking with Luther about our duties helps us discern what we are called to do as we live our lives.

Answering this question has as much to do with the roles and relationships that commend to us certain duties as it does with the spiritual guidance we find in Scripture. As employees, we look not only to our job description and employee handbooks but also to God's Word to understand what faithful service looks like in our roles. Scripture has much to say about parents, families, and households. Yet it doesn't say everything. This is true for many of our roles. Thus, practicing discernment about how we should live, work, and serve given our various roles should be a lively point of conversation and prayerful consideration among God's faithful followers. Much of the time, it might feel like we're muddling through, but there are anchors that help us not veer too far to the right or the left. And although many of us might be parents or employees or citizens, our specific roles are still unique to each of us, and how we live out those roles will always be a process of discernment in the church community over our lifetimes.

We began discussing institutions for the sake of recognizing institutional vulnerability as a key practice in renewing the church's social reputation in our society. Levin has helpfully guided us to see that renewing the church's social trust requires us experiencing the church's formative and molding work as a properly functioning institution. God does in fact use the church that way, as if it were any ordinary institution. Yet, in the eyes of God, the church is the very place where God works through its mechanisms and practices to form faithful followers of Jesus.

Having oriented our attention individually and corporately to helpful ways the church can recover from its trust deficit, let us now concern ourselves with forgiveness, a critical follow-up to these discussions of vulnerability.

THE CENTRALITY OF FORGIVENESS

Perhaps the paradigmatic nature of the church as an institution is defined by its practice of forgiveness. Beginning with God's approach to saving us, through Jesus' teaching on forgiveness as we've explored, and finally through the biblical guidance on vulnerability, confession, and forgiveness given to us as the people of God, no other institution's reputation is built on such a foundation. Everything about the church's social reputation should reflect this reality.

The magisterial reformers (the first leaders of the Protestant churches—Luther, Calvin, Zwingli, Knox, and so on) held that the true church is known most clearly when it is faithfully administering the forgiveness of sins. Jesus Christ was adamant about the primacy of this task (see Matthew 18:18; 28:18–20). Our entire existence as Jesus' followers hinges on the full awareness of our need for the Good News of the Gospel because we recognize that we need redemption. As the forgiven and redeemed children of God, then, we are empowered to forgive one another and practice Christian forgiveness with those who do not yet know Jesus. This is true not only because we are ambassadors of the ministry of reconciliation but also because the expression of forgiveness is simultaneously the expression of God's love for sinners. For those who don't know Jesus yet, the most concrete experience of His love is in knowing forgiveness.

Our society is desperate for the experience of forgiveness. Let me give just one example. For the last decade or so, various social campaigns have proliferated in which people are canceled, deplatformed, named, flamed, and shamed across various forms of media. What some consider to be ancient history in their own lives is discovered and dredged up from the depths of the past to be paraded in front of a watching public, only to settle just how bad the person in question is. Prominent leaders, media person-alities, celebrities, and yes, even influential Christians, many of whom were quite familiar to us, have simply disappeared from their public roles. For many, this is because they have been pushed out of those roles, exiled from the island of public life because of some sin that the media mob considered irredeemable. The #MeToo move-ment—while it's incredibly important not to dismiss its goals and positive outcomes—is just one of many that levied the toll of social excommunication based on the perceived irredeemability of some people's thoughts, opinions, or actions.

Another consequence of "cancel culture" and the exacerbation of public shaming has been the unintended diminishment in human vulnerability. Afraid of how others might react to their thoughts, opinions, or beliefs expressed out loud, many people have begun self-censoring. We lay low, and this is making our human interac-tions dull. Chine McDonald, head of the United Kingdom think tank Theos, points out that many of us think quite carefully and in calculating ways about what to write, post, or even speak out loud, wondering what the cost might be if our words are taken the wrong way. It's as if there are people on social media and elsewhere roaming like a lion and looking for vulnerable victims to devour. Jon Ronson, author of *So You've Been Publicly Shamed*, helpfully describes the consequences of all this calculating, editing, deleting, and so on when he concludes that the safest approach for surviving in our world seems simply to be bland.[9]

The social practice of treating some thoughts, opinions, relational associations, and behaviors as irredeemable cuts against the very claims of the Gospel. It is a worldly lie that the church should resist, not only by calling it what it is but also by treating even those we might consider despicable as nevertheless still redeemable. This is because God always treats humans as redeemable. Croatian theologian Miroslav Volf has referred to the cross of Christ as God's paradoxical monument to forgetting.[10] In the death of Christ, our past sins are erased. Every time we're absolved, they are erased again. God has chosen not to remember our sins on account of Jesus. We should apply the logic of Volf's image to the furthest extent.

That is, if Christ died for us while *we* were still His enemies, that truth is the same for all, whether that person was responsible for the Holocaust (Hitler), murdered and cannibalized people (Jeffrey Dahmer), or committed serial sexual abuse of children. Naming these calls out a sample of what our society tends to think are the "worst of the worst" kinds of sins. These examples often come up when Christians are wrestling with the question of whether God

---

9   See Chine McDonald, "Crossing the Divide in Unforgiving Times," *Theos*, June 28, 2023, https://www.theosthinktank.co.uk/comment/2023/06/28/crossing-the -divide-in-unforgiving-times (accessed April 17, 2024).

10   See Miroslav Volf, *Exclusion and Embrace: A Theological Exploration of Identity, Otherness, and Reconciliation* (Nashville: Abingdon, 1996), chap. 3.

would save someone who is *that* bad. The answer, like it or not, is unquestionably yes. He could, He would, and He likely has many times over. In the eyes of God, no hierarchy exists when it comes to sin or sinner. There is no "kinda bad" or "horribly, disgustingly, really, really bad." Rather, every sinner is on a level playing field—all are equally enemies of God. Yet the blood of Christ was shed for all, redeeming those who come to trust Him. The only unsalvageable are those who reject God's offer of grace. Yet even for them, if the Lord tarries and they continue to live, there is still time for the power of the Gospel to soften their hearts.

Volf's image of the cross as a monument to God's forgetting is powerful. Indeed, the cross is a monument not just for God but for us too. It is a concrete piece of human history; it really happened. We can go to the place of the crucifixion. We can see and touch other crosses like the one on which Jesus died. As Christians, we are told to look to the cross and remember what God has done to forgive our sins. There, He gave His only Son, the one born as a baby, born to die for you and me, for the very purpose of earning forgiveness for our sins and reconciling us to God, just as He had promised to Adam and Eve (Genesis 3:15). We come to the cross because, as the prophet Isaiah says, our sins are always before us (Isaiah 59:12). We are, as Augustine has suggested, a problem to ourselves, but a problem that we cannot do anything about (see Romans 7:7–25).[11] We are compelled to come to the cross because our own sins disgust us, causing us at times to wonder whether these things we struggle with will ever end. We wonder if we'll ever be enough.

---

11   The idea that humans are a problem to themselves I have borrowed from David Brooks in his chapter on Augustine in *The Road to Character* (New York: Random House, 2015), 195. See also Peter Brown, *Augustine of Hippo: A Biography* (Berkeley, CA: University of California, 1967), 173.

We are told to remember the cross. For us, the cross is like a standing stone that tells the story of God's work in the life of His people, a monument to what God has done for us. At the cross, our sins are separated from us as far as the east is from the west (Psalm 103:12), and as a result, we are no longer separated from God.

For God, the cross is the great monument to forgetting. Because His Son died there, God remembers our sins no more (Hebrews 8:12). That is, they no longer render judgment over us. The cross is the courtroom gavel after which we hear the words of God declared over us, "Not guilty." And in that moment, it's as if God's memory of everything bad we've ever done is erased. He remembers it no longer. And when He looks at us, He knows nothing of our sin, for He only sees us through the covering of Jesus' blood.[12]

A BRIGHT LIGHT SHINING

God offers the gift of forgiveness unconditionally on account of Jesus. The church, as the very Body of Christ in the world, stewards the gift of God's forgiveness in the world. A church that does not administer forgiveness unconditionally in the manner of God in Christ is, effectively, not the church. The society in which the church is immersed needs the redemptive work of God in their midst. That is why God has placed the church in the world: not to be *of* the world, but to be, as Christ was, *for* it.

Living faithfully as the church in our time means tending to our reputation. In other words, we must vulnerably examine whether we have been faithful to the charge we have received from our Lord.

---

12 The preceding four paragraphs are slightly edited and drawn from part four of Lutheran Hour Ministries' Nurturing Your Faith series on forgiveness, published in 2021. Visit the following link for more: https://www.lhm.org/studies/studydetail .asp?id=34454.

If the church has failed, the church ought to confess. Vulnerability of this sort will open a space for the world to perceive the church differently—not as an untrustworthy institution, but as one worthy of trust again because of its honesty about its own weaknesses and faults. A faithful church will also inculcate the practice of forgiveness, embodying God's redemptive work and offering His love to all who would receive it. For our own vulnerability before God begets His redemptive grace, and the church is His mechanism for delivering that grace to a world hiding in darkness.

Let us then always remember who we are as the church. We are not a lamp under a basket. We are a beacon on a hill, shining into and illuminating the world with the presence of its Creator and Redeemer among them. While the world may not recognize His presence in us, just as it did not know Christ in His first coming (John 1:10), the world may yet come to recognize Him, know Him, and finally trust in Him through the power of the Spirit as we live as Jesus did before the watching world. And as the Kingdom thus grows, more may be added as the light of the Gospel among us reaches into even more lives.

REFLECTION QUESTIONS

1. We have extensively reflected on that which can eclipse our winsome witness. What are some personal, local ways that a positive reputation for the church has been or can be built?

2. Think about a fruitful time of vulnerability (or if you are still working on this, what you imagine it would look like or feel like). What were some benefits of vulnerability shared through confession? What was a surprising outcome? Or what would you hope the outcomes would be?

CHAPTER 9

How to Avoid Mistakes That Prevent Engagement

RADICAL NEW CATEGORIES

Soon after Pentecost, something that God had long been foreshadowing became concrete. The apostle Peter's world was turned upside down again—as if encountering his resurrected Lord was not abrupt enough. In a vision, Peter learned an important lesson when God revealed to him that the Kingdom is for Gentiles too, not just the Jews. Peter expressed this radical new understanding while addressing those gathered at the house of Cornelius, saying, "Truly I understand that God shows no partiality" (Acts 10:34).

Several other times in the New Testament, this same kind of language is used, establishing a radical new way of thinking about human relations, especially in reference to the love of God as it reaches through us toward others. Each time the New Testament writers refer to the fact that God shows no partiality (see, for example, Galatians 2:6; Ephesians 6:9; 1 Timothy 5:21; James 2:9), there is a sense that because God does not, neither should we humans show partiality toward others.

Such impartiality—or lack of favoritism—was a drastic shift from the structure of relations as God arranged them in the Old Testament, where He very clearly "played favorites" with a limited group of people, the Israelites. This new and radical impartiality also went against the grain of the Greco-Roman cultural context of the early church.

A stark contrast between social classes was baked into that culture. There were the aristocratic elites, the plebeian commoners, and the poor, sick, and criminals. Even without the proper scholarly nuance, it's safe to say that this social stratification came with rules about who could associate with members of other classes and how those interactions were to be conducted. The rules generally prevented such cross-class association. Furthermore, the higher classes had the power, establishing which kinds of social interaction were possible, if any.

The new vision for social relations that emerged in the early Christian Church upended the expectations and imaginations of those who encountered its members and their practices. And as early Christians continued to enact those Kingdom-revealing practices, they helped establish a positive reputation for the church with the wider culture.

That same radical vision of social relations still applies in our time, despite the fact that, as sinners, we fail to consistently live it out. Rather, we're often captive to our modern society's vision of social relations, seeing our relationships with others through various cultural lenses that dictate whether and how we can relate to them.

Ironically, we tend to think that our cultural vision for social relations *is* the Christian vision for such relations. As we encounter the New Testament's repeated exhortation to show no partiality, perhaps we might even take offense at such a vision of the full human recognition of others and the equal treatment this Kingdom-based approach demands.

In our fallenness and blinded by our cultural lenses, we simply accept the social stratification embedded in our cultural imagination and thus unwittingly practice something other than the ways of the Kingdom. We fall into the trap of several modern category mistakes. A category mistake occurs when we confuse features or characteristics of one group of things with those of another group, as if the features are shared when they are not. For example, if we say the number 3 is red, we make a category mistake. Some category mistakes are obvious, like that example. Others, such as the ones I will highlight below, require closer reflection and analysis to detect. The ultimate consequence for us and the church is that these mistakes prevent our engagement with outsiders. I'll articulate five common ones below. In becoming aware of them, we will be without excuse when we wrongly engage in partiality and favoritism according to modern cultural rules, but even more, we can be empowered to live differently because we now know our mistakes.

LOVE ≠ AFFIRMATION

One thing that the people who are not members of the church still know about the church is that we emphasize love. And rightly so, for some of our most important and meaningful teachings have to do with God's love for us. For example, John writes succinctly in his first letter, "God is love" (1 John 4:8). Even more, God reveals Himself as love in His actions, as John articulates in his Gospel, telling us that it was out of love that Jesus came to save rather than condemn (John 3:16–17).

Because those outside the church know the centrality of our teaching on love, but not always the theological framework within which such teachings make coherent sense, they tend to hold us to a standard that is not fair or accurate to the teaching of Scripture and church tradition. Love, it is claimed, ought to result in full affirmation of every person. Christians can easily become captive to these ideas in two ways. First, in social settings with outsiders, Christians often feel obligated to affirm others in an absolute manner because Christians are to live according to the biblical standard of unconditional love. But unconditional affirmation is not the logical outcome of unconditional love, as we'll see. Second, Christians in some more progressive traditions mistakenly assume that the church and God Himself should simply love us as we are, thus eclipsing the church's teachings on sin and the specific way that God extends His love to sinners.

What is central to us here, however, is that God's love establishes a level playing field when the Kingdom arrives in Jesus and radical new social relations are made possible. While Christians are indeed called to love their neighbors, that love should not take the shape that the world demands. In fact, what the world demands is an impossible kind of love.

Take, for example, the fact that all of us were once children, having been raised by parents, guardians, other family members, and so on. While we ought to reasonably believe that those who raised us truly loved us, they did not absolutely affirm everything about us. They often told us no, scolded us for bad behavior, redirected us from things we inappropriately desired, sought to protect us from making choices that would lead to injury, and so on. And of course, the very reason they did this is *because* they loved us. Practically speaking, many of our relationships still work this way.

The worldly expectation that love will amount to full affirmation stems from the ideology of liberation that underlies our social norms. People expect that no one would stand in the way of whatever it is they might want (especially if it's not judged as harmful to anyone else). We often expect not to experience any barriers, boundaries, or limitations. We expect a "negative" kind of freedom, a freedom *from* whatever might prevent us from getting, doing, or being whatever we feel is good and right for us. So, anytime people do not experience that freedom from limitation, they interpret it as somehow unloving, mean, harmful, and the like. Lack of affirmation is experienced as lack of love. The category mistake here is making love equivalent to affirmation. But love has never been practiced that way.

As a social ethic, love in the kingdom of God tends to work itself out as a different form of freedom—a positive form, a freedom *for* a certain way of life. And as we've already discussed in our engagement with Dietrich Bonhoeffer, his extension of Paul and Luther amounts to a freedom *for* others. Love is a visible social practice in the church. Otherwise, Tertullian never could have recounted how outsiders speak about the church, saying, "See how they love one another." It was a visible action that went far beyond any live-and-let-live attitude that allows boundaries only according to the modern and supposedly banal ethic of "do no harm." Rather, the kingdom of God sets forth both an ethic of love and the guardrails for how it should be practiced—that is, loving others means we are to seek their good in all things. Likewise, the good of others is defined according to the Law of God, in which we are to delight (Psalm 1:1–2).

Love, then, is not total affirmation of others in all things but rather a God-ordained posture we maintain toward others for the sake of caring for them as our neighbors and people for whom Jesus Christ shed His blood. This kind of love offers a glimpse of the Kingdom to outsiders, exposing them to the love of God as He reaches down to care for them through the hands, feet, and mouths of ordinary Christians. Our mundane service to the people in our lives who might not know Jesus becomes fodder in the hands of the Holy Spirit, blowing as He will to produce faith in the hearts of those whom God calls.

DISAGREEMENT ≠ HATE

If love is not the same as affirmation, similarly, disagreement is not the same as hate. In fact, following the same example as above, those who raised us from childhood likely disagreed with us often, and through these experiences, we learned our errors and gained wisdom that has served us over the years.

Yet disagreement is often treated as the one boundary we are not allowed to cross in our present society. Disagreement violates the cultural expectation that we will be free from boundaries, the "negative" freedom that I noted above. When we disagree with someone, it is perceived as a boundary, as a form of "You cannot" or, perhaps more gently, "You should not." Our culture also suffers from a crisis of authority. The age of authenticity, as we've already explored, makes each individual an authority unto themselves, directing us inward to determine what is good, true, and fulfilling for us without any evaluative standard for really knowing the good, true, and meaningful. Despite the trouble that comes from following our hearts and being turned inward on ourselves, we still almost instinctively push back against boundaries of any sort. This is why disagreement is considered hateful.

In other words, disagreeing with someone is taken as a rejection of their humanity, of their "true selves" as they understand themselves. Of course, this is not likely what any of us intends. As we've said, disagreement could be motivated by very good intentions. Or perhaps we disagree because we have a different perspective, stemming from a different set of experiences that have provided us wisdom. Or maybe we have information that the other person may not that helps us anticipate the consequences of certain choices in a way they are not yet able to do.

Still, the power of claiming to be hated, of taking on the status of victim, is strong in our cultural moment.[1] To be a victim is a new form of elite status. As we noted in chapter 6, the marginalized and oppressed often seem to garner an exaggerated kind of attention in our time, with victimhood being the framework for the outcry against the harm of hate. Disagreement understood as hate allows people to claim that a kind of violence has been done to their person. They feel as if they are being limited and therefore are marginalized, oppressed, treated as second class, and so on.

To argue against these claims will likely prove futile. As we noted in a previous chapter, arguing against someone caught in an ideology like this will bear little or no fruit. Rather, the point of recognizing this category mistake is to help Christians not fall into the trap of claiming the status of victim for themselves, especially in terms of imagining our culture as hostile against Christians. (And as we noted earlier, some hostility might be a reasonable response to our antagonism toward outsiders.) This is the move we should

---

1   See Bradley Campbell and Jason Manning, *The Rise of Victimhood Culture: Micro-aggressions, Safe Spaces, and the New Culture Wars* (New York: Palgrave Macmillan, 2018).

not make; such a move only seeks power for ourselves. Instead, we claim that we are a people under authority, an authority to which we have been led by the Spirit to willingly submit. And it's quite possible that when we encounter disagreement—say, for example, from a fellow Christian who is seeking to keep us within Kingdom guardrails or, alternatively, from an outsider who is calling out unchristian behavior—we are experiencing not a violation of our person but rather the stern rebuke of God Himself through the love of another person.

Experiencing disagreement is one thing, but there are times when we have legitimate reasons to disagree with others and express that disagreement in public ways. So how can Christians disagree well? Let's answer that by imagining a more expansive way to disagree than we're used to working with. We tend to think that disagreement entails verbal or written proclamation against certain behaviors or ideas. These overt and often antagonistic forms of disagreement characterize our times. But there are subtler and more effective ways to express disagreement. For the early church, disagreement mostly took the form of a lived set of alternative social practices. That is, Christians "expressed" their disagreement with wider cultural values or ways of life by living their own lives according to a different standard. The Letter to Diognetus, a second-century point of reference that helps us understand how the early church lived and how it was perceived, details their alternative social practices:

> For the Christians are distinguished from other men
> neither by country, nor language, nor the customs
> which they observe. For they neither inhabit cities
> of their own, nor employ a peculiar form of speech,
> nor lead a life which is marked out by any singularity.

The course of conduct which they follow has not been devised by any speculation or deliberation of inquisitive men; nor do they, like some, proclaim themselves the advocates of any merely human doctrines. *But, inhabiting Greek as well as barbarian cities, according as the lot of each of them has determined, and following the customs of the natives in respect to clothing, food, and the rest of their ordinary conduct, they display to us their wonderful and confessedly striking method of life.* They dwell in their own countries, but simply as sojourners. As citizens, they share in all things with others, and yet endure all things as if foreigners. Every foreign land is to them as their native country, and every land of their birth as a land of strangers. They marry, as do all [others]; they beget children; but they do not destroy their offspring. They have a common table, but not a common bed. They are in the flesh, but they do not live after the flesh. They pass their days on earth, but they are citizens of heaven. They obey the prescribed laws, and at the same time surpass the laws by their lives.[2]

The church's alternative social practices are the kind of surprising and attractive phenomena that makes someone like the unbelieving historian Tom Holland take up the task of writing an account of Christianity over the last two thousand years.[3] Unable to ignore Christianity's formative power for shaping Western life

---

2   "Epistle of Mathetes to Diognetus," in *The Ante-Nicene Fathers*, vol. 1, ed. Alexander Roberts and James Donaldson (New York: Christian Literature Publishing, 1885), chap. 5. Emphasis mine.

3   See Tom Holland, *Dominion: How the Christian Revolution Remade the World* (New York: Basic Books, 2019).

and society as we know it, Holland tells story after story of how the church for centuries has been characterized by communities and remarkable individuals whose alternative forms of life garnered such a positive and attractive reputation that the world was permanently changed through them.

Disagreement, then, is best expressed not via argument or assertion but by presenting a lived alternative grounded in the historic traditions of the church, which are themselves grounded in Scripture and the life of Jesus. Expressing disagreement in this way safely avoids the accusations of hatred that often accompany antagonistic proclamations. It also allows for a more persuasive approach to a different way of life that others might experience as attractive and inviting. Living counterculturally in this way may create opportunities to answer for our faith (see 1 Peter 3:13–17), and having been asked, we are afforded an opportunity to winsomely explain what we're for rather than what we're against.

PEOPLE ≠ THEIR IDEAS OPINIONS, OR BELIEFS

There are sports rivalries all over the country. In Michigan, where I grew up, the major rivalry in college sports is between the University of Michigan Wolverines and the Michigan State Spartans. Perhaps felt more significantly, however, is the ongoing rivalry between the Wolverines and the Ohio State Buckeyes, particularly in football. If you were a fan (or alumnus) of either school, when you came across someone committed to your team's rival, relationships could become tense. At times, fans of opposing teams actually believe they cannot associate with one another. It is even the case that attending a game between the rivals while wearing the opposing team's garb might result in verbal abuse or physical violence.

It might seem silly that anyone would do such a thing, especially when, in the grand scheme of things, sports rivalries are rather trivial and benign. Nothing about them should merit the extreme measures some people take to avoid associating with opposing fans, spewing derogatory remarks, or even fomenting violence. And yet it happens.

Political rivalries might be a wider example, and disassociation (and even violence) based on politics occurs regularly. Yet it's not limited to politics and sports rivalries. As we discussed earlier, we treat countless differences in our time as such a big deal that we feel as if we *must* disassociate from others based on such differences. Violence against others because of such deep disagreement, while rare, also happens. And while these impulses are not new, our current social context exacerbates them to the point where it seems normal that we would at least choose to disassociate from those with whom we deeply disagree.

Underlying all of this is an unspoken category mistake. We have become used to treating people as if they are equivalent to the ideas, opinions, or beliefs they hold at any given moment. Those ideas, opinions, or beliefs become a kind of social standard delineating the boundaries between whom we can associate with and whom we can't.

Part of the reason this happens is because we tend to simplify our thinking, preferring to use neat, easy-to-understand categories that allow us to quickly make sense of our experiences in the world. But this move sometimes has unintended consequences, especially when it comes to making the wrong assumptions in human relationships. Rather than working through the complicated nature of, say, the relationship between what we believe about the world and the consequences those beliefs have for how we make choices, we tend to take a reductionistic approach and simply decide that if a person we know believes X, and if we believe X is somehow reprehensible, then we treat the person as if they are, in essence, also reprehensible. With this careless move, we've stuck a label to them that is unstickable.

Such reductionism is troubling because it ignores something about the nature of humans, especially within the Christian understanding of what it means to be human. That is, we ignore the fact that human beings are fallen. Fallen creatures are also fallible creatures. That means we all have incorrect views, beliefs, and ideas. And as we negotiate our way through life, we all change our minds many times over. We make mistakes and learn from them. Of course, while we may never change so drastically as to completely abandon something like our faith in Jesus, our understanding of God and His ways constantly undergoes formation. We learn to know God better over the seasons of our lives because God is molding and shaping our understanding. From Bible study to theological coursework to four thousand Sundays of hearing the Word preached,[4] we will never plumb the depths of the mysteries of God and His kingdom. We will always have more to learn and more mistakes to correct, simply because of the limitations of our knowing and understanding that are part and parcel of our fallenness.

This kind of learning and changing our minds is true of all human beings. From every follower of Jesus who is always only "on the way" to every person who has yet to know Jesus, we are all liable to be wrong about any number of things at any given time. So, to

---

4   The average human life span includes about four thousand weeks. See Oliver Burkeman, *Four Thousand Weeks: Time Management for Mortals* (New York: Farrar, Straus and Giroux, 2021).

reduce people to reprehensible and irredeemable simply because they adhere to a position we disagree with is itself a major error.

The radical new social arrangement established by the arrival of the kingdom of God effectively created a situation in which none of us has any advantage over another. Not only is everyone redeemable in principle, but God also revealed in sending His Son, Jesus, that everyone is worthy of redemption. How, then, can others experience the offer of redemption in Jesus if we, in our fallible ignorance, cut off relations with them? After all, just as in the early church, we who are its modern members are the ones through whom God has chosen to work to bring the message of Jesus to the ears of those who don't yet know Him.

In our era, we are sensing more and more that Christians occupy a minority status, much like in the days of the early church. Since the church's worldview is no longer dominant, we can more easily discern just how many ways of living and believing exist. Our time is pluralistic—that is, there is a manyness of beliefs, opinions, and ideas to which people adhere. Some of these beliefs are indeed wrong, even reprehensible, and so we (and others) *shouldn't* adhere to them. Nevertheless, our approach to wrong ideas is not to mount an aggressive defense but rather to live out a subtle kind of offense: a winsome witness to an alternative way of being. Peter's encouragement to the early church serves us well today:

> Now who is there to harm you if you are zealous for what is good? But even if you should suffer for righteousness' sake, you will be blessed. Have no fear of them, nor be troubled, but in your hearts honor Christ the Lord as holy, always being prepared to make a defense to anyone who asks you for a reason for the hope that is in you; yet do it with gentleness

and respect, having a good conscience, so that, when you are slandered, those who revile your good behavior in Christ may be put to shame. For it is better to suffer for doing good, if that should be God's will, than for doing evil. (1 Peter 3:13–17)

Our lives are meant to be a witness to the presence of the Kingdom. This is what Peter is after in his letter, having said already in an earlier chapter that we are "living stones," a "holy" and "royal priesthood" (1 Peter 2:5, 9). He emphasizes the point that our lives are a living witness when he says, "Keep your conduct among the Gentiles honorable, so that when they speak against you as evildoers, they may see your good deeds and glorify God on the day of visitation" (v. 12). So let us no longer remain captive to making the category mistake of thinking people are equivalent to their beliefs, opinions, or ideas. Rather, we are called to adopt the same perspective as Peter in Acts 10. Despite our differences, we show no partiality, just as God does not. For the sake of our witness, let us serve and love others by the power of God that all might come to a knowledge of salvation.

ASSOCIATION ≠ ADVOCACY

Our fourth category mistake is best described as "guilt by association." Jesus often experienced this. Every time Jesus sat down to dine with some person or group who was considered sinful and thus not to be associated with, the religious elite considered Him guilty by association.

In ancient Near Eastern culture, dining with others meant substantially more than it does to us today. To us, eating together is merely an act of friendliness. But for the people in Jesus' day, eating with others was an intimate form of sharing—so intimate, in fact, that sharing a meal effectively meant that a person identified affirmatively with those with whom they were eating. In other words, there was an unspoken sense that when people ate together, they were claiming, "You are one of us," to one another. To eat together in the culture of Jesus' time signaled the greatest kind of human solidarity. Every time Jesus shared food with people who were considered sinful—tax collectors, drunkards, prostitutes, and so on—those who saw or heard about the shared meals believed that He had self-identified with them. Since they were considered sinners, Jesus' association with them was suspect, because social rules of the day dictated that such association was forbidden. In the eyes of the culture, then, He was guilty by association.

Yet as we've already noted, Jesus never let an issue prevent a relationship. Nevertheless, it was His violation of the social rules that prohibited certain associations that got Him in trouble and eventually contributed to getting Him killed.

Jesus' followers today also experience this. For example, if we're part of a congregation or church body whose celebrity leader falls from grace, we may lose people's trust by our association. The same is true when a congregation or church body of which we're a part makes the evening news because of recently discovered sexual or financial improprieties or some other abuse of power.

At the same time, we Christians are often the worst offenders when it comes to making this category mistake. We tend to use the framework of guilt by association to determine whether our fellow Christians are behaving acceptably. Too often, Christians are chastised and even ostracized by fellow Christians because of their association with other sinners. Pastors are considered partially at fault for the decisions of their children, such as when pregnancy occurs outside of marriage or when their grandchildren are not baptized. Christians who build or maintain relationships with those who might be considered a gender or sexual minority are often looked down on. The same kind of judgments are rendered against Christians who spend time with the poor, sick, destitute, addicted, and so on.

What seems to be forgotten—or perhaps conveniently ignored—is the "other" part of the phrase. That is, "other sinners" rightly implies that we, too, are sinners. We are all on the same footing before God. Christ died for us while we were still His enemies, after all. Yet, when we want to start making distinctions about who are the "real" Christians, one of the easiest places to look is at one another. And the quickest way to make those distinctions within our own community is by observable behaviors. Other people can readily see who we associate with. If they believe we're associating with the wrong people, they may consider us "guilty" based on that association. The underlying assumption is that people whose lives reflect these and other observable realities (divorce, addiction, illicit relationships, perhaps an abortion, and more) are the kind of people with whom Christians should not associate. But this is no different than what the religious elite did to Jesus.

The category mistake here is to assume that associating with others (whoever they might be) and being in relationship with them is equivalent to advocating for their way of life or their beliefs in contradistinction to orthodox Christian commitments. Any number of circumstances could be considered here, but some common ones are those struggling with addiction or a failing marriage. When a grown child is getting married to someone of the same sex or someone of a different religion, parents are ostracized for trying to maintain the relationship with their child by attending the wedding. You're friends with a Christian who prefers this or that form of worship, while our church prefers the other? Not allowed. It's as if the knee-jerk Christian imperative is to react by telling those people that they are somehow being unfaithful to their beliefs when they are actually trying to live faithfully and follow Jesus' example by being supportive of the full humanity of their friend or family member.

But association is not the same as advocacy. And Christians need not be afraid of this accusation, much less live in such a way as to avoid it. Instead, the opposite is true. Jesus shows us this Himself. As He tells us, He came to *seek* and save the lost. Classic examples of this are His intentional seeking out of the Samaritan woman (John 4) or calling Zacchaeus down from the tree to dine in his home (Luke 19). We could name more. Consider Paul's admonition to the Corinthians, who were sorting themselves according to cultural standards instead of Kingdom standards, thus excluding some from the Lord's Supper (1 Corinthians 11). In none of these examples do we see Jesus or the early church leaders condoning a sinful way of life. Rather, we see the Son of God or the church demonstrating the importance of establishing a relationship for the sake of bringing others into contact with the saving work of Christ in the power of the Holy Spirit.

Associating with sinners is the very calling of Christians who will proclaim the presence of the Kingdom to others. We can't avoid it; we are all sinners, so any attempt to avoid such association is nothing more than choosing one sinner over another. Again, association is not advocacy. Instead, it's a kind of mutual support between humans, the kind we talked about in the previous chapter in our discussion of vulnerability and forgiveness. God uses our good works for just this purpose. Through relationships of this kind, we build trust. And from there, the Spirit may work through those relationships to bring about faith. It's just as Paul rhetorically recognizes: How can people hear unless someone is sent to speak the Good News (Romans 10:14–15)? While this passage is often most explicitly used in reference to pastors, it need not be so limited. For as a royal priesthood, we are all called to share the Good News of Jesus as a way of loving our neighbor as ourselves. In fact, as the missiologist Lesslie Newbigin has forcefully argued, proclaiming and witnessing to the Good News of Jesus is the primary vocation of the church.[5] So let us engage every sinner—whether a fellow pilgrim on the way with Jesus or someone yet to encounter the Gospel—as someone with whom we can fearlessly associate for the sake of the Kingdom.

ENGAGEMENT ≠ ENDORSEMENT

Writer David Dark says that all of us are at times fundamentalists in a selective way—that is, Christians have a common impulse to "protect" their faith by forbidding certain questions or avoiding certain kinds of media.[6] The assumption that Christians seem to work with is that faith is so fragile (and maybe God is so insecure) that we must do everything we can to shore up our faith (and protect God from serious questions). Perhaps it's obvious, but all of this is a rather unfaithful approach to following Jesus. We were never meant to seclude (and delude) ourselves into a kind of thoughtless, almost brainwashed faith that looks more like some

---

5   See Lesslie Newbigin, *The Gospel in a Pluralist Society* (Grand Rapids, MI: Eerdmans, 1989). See also Michael W. Goheen, *The Church and Its Vocation: Lesslie Newbigin's Missionary Ecclesiology* (Grand Rapids, MI: Baker Academic, 2018).

6   See David Dark, *The Sacredness of Questioning Everything* (Grand Rapids, MI: Zondervan, 2009).

strange, sectarian cult than the true church we see extending its reach into unfamiliar cultures and peoples in the book of Acts.

If we reflect on the approach of the earliest Christians, we can easily see the truth that none of us who are reading this would have been exposed to the Good News of the Gospel if those early Christians had not brought a different message into the world around them. We might never have met Jesus. Their willingness to engage with those who saw the world differently, considered different ideas, asked different kinds of questions, and so on is the very impulse of a faithful church seeking to bring the Good News to those who haven't heard it. And that approach required a kind of intellectual curiosity on the part of Christians themselves, as they learned about the alternative points of view, questions, and ways of life of others. Some Christians used this knowledge to find handles by which to introduce the story of the Kingdom. Paul demonstrated this well in Acts 13 as he talked with Jewish believers, and then in Acts 14 as he talked with pagans. Perhaps his most well-known witness is in Acts 17, when he shared the Gospel with those who were radically open to many different ideas as they carried on their discussions in the Areopagus. Paul offers us a model to follow.

Dark goes on to encourage readers toward curiosity and questions, similar to what the early church did. Without the curiosity and questions exhibited in relationship, the opportunities for sharing the Gospel might never have emerged. Still, Dark's encouragement doesn't go quite far enough. There's a more insidious version of the pressure not to explore certain ideas, ask certain questions, or expose ourselves to certain kinds of thinking, and it leads to our final category mistake. That is, we often work with the false assumption that entertaining or considering certain ideas, questions, or ways of life amounts to a tacit endorsement of them. If we're caught talking about, reading about, or asking about any of these ideas, we might be considered suspect, someone who can't be trusted with Christian orthodoxy or considered a true believer. Instead, we might be a doubter or, worse, a closet heretic—and therefore a possibly dangerous corrupter of the faith to those around us.

Yet engaging with ideas of all sorts is critical for our witness in the world. The alternative is to be seen as anti-intellectual, which Christians have often been accused of.[7] To be intellectually curious is not to somehow risk hollowing out our faith or allowing our cherished orthodoxy to be corrupted. Rather, we can be like the leaders of the early church, who engaged in some of the most historically significant intellectual pursuits to both answer the questions of outsiders about Christianity and clarify orthodox Christian teaching to insiders. Intellectual engagement with the ideas of the day allows us to better engage with those who adhere to those ideas and thus might open a door for us to help them wrestle with the differences Christian belief makes.

None of us should accept the premise that engaging with an idea—especially ideas that might be contrary to the Christian faith in some way, whether scientific, relational, sexual, ethical, political, theological, or otherwise—is to quietly endorse that idea. In fact, it's difficult to even know how and why an idea might be antithetical to our Christian confession of faith without knowing a good deal about what the alternative idea is and what consequences might come from adherence to it.

Furthermore, if we seek to be a collective body of people who serve faithfully in the world, then we will be required in many circumstances not only to know but also to work with ideas and

---

7   See David Kinnaman, *unChristian: What a New Generation Really Thinks about Christianity . . . and Why It Matters* (Grand Rapids, MI: Baker, 2007), chap. 6.

systems of ideas that are contrary to the Christian faith. Biologists require training in the scientific paradigms of biology, and that means that they will need to learn about and work with ideas concerning natural selection, evolution, and so on. This does not mean that they must set aside their Christian faith to work as a biologist.

The same is true for those of us with far less expertise. For example, as consumers, we live and breathe in a capitalist paradigm, one that seeks the exploitation of many for the gain of the few. Producers abuse their relationship with all of us by creating unnecessary desire through mechanisms of planned obsolescence. We're convinced to buy more or use more when companies exploit our psychological tendencies. Just think of how difficult it is to pull ourselves away from scrolling through our social media feeds or to resist the impulse to play just one more round of a casual game or to keep from pressing play on the next show in a series we're binge-watching when we ought to be getting some sleep.

We don't need to be experts in economics to recognize that we are always already engaged in a system of ideas in our capitalist society that implicates us in working against our neighbor, but from which we cannot fully extricate ourselves. Whereas one might accuse a biologist of endorsing ideas that oppose faithful Christian confession, hardly anyone is calling out our captivity to capitalist economics.

To consider and work with ideas may at any time be dangerous. Yet that's what we're called to do as followers of Jesus through the messiness of life in this world. Scripture does not prohibit the consideration of ideas, even those that teach something opposed to Scripture. Rather, we are called to discernment and empowered toward that end with the promised presence of the Spirit who will lead us into all truth (John 14:26). Let us not be afraid of ideas.

Let us not be afraid of people (including other Christians) who are willing to study, entertain, and discuss any kind of idea. Rather, let us engage them with discernment for the sake of bringing light and truth into our conversations and relationships, and even for deepening our own understanding of the grandeur of all creation. Let us use our understanding of ideas, even ones contrary to the Scripture, to find handles with which to make a faithful Gospel witness. A prime exemplar is Paul's engagement in the Areopagus concerning the idol to an "unknown god" (Acts 17:22–31). He used that idol as a handle, an object lesson of sorts, that allowed him to connect his proclamation of the Gospel to something familiar to his hearers. Those ideas that we dismiss as heretical may in fact open a space for us to connect with those who are outsiders in a manner they can understand. Paul's example is but one of many.[8]

FULLY AND FAITHFULLY ENGAGED

The radical new arrangement we see emerge in the New Testament creates for us a paradigm of freedom: freedom for and to witness winsomely with those in the world around us. That witness is empowered to be most faithful when we fearlessly pursue relationships with others. The category mistakes we've examined in this chapter can no longer prevent us from fully engaging with others who are far from the Kingdom. With the work we've done here, we're more prepared to handle worldly expectations for how Christians should behave. We're also more prepared to handle relationships with others and engagement with their beliefs, ideas, opinions, and more in a manner that allows us to compassionately

8   See Francis Rossow, *Gospel Handles: Finding New Connections in Biblical Texts* (St. Louis: Concordia Publishing House, 2001).

care for, support, and love them without fear. We need neither be worried that we're compromising nor concerned with others' perception of our engagements.

It may not always be easy for others to understand Christians and their posture of engagement with outsiders. But as we've noted more than once, Peter teaches us that that is part of the point. Our very lives will be a curiosity to those who don't yet know Jesus. Prompted by the Spirit, they may ask about why we're different. Led by the Spirit, may we be empowered and ready to respond well to anyone who asks about the hope that we have.

REFLECTION QUESTIONS

1. Consider the points from this chapter that Love ≠ Affirmation and Disagreement ≠ Hate. How have the category mistakes in these areas created challenges in your relationships? in your witness?

2. What are some challenges with living out the truth that People ≠ Their Ideas, Opinions, or Beliefs? What challenges have you faced when others have assumed that People = Their Ideas, Opinions, or Beliefs?

3. Were there times in your life when have you stayed away from someone primarily because you worked under the assumption that Association = Advocacy? Take a moment to say a prayer for those individuals—that they would meet Jesus in others and experience His grace and mercy. Boldly ask the Holy Spirit to guide you in this and future relationships, that you would not let issues prevent a relationship and would share a winsome witness.

4. In the church, certain discussions may feel like they are not possible or allowed because of the fear connected to the category mistake that Engagement = Endorsement. However, knowing that Engagement ≠ Endorsement, what intellectual curiosity would you like to see discussed in the church that you previously did not think would be possible to discuss? What benefit to the church or others would this discussion create?

CHAPTER 10

Three Goals for a Resilient Church

In the classic film *The Karate Kid*, Daniel asks his would-be mentor, Mr. Miyagi, to train him in karate. Daniel had been bullied and then beaten up by several of his peers who had been trained in the martial art but who had used it for aggressive rather than defensive purposes—a violation of the ethos of the martial arts, which encourage a wide sense of social responsibility and self-discipline rather than aggression and ego-advancement.

The training that Mr. Miyagi offers is contingent on making a pact with Daniel. Mr. Miyagi agrees to train Daniel, but Daniel is not to question the methods of his trainer. In his wisdom, Mr. Miyagi assigns Daniel several tasks that appear to be nothing more than getting Daniel to do chores on Mr. Miyagi's property. Waxing cars, sanding floors, painting fences, all in the blazing heat of the summertime—it's no surprise that Daniel is frustrated. We see him expressing impatience, wondering when he'll get to the *real* training. Daniel questions the ways of his mentor, revealing immaturity and a lack of humility to submit to those ways.

The film works so well up to this point that viewers can easily empathize with Daniel's frustration. Yet, little by little, as the drama of the film unfolds, we begin to see what Mr. Miyagi is up to. In each "chore," Daniel is growing stronger and more physically fit. He is also learning key bodily movements that will serve as the foundation for his training. Each "chore" involves a core movement that Daniel is slowly perfecting, albeit unwittingly. Mr. Miyagi is training Daniel in the virtues of movement and stance, as well as self-discipline, each of which is a key part of mastering karate.

Learning karate requires the same kind of discipline as learning a virtue. Practice is necessary, and sometimes we have to be coerced into practicing, either by a reward or by trusting those who nudge us to practice, telling us, like Mr. Miyagi, that it will be good for us. Eventually we experience the value of the practice because it begins to bear fruit. From that point on, we will likely carry on with the practice as if it's second nature, a habit we don't think about but which nevertheless shapes our lives. The habits we'll discuss in this chapter are the kind that will fruitfully elevate our Christian engagements with others as we seek to witness to Jesus and His kingdom.

In his book *Confident Pluralism*, legal scholar John Inazu helpfully recommends three "civic practices" that are meant to help anyone navigate our challenging society characterized by the deep differences that often exist between people and groups.[1] Inazu, writing as a Christian, is ultimately drawing on theological virtues without explicitly saying so, offering them to his world of readers as modern wisdom that is nevertheless extracted from the deep and ancient wells of the Christian tradition. Inazu sets out tolerance, humility, and patience as practices to which we can all aspire. With enough practice, they will become good habits from which

---

1   See John Inazu, *Confident Pluralism: Surviving and Thriving through Deep Difference* (Chicago: University of Chicago Press, 2016).

we can expect the fruit of winsome engagement. Each of these is yet another recoverable practice from the early church, all for the sake of a resilient witness in dark times.

PLURALISM: THE CHURCH'S SOCIAL CONTEXT

The title of Inazu's book gives us a clue as to one of the defining challenges we face in our age: pluralism. The early church also existed in a time of pluralism. And while it's not a perfect parallel, our two pluralistic ages have enough similarities to make learning from the early church helpful. *Pluralism* means "manyness"—a plurality of something. As the early church was emerging and establishing communities around the Mediterranean in the Roman Empire, pluralism flourished. Especially in locations of significant trade (such as port cities like Corinth) or in economic and political centers (such as Jerusalem, Athens, and Rome), people of many backgrounds and beliefs regularly gathered for life, work, leisure, and the like. Less significant cities, the ones that were not centers of commerce, economics, or political power, were less pluralistic and more homogeneous.

If you were a trader or a merchant, you might venture into a place like the Athenian Areopagus that Paul visited (Acts 17) and hear any number of ideas being discussed by leading thinkers and influencers of the time. If you were a Jewish believer living in Caesarea Philippi, perhaps you would run into various representatives of Roman political rule and their ideas—most often soldiers, but also tax collectors and members of the local civil ruling class. But if you were from a backwater town like Nazareth, despite the fact that you lived under Roman rule, it's possible you'd hardly ever have to deal with anyone other than people who lived and believed just as you did.

In our time, such homogeneous ways of life are far more difficult to come by. You may live in a place like Amish-populated rural Pennsylvania or predominantly Mormon-populated portions of Utah or Idaho and not have to interact in public with people who live according to a different worldview or set of sacred convictions. Even so, you still live in a world in which radio, television, and, most importantly, the internet exists. This radically increases your likelihood of being not only exposed to other ways of thinking and believing but also influenced by them. In our younger days, there is a sense of discovery in all this. People living differently than us were treated as a kind of curiosity at best or as anathema at worst. But as we grow up and continue to live in this world, each of us must find a way to negotiate how we will relate to people who are different from us.

This is the kind of situation Inazu speaks into. Inazu recognizes the "manyness" (pluralism) that we experience daily in our society, particularly the sort of manyness that exposes us to the deep differences that exist between individuals and groups on the basis of politics, religion, ethnicity, gender, economics, place of origin, native language, level of education, economic status, race, family dynamics, and many other influential issues that shape lives and communities. Inazu's stance is utterly realistic about our social circumstances, yet he envisions ways for us to confidently engage with other people in our time. To move forward as a society that is constituted by people of deep difference, we must find ways to promote working and speaking together so that all might flourish. To that end, he suggests three civic aspirations—that is, three characteristics that everyone, not just Christians, can practice as we exist together.[2]

Inazu calls them aspirations because he is well aware that we will never perfectly embody any of what he recommends. But without a target to aim for, we will never aspire to become better in our engagement across the deep differences of our society. Let's explore those aspirations together by looking at how the early church displayed them as a model for our own engagement.

TOLERANCE

To our modern ears, tolerance often rings of some progressive value that doesn't fit with the orthodox Christian tradition. But in the earliest days of the church, the practice of tolerance in the pluralistic culture of the Roman Empire benefited the church significantly, just as it did for the Jews under Roman occupation. When Rome would conquer nations, in the most basic sense, Rome required little from them in terms of major changes to their beliefs and practices. Rather, Rome wanted taxes, military conscripts, trade routes, and fealty to the emperor. Of course, that last one was quite troubling for the Jews and the emerging Christian Church since it's a clear violation of the First Commandment. Still, the tolerance that existed for the early church, especially as it established its roots among formerly Jewish believers and then Gentiles, with outposts in predominantly Jewish, Greek, and Roman cultural centers, was invaluable to the slow flourishing it experienced over its first three centuries.

Furthermore, as established Christian communities took shape within these cultural contexts, there was no aggressive agenda to

2   See Inazu, *Confident Pluralism*, chap. 5.

force others into following Jesus. Rather, the Christian communities were themselves tolerant of others. Their witness was gentle and winsome, while at the same time unbending in its confession. To the extent that Christians experienced social persecution, members of the early church were encouraged by the apostles and early church leaders to live in such a way that they could not be found guilty of any accusation leveled against them (see 1 Peter 3:13–17). As we've already seen in comments from Tertullian and the writer of the Letter to Diognetus, the early church eventually achieved a substantially positive reputation among outsiders.

If the church in the twenty-first century is to regain such a social reputation and thus build trust among outsiders, we should take seriously Inazu's suggestion of the civic virtue of tolerance. He's not talking about tolerating the things that don't matter much, like our favorite kinds of music, movies, books, food, or fashion. Nor is he talking about our commitments to our alma mater or our favorite professional sports team. Nor is Inazu signaling the relativistic sense of "anything goes" or "it's okay if it's consensual or not hurting anyone else."

Rather, Inazu suggests that tolerance means recognizing that people adhere to, promote, and live according to ideas that someone else might consider abhorrent.[3] For Christians, we would also include those things we consider unfaithful and "ungodly." Missionaries to foreign lands and unreached people often exhibit this posture well. That is, missionaries don't show up as strangers among a foreign people and immediately demand they change everything about how they live. Instead, they build relationships over a long period of time, finding ways to introduce people to Jesus and the ways of the Kingdom, all the while tolerating the differences they

---

3   See Inazu, *Confident Pluralism*, 87–88.

experience while working as missionaries. Inazu helpfully points out that the English word *tolerance* comes to us from a Latin word meaning "the enduring of something."[4] So perhaps Christians must tolerate—that is, *endure*—things we consider unfaithful, ungodly, and even abhorrent.

Inazu's background as a legal scholar comes to the forefront when he pushes us further on this issue. Inazu argues that tolerance only makes sense in the context of mutuality. That is, we might find others' ideas or ways of life completely abhorrent, but perhaps they harbor the same sentiment toward our ideas and ways of life. If we want to make a case for our way of life as the truth, we must allow for the alternative position to exist, and not only that, but also for those who adhere to it to believe with full conviction that their way is the truth. It is within this kind of situation that tolerance is most needed, Inazu says.[5] In other words, to be able to freely proclaim, promote, and advance what we love, we must also extend to others the same privilege. Of course, this opens a space for others to promote the exact opposite of what we hold sacred—they may love what we hate, and they may hate what we love. For the church in America, this is nothing other than enjoying the freedoms we have under the First Amendment of the Constitution while also allowing everyone else to enjoy their same freedoms.[6]

Tolerance of this sort recognizes that there will never be any sort of absolute tolerance (a logical impossibility because absolute tolerance requires intolerance of intolerance). Nor will there be any kind of absolute peace in which we all get along. Rather, as a civic "aspiration," tolerance suggests that differences can be and

---

4   See Inazu, *Confident Pluralism*, 87.

5   See Inazu, *Confident Pluralism*, 87–88.

6   See Inazu, *Confident Pluralism*, 16.

often are noted, taken into account, and respected, and that, to the extent those differences can be set aside for common goals, efforts ought to be made to do so. This approach is nothing other than what we regularly hear from Christian preachers, teachers, and writers as they reach back into the church's past to offer a way forward in our post-Christian era. They remind us that God called His followers through the prophet Jeremiah to live in such a way that benefited those around them so that all would flourish (see Jeremiah 29:4–14).[7] And while we will never achieve a utopian society as fallible humans, we can certainly enact tolerance in this way to aim for a "modest unity" with our civic neighbors, as Inazu terms it and as we discussed in chapter 6.[8] As Christians begin practicing this kind of tolerance, the modest unity that follows will build rapport and hopefully open relational doors for us to share the Good News (see Colossians 4:3).

HUMILITY

I used to serve as a university professor teaching theology and religion. This was during the rise of what has come to be known as cancel culture. A new kind of cultural orthodoxy was seeking to unseat traditional sensibilities about the very goal of education and university experience. A strong push had long been underway to move the purpose of education in general, and higher education specifically, from being about the pursuit of truth to being primarily about social reform, challenging existing power structures, and limiting what kinds of study and discourse were considered legitimate.

---

7   James Davison Hunter, for example, does this in his book *To Change the World: The Irony, Tragedy, and Possibility of Christianity in the Late Modern World* (Oxford: Oxford University Press, 2010), 276–84.

8   See Inazu, *Confident Pluralism*, 15.

Much of the driving force behind these efforts occurred because of the rise of social media and other forms of media promotion, which democratized voices that had long been suppressed, allowing them to be heard. Our discussion in chapter 6 noted how identitarian concerns became front and center in these efforts. Furthermore, subsequent endorsement of such cultural orthodoxies from consumer capitalist marketing also played a strong role; in other words, companies would outwardly show support for the *du jour* culturally orthodox positions in order to retain customers who supported these positions.

In wrestling with how to establish a classroom atmosphere that was resistant to using education merely for the sake of social reform, undermining power structures, or policing discourse, I focused substantially on an epistemological foundation that called all classroom participants (including myself) to a posture of intellectual humility—our second civic virtue. Such a posture is applicable far beyond the classroom, but by fostering it there, I was hoping that my students' classroom experience would be not only informative but also *formative* in terms of character. That is, I was aiming to convince my students of the importance of intellectual humility and, even more, to show them what it looks like and help them to experience it in a way that would guide their future engagement as servants of others in the world.

In light of that, I created a manual of sorts that I used to introduce students to new courses and establish an expected atmosphere and form of conduct with one another. In the manual, I explained the higher education environment we were operating in, tried to help students imagine what would be possible for their classroom experience, and laid out concrete ways to practice intellectual humility. The following paragraphs offer a glimpse of that manual. While my context was a university classroom, the concepts are easily adaptable to other contexts—households, workplaces, churches, social media, and so on. This is just one example of how a posture of humility can benefit us and is a necessary aspiration for our time.

In higher education, as in many places in our culture, we encounter ideas, forms of thinking, lifestyles, behaviors, and personalities that challenge us in our own perspectives, the way we use reason to think about the world, and how we believe the world should be. In higher education, we are privileged to have these sorts of encounters. This environment presents us not only with a variety of ideas, people, and ways of being that are radically different than our own but also with the opportunity to try to understand them through conversation, deep investigation, intellectual wrestling, and an attitude that begins with hospitality and respect. We're offered the chance to learn how to dialogue in healthy ways about things with which we may not initially (or ever) agree or fully understand.

In this course, you will likely find yourself encountering ideas, people, and ways of being that do not necessarily match your own perspectives, beliefs, ethics, or overall approach to life. You are attending a Lutheran Christian university, but you are not expected to be Lutheran, Christian, or believe in Jesus to get an A or even to pass this course. You are not required to accept or adopt anything you encounter in this class. But you are required to engage the course content with vigor and a critical perspective and to interact with your fellow students in a manner that demonstrates preparedness and a spirit of listening, learning, conviviality, and civility.

In order to promote this, the posture of this course is one of trying to put as much critical distance as possible between ourselves and all ideas, worldviews, behaviors, lifestyles, backgrounds, and so on. That means, ultimately, that the first person we question is ourselves. We do not begin with the assumption that the way we see things is the only way to see things, or even the right way. Only after being able to critique ourselves and embody the posture of believing that we could indeed be wrong (and it's likely we *are* wrong in some respects) are we able to engage in questions and dialogue with others. If we don't understand ourselves, how can we help others understand us? If we do not at least understand ourselves in this basic manner, how can we engage in fruitful dialogue with others, especially when there might be disagreement or misunderstanding in our dialogue? Only by being able to articulate our own perspectives well and, furthermore, to critically evaluate them are we then able to offer our best contributions in our dialogue and learning with others.

One working assumption I used as I set the tone for students in my courses is anthropological. That is, as Christians, we have a certain understanding of what it means to be human. And part of that understanding has to do with our fallenness. As people in need of redemption, we usually discuss our fallenness in terms of sin, behavior, opposition to the ways of God, and so on. Far less often do we talk about how our fallenness affects our ability to clearly discern and know the truth. As Paul helpfully acknowledges, humans only ever see "in a mirror dimly," or as other translations put it, "through a glass darkly" (1 Corinthians 13:12 ESV; KJV). By this he means that we always see in a distorted way, in part but not in full. Our knowledge, perception, understanding, and ability to learn are always hampered by the fallibility that comes from our fallenness. We've noted this already in several places earlier in the book. We humans always need help. Thank God that we can rely on the Holy Spirit to lead us into all truth (see John 16:24).

Humility, then, is the recognition that our own positions are challengeable and that we are not infallible creatures who are always right. Humility opens us up to being able to dialogue in confidence about our own perspective while also recognizing that we do not see things perfectly and, furthermore, that others may know better. We can learn from others, whether fellow followers of Jesus or those who do not yet know Him. Humility also presses us to treat others as more important than ourselves (see Philippians 2:3–4), which helps shape us to be listeners before we are speakers. And our listening, as we've discussed in a previous chapter, should take the shape of listening in order to understand rather than listening in order to react or respond.

If the church and its members can embody humility in this way, our engagement with others in our pluralistic world can be confident and winsome as a form of witness.

PATIENCE

Patience is the final civic aspiration that helps us live and interact with others amid our deep differences. Let us acknowledge right away that discussing patience in modern times is difficult. Many of us likely approach patience with trepidation. We've heard the warning that to ask God to teach us patience is to ask for trouble. Even more, we often know that we're not patient people, and frankly, we don't want to be. This makes patience difficult to discuss. Yet it may also signal important reasons to discuss it.

In our day, patience is a virtue that's almost unheard of. Collectively, as members of our society, we do not practice patience very well, even if we acknowledge that patience is a good thing. We are a demanding, impatient, and often bored people. We tend to expect to get things when we want them. Few of us are good at delaying gratification, and our lack of patience seems only to get worse over time.

Patience is the sort of thing that takes constant practice. But practicing patience is unusual for us. Rather, we've been shaped by other practices that we engage in, leading to habits that expect instant gratification, such as restaurant drive-throughs, on-demand media, faster computer processors, and self-checkout lanes. Our expectation for nearly instant gratification reveals itself whenever we have to wait and things are going slower than we want them to, from having appointment delays to enduring slow traffic, from putting up with staff shortages at restaurants to waiting more than two days for our package to arrive, or maybe worst of them all, having to watch the three blinking dots in a text message conversation, eagerly anticipating an incoming message that seems to take forever to arrive.

Lacking patience, we often react with anger and frustration to circumstances that require us to wait. We're mad when we find out the new season of the show we planned to binge-watch over a weekend ends up being slated for serial release over a period of ten weeks. Sometimes our reactions even hurt others—there has been a marked increase in road rage in recent years.

We're impatient about the world too. Why does justice take so long? Why can't people and nations find ways to get along? Why do diseases, terminal illnesses, moral improprieties, betrayals, violence, natural disasters, and all other sources of pain persist in spite of our best efforts to mitigate them? When will there be peace? We are impatient for peace.

THE PATIENCE OF ADVENT PEOPLE

Inazu's recommendation for patience as a civic aspiration has deep Christian roots.[9] Christians are, after all, an Advent kind of people. Traditionally, the season of Advent is celebrated as a retelling of one of the most important parts of our story as God's people—waiting for the arrival of the Messiah, the child Jesus, born in Nazareth. Yet there is another sense in which we continue to wait, just as we did for that first Advent. All Christians are living in a perpetual Advent as we await the return of the King. The fulfillment of our final hope and the eternal promises of God rest on Christ's second coming, bringing about the consummation of this age. We wait for what we confess in hope as we say the Nicene Creed together with the historic, contemporary, and—while the Lord tarries—future church when we say, "I look for the resurrection of the dead and the life of the world to come."

---

9   See Inazu, *Confident Pluralism*, 90.

When we remember that we are Advent people, our impatience with the situations and circumstances I noted above seems trivial. Waiting for a text message is hardly comparable to waiting for the resurrection of our bodies or the establishment of the new heavens and new earth. The confession we make together in the Creed orients our imagination concerning *what* we're waiting for and *how* we wait for it. The waiting game of Advent-oriented Christians is radically different from how the world plays at waiting. Followers of Jesus are perpetually engaged in a long game, as it were. Waiting for the return of the King relativizes all other waiting.

Changing our imagination about how we wait and what we wait for—the long Advent of waiting for Jesus to come again—motivates us to wait differently for the things in this world. Christians learn to wait differently together as they gather around Christ's Word and His promises. Yet as we wait for the Messiah to come again, we are also learning how to wait for His work in the world around us. This begins with our prayer for daily bread. And as we experience and then thank God for His provision, we are empowered to see how He provides so much more than mere bread and gives us the gifts of skill, talent, time, treasure, friendship, community, beauty, and so much more. Furthermore, we see how important it is for God to involve us in the delivery and use of all these things for the blessing of human life on earth in the here and now—a glimpse of the presence of the Kingdom among us, inaugurated in the first Advent when God took on flesh and became one of us.

To be patient means we are waiting not only for God to bring about the end of the age but also for God to work in our midst here and now. He does this by bringing about human flourishing in various ways (e.g., through our daily bread) and by bringing about increasing amounts of comfort and healing in the midst of suffering and injustice, peace that surpasses understanding, and joy that surpasses the false contentment of the world in the lives of people around us.

Inazu encourages us to be patient because he recognizes that learning to live together amid deep difference will not happen overnight. One conversation is not likely to bring about agreement, generate friendship, or exhaust the possibilities of understanding. Inazu believes that if we have in mind not just our own flourishing but that of others, we will exhibit patience in our pursuit of living together in our pluralistic culture. Patience of this sort might look like maintaining a commitment to solving a problem, even if we aren't around to see the resolution—to devote our lives to finding solutions that may only bear significant fruit after we are gone. That is, our patient efforts might only have results for our children or their children.

In this way, Inazu's suggestion certainly challenges us in our instant-gratification culture. But he is convincing, and we often recognize many people of the past who have become heroic icons of patience for their cause, including for issues that are not yet fully resolved, such as civil rights. We think of Abraham Lincoln and Martin Luther King Jr., both of whom invested in something that was worth their very lives and cost them as much. We can add to this the story of Francis Perkins, the first woman to become secretary of state, who advocated substantially for workers' and women's rights. Yet all of their work was continued in later generations and endures today. We have made much progress, but there is clearly much more to be done. Patience will be crucial in advancing this cause.

Patience is required in this kind of Kingdom living—the kind that not only looks for the arrival of the King and the end of this age but also seeks to invest in our social architecture here and now.

This is what God instructed His people to do during the Babylonian captivity so that all might flourish and see it as the gift from God that it is.

THE PATIENCE OF THE EARLY CHURCH

It is this kind of patience that characterized the earliest citizens of the Kingdom. The early church doubled down on patience. Tertullian (whom we heard from before) and Cyprian, two major voices of the early church, both wrote substantive works on patience. Both writers were leaders of the early church in North Africa. Cyprian, for example, who was bishop of Carthage, encouraged his people, saying, "Let us, as servants and worshippers of God, show, in our spiritual obedience, the patience which we learn from heavenly teachings. For we have this virtue in common with God. From Him patience begins; from Him its glory and its dignity take their rise."[10]

God's patience, which we constantly experience through His ongoing willingness to endure our rebelliousness, is the model the early church used as a foundation for its way of life in a society in which they were a backwater minority. During the time of Tertullian and Cyprian, the early Christians did not enjoy the privilege of recognition in the Roman Empire that would come later, following Constantine's conversion. Nevertheless, those first church leaders, living and teaching in the century after the apostles, emphasized patience. The second-century writer Justin Martyr believed that "the effectiveness of Christian witness depends on the integrity of the believers' lifestyles."[11] The simple idea is that patience is

10   Cyprian, "Treatise IX: On the Advantage of Patience," in *The Ante-Nicene Fathers*, vol. 5, ed. Alexander Roberts and James Donaldson (New York: Christian Literature Publishing Co., 1886), 484.

11   Alan Kreider, *The Patient Ferment of the Early Church: The Improbable Rise of Chris-*

attractive. It reflects the beautiful ways of the Kingdom and the King in contrast to those of the world.

The church historian Alan Kreider helps us to see this in his brief comments about Justin Martyr's encouragement to the second-century Christian community in Rome concerning patience:

> According to Justin, patience is central to the life of his community in Rome. Justin uses various sayings of Jesus to illustrate the significance of patience for members of his community: turning the other cheek when someone hits them in the face; giving their tunics to someone who takes their cloak; avoiding the incendiary sin of anger; and, if they are compelled to go one mile, going two miles. When people see Christians behaving like this, Justin comments, people are intrigued; they "wonder" at the God whom the Christians say motivates their behavior. So it is important for Christians not to quarrel like other people, and it is essential that they live their "good works" visibly in the sight of others. Then, when Christians live with integrity and visibility, "by our patience and meekness [Christians will] draw all men from shame and evil desires." According to Justin, patience attracts people.[12]

This wisdom from the early church is apt for our own time. Practicing the virtue of patience in our pluralistic culture, when it

tianity in the Roman Empire (Grand Rapids, MI: Baker Academic, 2010), 15. Quotations from Justin Martyr within Kreider's quotation are from First Apology of Justin, 14.3, trans. E. R. Hardy, in Early Christian Fathers, ed. Cyril C. Richardson, vol. 1, Library of Christian Classics (Philadelphia: Westminster Press, 1953), 242–89.

12 Kreider, The Patient Ferment of the Early Church, 16. Brackets in original.

often feels like the Christian Church is returning to something of a minority status, is still powerfully attractive. As we've noted in an earlier chapter, it is not just Christians who are frustrated and exhausted by how divided we seem to be in our society. Many outsiders share our frustration and exhaustion. We can shine a hopeful light of Christian witness as we endure together our divisions and differences with patience.

Furthermore, with the same patience that awaits the return of the King, we Advent people can seek the good of those around us, not because we agree on everything or share the same worldview, but because we are Christians and to live this way is to live as Jesus, as He showed us in His life and then called us to imitate. In this way, as we've noted time and again in this book, the world might actually meet Jesus in us (see Galatians 2:20). This is our hope and prayer.

THAT THE WORLD MAY KNOW

It's unlikely any of us will become a master in the Christian way of life and serve as a perfect exemplar, as Mr. Miyagi was for Daniel in the martial arts. But there's no need for such a thing. Instead, it's more than enough that we are followers of the great Master, the Lord of all, the King of creation—Jesus Christ.

My purpose in this book was to help us better understand the world we live in as Christians. For some time, many of us have felt that things have changed. Our articulation of what has changed has been lacking, as have our responses to it. That lack has produced a vacuum in which alarmism, fear, resentment, anger, and reactionariness have become primary responses. I pray that this book has helped fill that void and thus equips the church to embody a more hopeful, faithful, fearless, and resilient response.

As we gather together regularly as God's people, we are shaped as those who shine the light of the Gospel into the darkness of the world. Our lives are watched by outsiders. We are always, whether intentionally or not, Christ's witness. I pray this book will help the church recognize this fact and aim for a winsome posture in our witness.

May the Holy Spirit lead us as witnesses for the Kingdom, helping us develop relationships of trust within which people might meet Jesus in us and thus come to know the grandeur of His love for them.

REFLECTION QUESTIONS

1. This chapter examined a different way to understand tolerance: "Tolerance suggests that differences can be and often are noted, taken into account, and respected, and that, to the extent those differences can be set aside for common goals, efforts ought to be made to do so." Has anyone ever done that for you? How did it affect your willingness to enter into or maintain a relationship with that person? What are some practical examples of how you can do this for others in your life?

2. Treating others as more important than ourselves is counter-cultural in the United States. How have you seen others live this out?

Acknowledgments

This book started to come together before I was even aware of it. Almost ten years ago, a radical shift began on college campuses that eventually trickled down into popular culture. Today that shift, among others, has greatly contributed to the fractured, confused, and polarized social landscape we're all trying to navigate. Trying to get a handle on how to respond faithfully as a Christian to the social fissures that were forming and growing into seemingly uncrossable chasms was the impetus for much of the thinking I've included here. That said, I was not alone in the social crucible where these ideas were coming together.

Reaching back to those days as a faculty member at Concordia University in Portland, Oregon, there are a number of people who served as thought partners and wrestled with me and others on how best to serve our students and faithfully follow Jesus. I want to thank Megan Bouslaugh, Phil Brandt, Steve DeKlotz, Ted Engelbrecht, Paul Linnemann, Erin and Reed Mueller, Dave Sadler, Michael Thomas, and more. Our time spent working closely together has informed much of what I've written here.

While there and since, I've continued to develop this work, presenting pieces of it publicly here and there. The reception has been surprisingly good. It began to strike me that perhaps this content was hitting a nerve and needed a larger and more comprehensive form of presentation. Concordia Publishing House was willing to take that on, recognizing along with me the need for this material to serve the life of the church.

The process of bringing this book to fruition has been shepherded by a number of talented folks at CPH. Jonathan Schultz,

Laura Lane, and Elizabeth Pittman have been excited from the moment I shared the proposal and they expressed a desire to take on the project. Jamie Moldenhauer has been a tremendous editor who has improved every page. Anna Johnson, Erica Sontag, and others have worked hard to make sure the book will get into the hands of those we believe need it most. To all of them, thank you.

In the background has always been a supportive foundation for me. My wife, Bethany, has not only been a constant thought partner, but as someone who has been alongside me in the development of these ideas and the writing of this book, she has been invaluably helpful in crafting the discussion questions for each chapter. My and my wife's parents are walways present with cheers of encouragement, as are our siblings. My young children have been curious about what writing a book is about and excited about what it will mean when it's finally published, and I'm eager for them to share in the fruit I hope it bears. I also want to thank my current colleagues, Jeffrey Craig-Meyer, Nicole Heerlein, Beatriz Hoppe, Becky Pagel, and Mike Zeigler for their support as I've quietly worked on this project while serving alongside them at Lutheran Hour Ministries.

Finally, two others. First, Dale Meyer, who also believed in this book as soon as I told him what I was working on. He was incredibly generous in writing the foreword. Second, Joel Okamoto, my doctoral advisor and now friend and thought partner. His mentorship has shaped my thinking and approach to writing and service in the church in an unspeakable number of ways. To each of them, thank you for how you've poured into me over the years.

Chad Lakies
April 25, 2024
Feast of St. Mark the Evangelist